THE HIDDEN PLEASURES
OF LIFE

By the same author

Conversation
An Intimate History of Humanity
Happiness
The French
A History of French Passions
in five volumes:
Ambition and Love
Intellect and Pride
Taste and Corruption
Politics and Anger
Anxiety and Hypocrisy

Emile Ollivier and the Liberal Empire
The Political System of Napoleon III
Etc.

Theodore Zeldin

THE HIDDEN PLEASURES OF LIFE

A New Way of Remembering the Past
and Imagining the Future

MACLEHOSE PRESS
QUERCUS · LONDON

First published in Great Britain in 2015 by

MacLehose Press
An imprint of Quercus Publishing Ltd
Carmelite House
50 Victoria Embankment
London EC4Y 0DZ

A CIP catalogue record for this book is available
from the British Library.

ISBN (HB) 978 0 85705 368 8
ISBN (TPB) 978 0 85705 370 1
ISBN (Ebook) 978 0 85705 367 1

10 9 8 7 6 5 4 3 2 1

Designed and typeset in Miller by Libanus Press, Marlborough
Printed and bound in Italy by Graphicom

To Deirdre Wilson

Contents

Preface

FIGHT FOR YOUR RIGHTS! PROTEST! Ignore the horrors around you, amuse yourself, be happy! Make money, work hard, win power! Hide your wrinkles! Are these and their likes the only weapons with which we can defend ourselves against the cruelties of life? Humanity is no longer what it was when these now ancient forms of protection were invented. We know more than we ever did, and have suffered more disappointments than we can remember. We are now free to extricate ourselves from reliance on corrupted versions of ideals that once seemed to radiate only beauty and hope. So I have set out to find others, hidden, unspoken or forgotten, by approaching the history of human experience from a personal angle.

Each of my chapters begins with the voice of a person from a different epoch and civilisation confronting one of the big decisions that everyone has to make, and responding with a story of their own experience. This draws me into a conversation in which I ask what other answers might be available today, what opportunities were missed in the past, and what possibilities have opened up since then. The characters in this book are not heroes to emulate. I have chosen them partly because they have left particularly frank personal testimonies, suggesting that it is sometimes easier to get to know more about the dead – when their private secrets are revealed – than the living – who take so much care to conceal theirs – and partly because they have inspired me with unexpected thoughts about what humans could attempt in the future. They have stimulated me to search in new directions for what life can contain, to become aware of what I have missed, and to distinguish between what humans are and the labels they stick on themselves. History is not just a record of what happened and why it happened, but above all a provocation of the imagination.

I begin by investigating the untried options individuals have when they feel powerless, or isolated, or not valued at their true worth, or frustrated that civilisation's arrangements do not suit them. I explore neglected paths that cross the boundaries erected by money, prejudice, pretence and misunderstanding, I focus on what happens when two strangers meet, expanding the notion of the couple to include not only people who fall in and out of love, or live together, but also 'couples of the mind', who form independently of physical union, time or place. Curiosity can generate a desire as powerful and insistent as the desire of the body. Ideas can forge long-lasting bonds, even if these are fashioned out of illusions about oneself or about others (chapters 1–7).

Next, I meet people as they appear when they belong to large groups, to a nation or a religion (chapters 8–16). The deeper I go into the history of how these groups became what they are, very different from how they started, the more I realise that the seemingly formidable barriers around each one are less immovable than they appear. Numerous uncertainties are hidden beneath the surface of the metaphors they use to differentiate themselves and the slogans that conceal internal conflicts or distract from abandoned ideals. Is it inevitable that people should repeatedly forget that, in retrospect, they regret the violence to which their passionate loyalties lead? Why has pleasure in laughing at human follies achieved so little in preventing them? In the history of the relations between men and women (chapters 17–19) I find pointers to how stultifying habits might slowly be dissolved.

Then I confront the great puzzle of why so many individuals spend such a large proportion of their waking hours in boring, futile and sometimes servile employment, why there are not enough worthwhile and life-enhancing jobs to suit the talents of new generations, and why there is often more disillusionment, more betrayal, more back-stabbing at work than in families (chapters 20–25). My adventures inside corporations and governments have impressed upon me how difficult it is for them to change, but also suggest they could be different. The original meaning of the word 'business' was anxiety, distress, officiousness, difficulty. So I investigate the possibility that business could find a new meaning again, and a more exhilarating philosophy. The triumphs of technology and medicine have been achieved by endless experimentation, 'research and development', so I show how professions and firms could each have, side by side with their existing practices, the equivalent of a laboratory to try out, on a small scale, different possible ways of reinventing themselves, to fulfil a wider range of present-day aspirations.

My final chapters (26–28) are about the art of reflecting on the passing of time. I find it is even possible to see the process of ageing and the prospect of dying in a less blinding light.

How then could human energies begin to be divided differently between sexual intercourse, commercial intercourse and verbal intercourse? The mistrust and misunderstanding that plague people's lives have often been resolved by intimate, face-to-face conversations, but many conversations are trivial, or hurried, or monologues, or human versions of birdsong without the beauty, endlessly repeating the same refrain to the same narrow circle. A book is an invitation to engage in a silent conversation with an author and the characters in his book, at a rhythm that suits the reader. This book is not a thriller designed to make it impossible for you to put it down; on the contrary, it invites you to pause and reflect after each chapter, and start your own conversation about it. I should like to know what you can see and understand that I cannot. If, as a result, we say what we have not said before, we might be able to think about the future more fruitfully.

However, Thomas Edison put this warning on the door of his laboratory: 'There is no expedient to which a man will not resort to avoid the real labour of thinking.' A wit replied: 'Well, why should a man think when Mr. Edison reaches conclusions for him? Personally, we'd resort to any amount of thinking to avoid real labour.' I prefer to regard thinking as a sociable activity. Bringing ideas and people from separate domains together is one of the main ways in which thinking develops and discoveries are made. Finding unsuspected links between dissimilar individuals, between apparently incompatible opinions, and between the past and the present is one of the first steps on the path to hidden pleasures. It is sometimes salutary to see the world not only in bright and contrasting colours, but also in sepia, with the frontiers blurred by unexpected commonalities.

[1]

What is the great adventure of our time?

IN 1859, AT THE AGE OF twenty-three, an Iranian student walked out of his home in Sultanabad because he was unwilling to get married. His parents were pressuring him to, but settling down while still young, he said, would mean that 'I would spend all my life in the same place and would not learn anything about the world.' Taking only three loaves of bread with him, and wearing only summer clothes, he walked northwards, not quite sure where he was heading. Eventually he reached Russia. He kept on walking and travelling for eighteen years through most of the countries of Europe, the U.S., Japan, China, India and Egypt. He joined the pilgrimage to Mecca nine times. 'No handicap in the world is worse than ignorance,' he wrote in his diary.

'No handicap is worse than ignorance'

There may be backpackers who have journeyed as far, but who among them has learned the language of almost every country visited, as Hajj Sayyah did, and earned his keep as a translator? Though he had no money, no letters of recommendation, no influential family behind him, he obtained audiences with the Tsar of Russia, the Pope, the Kings of Greece and Belgium, Bismarck, Garibaldi, and repeatedly met President Ulysses Grant in the U.S.A. He was the first Iranian to become an American citizen. He demonstrated what gentleness, politeness and unpretentiousness could achieve. He was welcomed everywhere. Only once was he assaulted, in Naples. Only once was he insulted, by the Ottoman consul there who said, 'He is an Iranian; how can we believe him?' But the consul later apologised, when he got to know him better. Even the pickpockets of Naples befriended him, and gave him free lodging in the house where they trained novice pickpockets. He bore no grudges, only asking himself: 'How could there be such extreme differences among mankind? How could man be mean to such a degree, or on the contrary so noble?'

His insatiable curiosity took him not just to the museums of every city, but to its schools, libraries, churches, factories, botanical gardens, zoos, prisons, theatres. When asked who he was, he would reply, 'A creature of God and a stranger to this city.' His favourite proverb was: 'Keep secret your wealth, your destination and your religion.' He delighted in being 'a common man', able to discover how uncommon every common man was. 'If I were a king, I would never see things that way, because kings cannot be in the society of the poor. The purpose of the king is to show his appearance to the people, but the purpose of the poor is to see the people the way they are. They move about freely without fear. Nobody notices them, but they see everything and everybody.'

People were so kind to him and invited him to their homes, to the theatre, and to join them on their outings, because they reciprocated his interest in them. Not that he approved of everything. He openly criticised the manufacture of arms when he met the King of Belgium. He recorded the bitter complaints he heard about poverty and oppression. But in

Paris he wrote, 'People here enjoy liberty. They freely say what they want. No-one interferes in other people's business . . . Sorrow makes life short. These people have no sorrow, they should never die.'

When he finally returned to Iran, he entered the quite different adventure of politics, the search for political solutions to humanity's ills. Protesting against the 'undeserved hardships and atrocities which were beyond the endurance of beasts, let alone men, inflicted on poor, hapless and ignorant Persian subjects like myself', he joined the movement against corruption and misgovernment that led to his country's revolution of 1905. He was active in the most influential secret society plotting change, was sent to prison and rural exile, and, when his life seemed to be in danger, he took refuge for five months in the American embassy. After the revolution, widely admired for his wisdom and humility, he was called the Secret Harbinger of the Humanist Movement. The Persian word translated as 'humanist' is '*Adamiyat*'. Hajj Sayyah was a protagonist of the 'fellowship of humanity' (*ashab-e adamiyat*). But politics proved to be too full of rivalries and animosities to achieve his ideals, and it still has not achieved them. On the other hand, backpackers usually seek only a temporary solution, postponing the day when the straitjacket that rigid institutions favour has to be donned. What other path then is there to take?

Undeserved hardships and atrocities

Hajj Sayyah's eighteen-year journey was an adventure, the opposite of a career. He differed from adventurers like Cortez – in search of a kingdom, using traditional weapons, force and guile – or Columbus – greedy for the fabled gold of India. He had nothing in common with the pirates

The opposite of a career

and courtesans, the mercenary soldiers or the Californian gold-diggers who used to be the archetypal adventurers, nor with the French Academy's 1823 definition of the adventurer as a person without fortune or status who lives by intrigue. Only in recent times has being called an adventurer ceased to be an insult, suggesting instead an idealistic person searching for what society does not offer; but this has often meant only a vague longing for the exotic, for new sensations or for primitive simplicity, or a contempt for worldly ambitions, even rejecting all ambition, following the poet Rimbaud's maxim that 'goals are inane'. The spirit of adventure could be interpreted as an escape, or a purely personal achievement, or a triumph of technology, like the journey to the moon.

The spirit of adventure

Almost exactly a century after Hajj Sayyah embarked on his long journey, Simon Murray, a nineteen-year-old Briton, jilted by his girl-friend and bored by his job in a Manchester iron foundry, walked away and joined the French Foreign Legion. He wanted to prove to himself that he deserved a better destiny, that he had the strength to survive the extremes of cruelty and war. Self-confidence was his reward. He wrote a book, with remarkable literary skill, about how he overcame the cruelties and dangers of the desert, which was so gripping that it was made into a film. Then he went into business, became head of huge corporations and grew very rich. However, that was not enough for him. In his sixties, he repeated his youthful act of defiance by walking alone to the Antarctic. But his adventures were in the tradition of doing things because they were difficult and challenging. They were a supplement to life, like sport, an escape from the ordinariness of life, but they did not change life. They

Escape from the ordinariness of life

were important to him, but for others ordinary life continues as before. Other kinds of adventure are possible.

If you and I had met in the sixteenth century, I would have said to you: The great adventure of our time is to discover new continents and new oceans. Let us stop grumbling about our discontents and seek a more exhilarating purpose. Come to America. And after that, let us explore the whole world. We cannot think we have really lived until we have seen the full extent of humanity's home.

A more exhilarating purpose

A century later, I would have said to you, the great adventure of our time is science. It is going to reveal that behind what we can see and touch and hear, there is an even more amazing world. No object is what it appears to be. Let us discover the secrets of nature: they promise to be much more amazing than the fantasies of magic.

The fantasies of magic

In the eighteenth century, a wonderful adventure held out the promise of a completely new era of equality. Come and join in the struggle against public and private tyrannies. Let us overthrow despots and proclaim freedom for everybody. Let us ensure that each and every person has the right to aim for every kind of achievement, however poor their parents were.

There are also adventures that have existed since the beginning of time. One is the search for purpose and a less self-centred existence, which is what religions and ideologies teach. Another, just as ancient but neglected until its recent revival, involves finding ways of living harmoniously with all the earth's creatures and plants, the sea and the landscape, as they constantly renew themselves. A third is the quest for beauty, and its appreciation in many forms, to reveal that the imagination has no limits.

Each of these adventures remains attractive enough to absorb a person for a whole lifetime, but since they were conceived, a new horizon has come into sight. Understanding of the huge universe and of its minute particles has been completely transformed. Men and women have been reshaped by education and information and experiences and expectations that never existed before. The world is filling up with a new kind of human being. Many are no longer comfortable struggling to earn a living using only a fraction of their talents, in ways invented long ago for much more subservient creatures. Each has been trained to be a specialist in a single domain, with skills that can bring deep satisfactions, but which can also narrow the imagination. The 'meaning of life' is no longer as clear as it was once supposed to have been. Never have so many humans been uncertain about their larger purpose beyond their daily grind and nightly pleasures. Old assumptions threaten to collapse, leaving one naked. Many people's assumptions have already collapsed and they are naked.

A new kind of human being

I am not content to clothe my nakedness with borrowed or worn-out clothes. I would like to know what alternatives there could be to 'alternative living' and 'dropping out of the rat race'. Utopias and dystopias have led nowhere, so where else can one go if one can no longer believe promises about a better future and one is tired of prophets of gloom and despair? Ideologies which once radiated hope have lost their lustre. Too many people have been left at the wayside by progress, too many do not know how to find their place in it, too many are unsure where it is taking them.

Being left at the wayside by progress

New laws, new structures, new theories, new instant cures for troubled souls proliferate, and yet innumerable people still feel frustrated.

There is of course no shortage of certified and uncertified experts providing advice on how to manoeuvre through all rocks and shallows, real or imagined. A vast choice of remedies is available to help people, however lost or perplexed, to become happy, or rich, or successful or whatever. An overwhelming variety of business solutions, political programmes and psychological therapies already exist. So there is no need for yet another formula to enable you to get what you want. Besides, most people do not get what they want. Many people do not know what they want. Some people might want entirely different pleasures if only they knew about them.

Finding entirely different pleasures

When stripped of their certainties, humans have always rushed to find new certainties to replace those they have lost. When it is no longer possible to go on doing what one has always done, and when, for example, a steady career with promotion and a secure pension becomes an unrealistic dream, the yearning for security becomes a dominant preoccupation. But I do not find it exhilarating enough to devote myself to propping up and repairing ailing institutions, which keep on breaking down like an old car, when it is obvious that they will sooner or later collapse in crisis again.

The unrealistic dream of a steady career

I do not wish to spend my time on earth as a bewildered tourist surrounded by strangers, on holiday from nothingness, in the dark as to when the holiday will end, stuck in a queue waiting for another dollop of ice-cream happiness. I am conscious that I have tasted too few foods,

experienced too few forms of work, nibbled too hesitantly at the mountains of knowledge that surround me, loved too few people, understood
too few nations and places. I have only partly lived and my only qualification for writing this book is that I would like to know more clearly what a
full life could be. Am I fully alive, or do I merely survive, when I just repeat
the same gestures, the same breathing in and out, following an itinerary
that others have fixed for me, commuting to the same office every day?
Or do I need to be renewing myself, not just listening to others sing,
not just being entertained by them but composing a song myself that
gives inspiration to others, not just being amused, but being a muse
myself?

*What a full
life could be*

Instead of searching for a niche in which I would be safe, instead of
torturing myself with questions about what my true passions or talents
are, I shall aim to get a taste, even just a nibble, of what it is possible to
experience as a human being. What I cannot experience personally, I
wish to imagine by getting to know others who have gone where I have
not been. Rather than being immobilised by being unable to choose
between all the options paraded before me, and rather than ignoring what
seems too remote or unpalatable, my starting point is that everybody's
experience is of interest to me. A lost soul is one for whom the thoughts
of others are a mystery, and to whom no-one listens.

Lost souls

The great adventure of our time is to discover who inhabits the earth.
Though much has been said about the classes and categories into which
humans can be more or less uncomfortably fitted, the intimate thoughts
and muddled feelings of each of seven billion unique individuals remain

largely hidden. The minute discrepancies in the experience and attitudes of each one, which distinguish them from the statistical 'average person', are the essence and torment of each life, what attracts and repels, and what makes one who one is. But though people say they are interested above all in people, they do not know one another. All too often, they consider that their intentions or character are misinterpreted and that mistaken conclusions are drawn from superficial appearances.

A start on this adventure can be made by setting out to explore three neglected places, and first of all the part of life that is most hidden from view. I see private life as emerging from obscurity and challenging public life as the centre of attention. Instead of being obsessed with rules and regulations and the pecking order of organisations, I prefer to explore the consequences that follow from intimate personal relationships increasingly determining the quality of an existence. As families cease to be so dominated by property, as kinship feuds cease to be so bloody, and as the search for congenial partners becomes ever more absorbing and challenging, private life is becoming a source of a new kind of energy and of new priorities. As people have more contacts outside their neighbourhoods, relationships of many more kinds, both transient and long-term, are reshaping the landscape.

What is most hidden from view

The interaction between two individuals who develop emotional, intellectual or cultural links is producing a new motor of change. The duo or couple is as significant an influence as the solitary soul or the irrational crowd. Humans are not limited to a choice between individual self-reliance and collective struggle. One-to-one relationships now have a

A new motor of change

more central place in life than ever before, and have also been recognised as the source of many extraordinary achievements in varied fields of endeavour. It was prescient of the Chinese to write the word 'humaneness' (*ren*) with a picture of two human beings, recognising that its essence is in the relationship. Intimacy is a microscope which reveals a hitherto invisible universe that the culture of hierarchy and pretence conceals. Though many may be desperate to preserve their privacy, they also want to be recognised as being special. A new agenda is being opened up by the clash of these sensitivities, the desire to cover oneself up, and the occasional eagerness to undress and be seen as one really is.

A hitherto invisible universe

Secondly, I shall cross the most formidable barrier that separates humans, the barrier of death. I see people as living in the past as much as in the present, perpetuating ideas and habits from long ago, though often without being aware of it. To be poor is not only to be short of money, but also to possess only one's own memories. The originality of our time is that the world is today richer in memories than it has ever been, more than traditional societies ever lived by, but it is making little use of them. There is a huge inheritance of memories waiting to be shared out. Never have there been so many scholars, books, museums, archives and mementos resurrecting all the civilisations that ever existed. Never has so much of the past been alive. Television has even brought it, with all its turpitudes and illusions, into many homes. We can now know about everybody's ancestors, not just our own tribal ones. Moreover, though to be modern was supposed to mean living in the present and liberating oneself from ancient tyrannies by banishing and forgetting the past, old traditions

To be poor is to possess only one's own memories

have survived with a tenaciousness that was never expected. Adding other people's memories to one's own memories transforms one's ideas of what it is possible to do in a lifetime. A new vision of the past makes possible a new vision of the future. History is not a coffin with no escape. On the contrary, it is liberation, a bunch of keys that opens doors to places one never knew existed.

History is not a coffin with no escape

I see each individual as having a philosophy of history – though it is seldom given such a grand name – that explains for them why they are being swept along by events they cannot control: it may be economic forces or cycles of revolution and reaction, or a spiritual power, or the influence of exceptional people, or the blight of personal traumas. Most people are wrapped up in a patchwork of philosophies, inherited from different centuries, which each has put together in a slightly different pattern. The mind-set they adopt may change a little in response to the harsh knocks of existence, but fragments of old attitudes almost always survive beneath the surface. Nothing limits a person more than these inherited convictions about what is possible and what is not. But history need not be seen as a final judgement on what men and women and children can do. On the contrary, it is a series of unfinished experiments, of missed turnings, of inventions ignored, where trivial accidents often diverted events into directions which have been far from inevitable. Moreover, memories of one's childhood or of the achievements of one's ancestors are not enough to form comprehensive judgements about one's destiny. One can also acquire other memories.

Convictions about what is impossible

Thirdly, I look at humanity from a different perspective by moving my focus away from its traditional ambitions, victory in war or harmony in peace. Wars which kill and destroy have ceased to be as glamorous as they once were. Success, which everyone is expected to aim for, is ever more difficult to achieve in work and wealth, and the compensations of victories in sport are feeble consolations. Peace, alas, seems to be a chimera. Humans have never been able to achieve harmony for very long, either with their fellows, or with nature, or with the supernatural, even when they claimed to be obeying the sages who preach brotherly love. Consensus is becoming ever more elusive, for reasons that will become clear in later chapters. I am searching for a new attitude to disagreement, a new skill, new ways of putting disagreement to better use. Instead of focusing on what people or nations or groups have in common, I propose to confront the innumerable minute differences, often seemingly trivial, that keep them apart, and investigate how these can become fertile rather than sterile.

Of course, no person can know seven billion people, but that number should not be any more intimidating than the many more billions of neurons and molecules invisible to the naked eye that scientists confront, which are just as difficult to comprehend and whose secrets, as they emerge in dribbles, are transforming understanding of the world. To set out on a road that has no end, with no expectation of finding all the answers, has always been more eye-opening than travelling to a fixed destination, because it leaves freedom to stray into by-ways that may prove more rewarding than preordained goals. Humanity's great adventures were undertaken by a few determined people who disagreed with almost

A new attitude to disagreement

Travel with no fixed destination

everyone else. We shall see whether benefiting from their experience is more difficult than getting to the moon.

Humans are not born free. No one is born free of the fear of strangers and the unfamiliar. But history is a record not only of terror and submission but also of danger defied, inspired above all by curiosity. Curiosity is my compass, surprise is my nourishment, boredom is my bane. Curiosity is the best route I know out of the many kinds of fear that turn the light into night, dissolving problems into microscopic particles, each of which becomes an object of wonder rather than a threat. I cherish surprise because it mixes the possible with the impossible and occasionally finds that opposites need not be enemies. Boredom is the groan of the exhausted and the scream of the impatient, and the wailing noise that hope makes when it dies. I have written this book in an attempt to keep hope alive, but not false hope, and not the kind that is mocked by sceptics, cynics and comics. Is that possible if life is no more than a brief candle, a tale told by an idiot, signifying nothing?

Where can curiosity lead?

About one hundred billion lives have been brief candles, snuffed out, with few exceptions, into complete oblivion. That is the best guess as to how many humans there have been since they first appeared on earth. Of course, many departed convinced that they were starting a new existence in another world. Many now succeed in living much longer in this world, but they differ a great deal in how much of life they experience, and how much of life they illuminate. What can one do today not to be just a brief candle?

An idiot now has the chance to tell a tale that has not been heard before.

What does it mean to be an idiot?

People were called idiots, when the word was first invented, simply because they were regarded as not a having an indispensable place in society and were not habitual orators in the public assembly, meaning that they were private persons. Today, in that sense, most of us are idiots. People were also called idiots not because they were stupid, but because they were un-educated or ignorant. Today, there is so much knowledge too complicated to master that we have to admit to being idiots in this sense too. All who are isolated socially from those with different incomes and education, or culturally from tastes and languages that mean nothing to them, or profes-sionally because their skills are so specialised, have increasingly become strangers to one another: they may have the technology to communicate, but are far from fully appreciating or liking one another. So I have been trying to find out what kind of conversations could liberate us from the idiocy of our isolation.

What is a significant life?

A life becomes significant when it responds to a quandary from which an escape route has not yet been found. At the meeting of the 18th and 19th centuries, when the old monarchical order was crashing under the onslaught of industrial and political revolutions, our forebears invented a new way of looking at the world: the enlightenment and romanticism appeased bewilderment and re-ignited enthusiasm, at least for a time. But today, in response to technology's overturning of old habits and the discred-iting of once seemingly impregnable institutions, no comparable emotional or rational buffer has emerged to protect us from these shocks. That leaves

What can reignite enthusiasm?

us free to think about what adventures you or I could embark on today that we could not in the past. What new priorities can we give to our private lives? If we cannot become rich, what could be a substitute for prosperity? If religions disagree, what other outcomes are possible beyond strife or doubt? Where there is too little freedom, what is the alternative to rebellion? When there are not enough exciting jobs, what new ways of working could be invented? When romance is disappointing, how else can affections be cultivated? What wisdom can be salvaged from crumbling institutions? When so much is unpredictable, what can replace ambition?

I do not wish to pontificate about what you should do or believe. I prefer to know what you believe, what other people believe or have believed, how the world appears to others apart from myself, and what would happen if people got to know more about what went on in other people's heads. It makes no sense to decide what to do with one's life without knowing what others have done with theirs, and with what results. Persuading you to think as I do would limit the benefit I would gain from listening to you, and it would in any case be pointless, because ideas nearly always change when they move into another mind.

What goes on in other people's heads

I appreciate that the last thing many people want is an adventure into the unknown, that life contains stresses too hard to bear, and that withdrawal from the hurly-burly, or taming the mind into quietude, or cultivating contentment, seem the best kind of defence. The world is indeed often terrifying, disgusting and tragic, but it is also beautiful. I should like to know how exactly each person would make it a tiny bit less disgusting and a tiny bit more beautiful, or else declare such a task to be impossible. I never forget that a huge proportion of past efforts to find solutions that please everybody has produced undesired and occasionally

Turning disappoint-ment into an invitation

catastrophic results, and that turning disappointment into an invitation to search for a new direction is easier said than done. I know how futile so many attempts to diminish humanity's seemingly ineradicable cruelty have been, but I have felt constantly renewed by its ingenuity, its ability to get out of the mess it creates, and its unceasing discovery of unsuspected wonders and possibilities in both people and the natural world.

So instead of arguing about whether things are getting better or worse, which they doubtless are, I prefer to devote that time to finding a gift that will express my gratitude to the world for tolerating my presence in it; obviously it will have to be something it does not already possess. That is

Searching for a clue

my treasure hunt. Each of my chapters is a search for a clue.

[2]

What is a wasted life?

WHAT CAN A PERSON AIM TO DO today, beyond passing examinations, and establishing a career, and finding a perfect partner, and having a loving family, and enjoying absorbing hobbies? Are there other ambitions that can lead in new directions and compensate for the disappointments that tarnish even the best laid plans?

Mao Ch'i Ling, a one-time Chinese celebrity, climbed the ladder of success to become a respected public official, and also won esteem as a playwright, poet, painter and musician. Despite his many accomplishments, he felt he had wasted his life. His exciting existence included ten years devoted to what he believed was a worthy cause, armed resistance to a foreign invasion. Many of his friends and relatives died in that war, while he assumed a whole variety of disguises to escape arrest and execution, moving endlessly between the most bizarre hiding places. He ended up exhausted by his wanderings, desperate for rest. So he toadied to the government he did not respect, and despised himself for doing so. He survived into old age, but that did not seem to him to be a sufficiently laudable achievement. He could not suppress the feeling that 'I have not established myself as a virtuous man . . . I failed to make any real contribution . . . My empty words served no purpose . . . My heart is anguished.'

Failing to make any contribution

He told his descendants to destroy all his poetry and save only one-tenth of the numerous books he had written. His pitiless obituary, which he wrote himself, ended with these words: 'His life was lived in vain.'

If Mao Ch'i Ling (1627–1716) were alive today, would he reach the same pessimistic conclusion, despite being supported by all the advances of medicine and technology, the service society, the entertainment industry and the welfare state? Would therapists and counsellors have purged

Melancholy   him of his melancholy? Would insurance salesmen have convinced him that his troubles were trivial compared to the disasters he had so far avoided, and from which they could protect him? Would his computer have opened his mind to international opportunities, and would spam

Libido   emails have encouraged him to try to restore his libido? Would he have cleared his conscience by writing a cheque to alleviate the suffering of distant lands too uncomfortable to visit? Would he have rejoiced at being able to cast a vote every four years so that professional politicians could make the world a better place, which philosophers like him had so signally failed to do? Or would he have been satisfied with attaining a different kind of immortality, as a statistic in the database of a marketing company, commemorating every purchase he had made?

Modernity   It may be that, despite all the achievements of modernity, there are more people than ever before feeling they have wasted their life. However, they have been learning to talk about their deepest concerns, instead of saying what those in power demanded that they should say. Mao Ch'i Ling's self-portrait obituary was as courageous an act as the Charge of the Light Brigade or any other military assault that could only end in death. It was, for him, the suicide of his reputation. With some remarkable exceptions, most biographies written before him were hagiography, raising humans to the status of heroes and saints, presenting them as specimens of virtue and models to be imitated, while ignoring their human defects. Or else they were turgid recitals of career advancement, presenting life as a string of events embellished with anecdotes. By contrast, Mao Ch'i Ling was one of a small number of writers who appeared almost simultaneously in China and Europe around the sixteenth and seventeenth centuries, producing a different kind of autobiography, searching their idiosyncrasies for meaning, and reflecting on their weaknesses with merciless frankness, instead of holding themselves up as holy models. *A different kind of autobiography* They were explorers of the significance and difficulties of individuality. They made it possible to get a glimpse of what individuals were thinking privately, what went on in their heads when they were not playing the role society expected. They offered only a glimpse of a part of the truth, and it is never certain what the whole truth might be. But to discover what ambitions are worth cultivating, it is useful to hear the evidence of those who have had ambitions and have tried to describe them.

It is not easy to find records of the deep feelings of ordinary people, and of thoughts too dangerous or painful to reveal. Autobiographies are a rare cactus that flowers spasmodically in the desert of pretence, appearing briefly and then disappearing, in the same way that epochs of promiscuity and puritanism come and go. Autobiography remained a very minor form of literature so long as tribes, clans and armies commanded all loyalties, while most individuals were regarded as insignificant elements in them. *A cactus in the desert of pretence*

It took a long time for the singular life to be seen as an independent force, just as it took centuries for the atom to emerge as a prime source of energy.

Fashions in honesty

Soon after Mao Ch'i Ling's death, China's political climate changed and autobiographies almost stopped being written for two centuries, not reviving until the student uprising of 4 May, 1919, one of the most important revolutions in Chinese history, foreshadowing the Western world's May Days of 1968. Suddenly, autobiographies became a widespread passion. A new form of writing was introduced based on the way the language was spoken, abandoning classical conventions, so it became possible to say things that had not been said before, and to be more easily understood. The tyranny of ancient forms of expression was suddenly broken by the manifesto of Hu Shi (1891–1962), the intellectual leader of China's renaissance. Speak what you want to say, speak your own thoughts, do not imitate the ancients, eliminate cliché, reject melancholy, express your immediate emotions. Hu Shi urged his contemporaries to write autobiographies, and he set a personal example. In the 1920s and 1930s almost all Chinese writers, famous or not, wrote some form of autobiography.

One woman, significantly, took the lead. Chen Hengzhe (1890–1976), who had studied at Vassar and Chicago and was the first woman professor at Beijing University, published an autobiographical short story in the new vernacular, in the first person, presenting students talking to one another freely, without revealing what class, place or family they came from, liberating them from the tradition of being categorised as daughters, mothers or wives. The only way her characters could be identified

Categorised as daughters, mothers or wives

was by what they said. Her aim was 'to capture the human sentiments that arise in the course of human interactions'. She went far beyond anything attempted in the past. For long she resisted the pressure to marry, and when she finally did at thirty, publicly questioned whether it was a good idea. Writing about oneself became an instrument of rebellion. But this only lasted two decades, until the government, worried that people were thinking for themselves, once again imposed silence.

Autobiography as an instrument of rebellion

Exceptional conditions were needed to allow people to speak openly and imagine a different kind of life for themselves. That had already happened briefly in tenth-century Japan, when for a time aristocratic women enjoyed economic independence, living separately from their husbands in their own homes, able to use their ample leisure to reflect on the inadequacies of men. In A.D. 905 Japanese women began writing the language they spoke instead of Chinese – the official language – and they put what they felt into diaries and autobiographies. One of the most remarkable of these women, known only as Michisuna's Mother, believed, as Mao Ch'i Ling was to believe after her, that she had lived 'a vain existence', doing nothing significant, just 'living, lying down, getting up, dawn to dusk'. She decided it might be worth describing what it is like to be 'a nobody . . . a woman married to a highly placed man'. She did so with brilliant literary and poetic skill, deliberately producing a dazzling alternative to fictional romances, which she despised as 'fantasy'. Her book was about sorrow and suffering, the equivalent of the blues. Of her husband she wrote: 'Our hearts did not melt towards one another, so we drew further apart.' Her husband, on one of his ever-rarer visits – because

Being a nobody

he had, according to accepted custom, other wives and concubines –

'Have I done anything wrong?'

exclaimed: 'Have I done anything wrong?' She wrote: 'I was so upset I could not say anything at all.' Nor could she do anything but write about it. But she was mistaken to think of herself as a nobody; her book showed she was not a nobody. And yet it took another ten centuries for the relationships between men and women to be reshaped, and the reshaping continues.

Sometimes investigators of their own inner feelings were blinded not by modesty but by vanity. During the middle ages the personal voice made itself heard mainly in the Middle East, where over a thousand Arabic autobiographies were written (as has only recently been discovered). A sentence in the Quran was reinterpreted to encourage people to write them. 'And as for the bounty of your Lord, speak' was taken to mean that it is desirable to thank God, even for painful misadventures which always contain a lesson. Apologies, theories, ideals, emotional and intellectual conflicts and memories poured out in extraordinary variety, contrasting strongly with the lives of saints that nourished European tastes. One author stands out for being totally obsessed with himself and paying the

The penalty for arrogance

penalty of arrogance. The Egyptian Jalal al-Din al-Suyuti (1445–1505) boldly asserted his right to judge his own life, publicly challenging the opinions of all authority, even his father's. 'I have no equal, no-one else living has mastered the number of disciplines which I have.' He published some 600 books and articles on every possible subject (except mathematics, which he dismissed as 'disagreeable to his nature'). His learning, he believed, qualified him to exercise *ijtihad*, meaning the right to express an independent opinion, to personally clarify the teachings of religion, and he demanded recognition as a *mujaddid,* a Renewer of the Faith. People flocked to him seeking fatwas to decide upon disputed matters of religious law, but he infuriated his colleagues by condemning them as ignorant and stupid when they disagreed with him. Chapter 17 of his autobiography was entitled: 'How God blessed me by setting enemies against me and tested me with the false accusations of an ignoramus' (meaning a rival scholar). In the end, his enemies got so cross they threw him fully clothed into a pond, nearly killing him. So he retired and wrote his memoirs, unable to see himself as others saw him, but bequeathing a dramatic black-and-white Dürer-like picture of academic bitterness and megalomania, protesting, even then, at falling educational standards. *Academic megalo- mania* Egypt had to wait till the twentieth century for autobiography to be revived and a new model to be set by the blind novelist, historian and minister of education Taha Hussayn (1889–1973), whose masterpiece, *An Egyptian Childhood,* not only became a landmark in literature and a compulsory text in all schools, but encouraged a flood of personal reflections by both women and men.

Autobiographies can of course be written to wipe out painful mem- ories. Banarasidas, a seventeenth-century Indian playboy, the son of an *What is left unsaid* Agra merchant, gave the outward impression that he was speaking frankly. He said he knew he was wasting his life, and he was not worried by that: 'I hovered between earth and heaven befouling the air like a camel's fart.' He describes his failings without contrition, saying of himself: 'He cannot desist from falsehood . . . and he avidly studies indecent literature.' Of his 'meagre qualities . . . none are excellent or free from blemish'. Deep emotion wells up in him, however, when he remembers that all his nine

The loss of children

children have died, and 'the parents, like trees at leaf-fall, remain as stumps.' That little phrase reveals that his bravado concealed despair. Without his children, he truly felt that he was a nobody.

In modern times, the novel has become the main outlet for personal but indirect revelation of desire and disappointment. But why is it said that everybody has a novel rather than an autobiography in them? Margaret Cavendish (1623–1673) was perhaps the first to show how much is gained by telling both her life story and the story of a different existence she would like to have lived. 'Why hath this lady writ her life?' she asks. Because 'I am as ambitious as any of my sex was or can be, which makes that though I cannot be Henry the Fifth or Charles the Second, yet I endeavour to be Margaret the First, and though I have neither power nor time nor occasion to conquer the world as Alexander the Great and Caesar did, yet rather than not to be the Mistress of One, since Fortune and the fates would give me none, I have made a world of my own for which nobody I hope will blame me, since it is in everyone's power.' So she supplemented her autobiography by inventing an imaginary life, *The Description of the New World, called the Blazing World*, a sort of utopia where she can do anything she pleases. And to that she added *Observations upon Experimental Philosophy*, which gave her a scientific reputation and got her invited to the Royal Society. At the same time, she says

The fear of oblivion

she is really quite 'bashful'. She fears oblivion. She says she writes for pleasure, but she is desperate to become famous. She does not want to live in vain. What would Mao Ch'i Ling think about living in vain if he could listen to all these many brave people worrying about living in vain?

In South Africa during apartheid, Dugmore Boetie (1926–1966) showed how autobiography could provide a sort of answer to despair. He became almost a celebrity when he described how he had murdered his mother, lost a leg during his military service and been jailed seventeen times for crimes of every kind that he joyfully recounted. He said he was proud to be a confidence trickster who 'gets his stimulants from the vitamins of an empty stomach. Why stand in judgement on yourself?' But it turned out that his adventures were fantasies. He claimed he had no family, but numerous relatives came to see him in hospital when he was dying of lung cancer. They revealed that he had lost his leg from an infection at the age of eight, that he had never been in the army and only briefly in prison. His autobiography, he finally admitted, expressed his 'wrath against a police-infested' country. It served to blot out his suffering by replacing it with delight in his own ingenuity: his imaginary escapades were as effective a method as any to enable penniless people like himself to survive. Only his poverty was real. At the end he said, 'lying to yourself is the biggest sin of all.' Perhaps it is the most widespread sin too.

An answer to despair

Lying to yourself the most widespread sin

Nothing has been more difficult than judging one's own life. How differently would Mao Ch'i Ling have looked on his life if he had known there were people in other countries who shared his ideas? He lived at a time when pedantry was an admired sign of distinction in China, and he hated that. He felt powerless against it. He despised the bureaucrats who memorised the classics and showed off their knowledge writing

Inspiration from foreigners

'eight-legged essays'. He needed encouragement, and it was available but he could not obtain it, as he might today. Inspiration from foreigners has repeatedly sustained dissenters who would otherwise have been led to despair by their isolation. Mao Ch'i Ling would have been heartened if he had been able to read what, five years before his death, was being said in a popular London magazine, the *Spectator*, which was shooting at the same target as he was. The pedant, wrote its editor Addison (1672–1719), was a person who is able to talk of nothing else but the books he has read, and 'does not know to think out of his profession and particular way of life'. Mao Ch'i Ling may even have been tempted to revise his opinion of himself if he had been able to converse with the optimistic German mathematician, philosopher and diplomat Gottfried Leibniz (1646–1716),

Being different abroad

passionately interested in China, who insisted that Europe had a great deal to learn from Confucian civilisation. A life may seem futile in one's own country, but appear in a quite different light abroad.

Mao Ch'i Ling was one of those who, disenchanted with the chaos and corruption of government, was searching for ways of introducing more imagination and passion into daily existence, advancing beyond self-serving ambition, empty rituals and sterile controversies. But he did not know that England was waging a Civil War and questioning almost every-

Bringing adventurous minds together

thing in politics and religion at about the same time as China's Society for Renewal (Fu-she) was bringing together adventurous minds to invent new priorities. Nor could he sense that the European Enlightenment would soon be questioning age-old dogmas, and opening up new scientific perspectives, at the same time as China's movement for Evidential Learning would be demanding more rigorous historical evidence in all branches of knowledge, replacing metaphysical speculation by the pursuit of novel solutions to ethical, social and practical issues. Above all, he could not imagine that his brave reflections on his experiences, which were more varied than most people's, might be valued by succeeding generations, who would disagree that he had lived in vain.

What succeeding generations value

A wasted life talks only to itself and ruminates only on its own doubts. But there is no longer any need to remain trapped in one's own time and space. Placing different lives side by side transforms one's understanding of them. I want more than to hear people telling their own story, taking the traditional path of confession on which autobiography, oral history and various forms of therapy continue to tread. I am more interested by how people affect each other by what they say, and also how they resist being changed by what they hear. The more profound the conversations between them, the more likely they are to reach destinations they believed to be beyond them. For the first time in history, they can hear each other speak from a great distance, which means they can find allies where they once imagined there were only strangers, and when that happens, the temptation to see themselves as victims is no longer so overwhelming. If relationships between different lives generate the surprises out of which the future is made, the gloomy prophecy that 'clinical depression' will be the great epidemic of the coming century may not be fulfilled.

Strangers, allies and victims

'Read no history, only biography, for that is life without theory.' So said Disraeli (1804–1881), a novelist as well as a prime minister, but he must have known how much fiction there is in biography as well as in history, deliberately or unwittingly. Biography is meaningless without history, which is a painting of the landscape that surrounds every life, and biography is worthless without autobiography, which is the mirror that reveals what a person imagines himself or herself to be. Critics point out what is wrong and flatterers what is fashionable, but every individual remains to some extent an enigma. Innumerable autobiographies are never revealed or written down, and exist only in the imagination; others are so simplified that they are misleading. A popular magazine specialising in the cult of minor celebrities, for example, advises its readers that they are 'spiritual' because they 'look into their inner self', 'authentic' because 'they do not worry about what other people think or say about them', 'sensual' because they know what 'makes them hot and go for it', and 'sensational' because they pay themselves compliments and 'make a declaration of love to themselves'. This is the doctrine that has been *The solitary* evolved for the solitary self, who is justified in not needing any input from *self* anyone or anything else, and can remain unchanged for ever.

However, it is also possible to see every life as an experiment, which has questions to ask and something interesting to say to those who have not yet shut down their sense of wonder at the variety and unpredictability of *Every life* human waywardness. In this perspective, a life is wasted if what it discov-*as an* ers is never pondered over, never shared, and remains ignorant of how it *experiment* appears in contrast to the lives of others, in different places and different centuries. This book is my way of reflecting on the gaps in my life and on what else I could be doing. If as a result anyone is stimulated to reflect on their experience in ways that lead to thoughts that would not otherwise have been born, then my own life may not be totally wasted. A large part of the art of being a couple revolves around discovering what to give to others and cultivating the sensitivities that enable one to receive from others.

How can people lose their illusions about themselves?

WHEN PAINTING A PORTRAIT, Lucian Freud (1922–2011) often used to shade his eyes and look at his sitter's face and body a few yards away, as though he was a sailor searching for a distant land or an explorer confronted by an impenetrable forest. Every detail held his attention, every texture, every fragment of clothing was special; nothing was seen as an example of something more general or ideal. Even when painting an egg, he found that each egg was different. A sitter was a mystery, a puzzle to be solved. He made no plans in advance as to how his painting would take shape. 'The point of painting a picture is that you don't know what will happen.' The aim was certainly not to produce a resemblance. Instead, he wanted to create a figure that was 'disturbing, by which I mean alive'.

Seeing oneself in others

To be 'alive', a portrait had to 'involve' those who looked at it, making them imagine that there was something of themselves in the painting. He himself was less concerned with looking at his models than with 'being them'. Likewise, he appreciated a novel when it made him 'almost feel as if I had written it myself'. Did he mean that making a portrait of other people is the way to discover oneself, or to become a different person?

Though he conceded that shocking the public might sometimes be necessary to get its attention, 'I always thought truth-telling was more *The* exciting.' He wanted above all to know the truth, 'to see things as they *excitement of truth-telling* really are'. But what truth was that? He said of his wife Caroline, whom he famously painted several times, 'I never knew Caroline that well.' How then does one get to know another person well, or indeed to know oneself well? 'Being in love', he said, 'is complete, absolute concern, where every-thing about the other person interests, worries or pleases you.' But how mistaken can one be about the person with whom one is in love?

Lucian Freud often took a year or even longer to finish a painting, watching his sitters with 'piercing eyes', charming and entertaining them with wide-ranging talk, sometimes turning them into lovers, and father-ing fourteen children in the process. He observed their every gesture, even when they were hungry, tired or drunk, searching for the 'glow'. The woman fifty years his junior who was the subject of his 'Naked Portrait' remembered that sitting for him went on for seven days a week, night and day, for a whole year; they became lovers, but when the sittings ended, so did the affair. Though Lucian Freud often began a conversation by saying *Two Freuds* 'Tell me about your childhood', and though genitals feature so often in his pictures, his purpose and method were different from that of his grandfather Sigmund, the inventor of psychoanalysis. Not only did he tell his sitters a great deal about himself, and try to include a joke in every painting, but he shunned making judgements, let alone finding cures, and once he had finished a painting, he was not interested in thinking any more about it. 'My work is purely autobiographical. It is about myself and my surroundings. It is an attempt at a record.' It was, however, about himself only insofar as it was about what he chose to observe and notice. 'I don't want the picture to come from me. I want it to come from them.' There was no message he wished to convey, no symbolism or rhetoric. 'I like it if people say very contradictory things about my work.'

A new kind of portrait This is one of the crossroads, not pointing in any clear direction, at which the art of portraiture arrived in the twenty-first century. Whenever people develop new aspirations, they need a new kind of portrait. In the Middle Ages, when they were more concerned with a person's ancestors and property than individual talent, it was enough to have a coat of arms rather than the likeness of a face. The flattering portrait, making one look as rich and beautiful as possible, was invented to satisfy the search for higher status and the hunger for admiration. A longing for immortality produces the impassive boardroom portraits which are like tombstones made to be hung on a wall. When every individual is perceived as a psychological enigma, the artist becomes an interpreter of the mystery, and is glorified even more than the subject. The instant photographic snapshot coincides with the belief that everyone can be interesting, but also that everything is relative and disposable.

The rejection of role-playing Today, the rejection of role-playing and deception in relationships, the discrediting of political and business heroes who lie, the condemnation of racism and discrimination, mean that appearances count for much less than they used to. A portrait has to say much more when transparency and honesty become supreme values, and when there is a growing awareness that humans are infinitely complicated, that they are not entirely, or even remotely, what they appear to be.

However, we are all obliged to have a portrait of ourselves in a passport or identity card in which our government describes what it thinks is important about us. Why is it not possible for us to create our own passports, saying what we want others to understand or appreciate about us? Why may we not add new pages and pictures as we meet more people who enrich or modify our view of our place in the world? Why cannot we cut pages out when our hopes die? Of course we may mislead or lie, or be misunderstood. But why cannot our self-portrait passport be accepted as our own original work of art, which says something about our illusions and our dreams and what is not normally obvious? Why cannot we choose the shape of our passport for ourselves, and encase or frame or bind it in whatever idea of beauty we have? Why cannot we draw inspiration from the painter Wan Shou-ch'i (1603–1652), who was also a furniture designer, porcelain manufacturer, carpenter, gardener, temple renovator, poet and musician, and who left thirty-four self-portraits in different costumes to record his many and varied personalities?

Creating one's own passport

Thirty-four self-portraits

It is possible to conceive a passport that would be more useful than a curriculum vitae, which is a misleading boast, excluding any hopes or opinions which might make one unemployable. A passport could be more informative than a business card, which is an advertisement of status, and proof that one is the property of an organisation more worthy of respect than oneself. The compulsory national passport, a relic of monarchical despotism, was abolished as an insult to freedom by the French Revolution, and by many countries subsequently, so that in the nineteenth century people prided themselves on not having a certificate from a bureaucrat judged a better proof of who one was than one's own word. Even Napoleon III declared that the passport never stops the criminal but merely obstructs the free passage of the innocent. But paranoia about spies in the First World War resurrected passports; and they gradually resumed their role as instruments of control rather than of enlightenment.

A passport to the imagination

This book is my own kind of passport, which allows you to enter my imagination. I need your visit, because my thoughts are nourished by those who cross my path, for otherwise I would be a stagnant swamp of prejudices. My passport is the product of conversations which stimulate my preoccupations and sympathies, and make me aware of other forms of existence. I offer you my passport because I should like to see yours. The world is what is revealed when we each say what we see, when we all shine our faint torches on it.

But why reveal who you really are? The world is filled with polite, shy, inscrutable, unintelligible, tight-lipped, superficial, dishonest and also honest people who are increasingly difficult to decipher, and who for one reason or another do not make public what goes on inside them. Many do not reveal their thoughts or feelings because they are not sure what they think or feel. Many would be braver in their speech if they were more certain of a sympathetic hearing. Many are schooled to believe that they need to be hypocrites. The hidden thoughts in other people's heads are the great darkness that surrounds us.

The great darkness that surrounds us

According to the teaching of the European Enlightenment, superstition and prejudice are the main obstacles to discovering what the world is really like, and education and legislation can eliminate them. But it is still very difficult to understand the motivations and implications of what others say and feel. The many darknesses that remain still await a second and more ambitious Enlightenment.

A more ambitious Enlighten-ment

There are thoughts that are still-born because the mind is not sufficiently stimulated to bring them fully into being. The pressures of ordinary life are so preoccupying that the more fundamental problems of the art of living are avoided in normal conversation. What is most important is often least discussed. The struggle against censorship is never won, but self-censorship is even more insidious. From the beginning of time, people have wittingly or unwittingly been using contraceptives against thought.

Contracep-tives against thought

If thoughts are left to themselves, they remain lonely and limp. They become meaningful to others only when they are fertilised by interaction. Throughout history the focus has been on instilling conventional ideas into supposedly empty heads, failing to realise that making ideas is like making love. Ideas cannot just be fed into people. Every individual has sensitivities and memories that shape what they absorb. And until ideas have met many different kinds of ideas, they cannot know their own value. The thoughts that the world hides in its head are only very superficially glimpsed in votes and polls. Only a tiny minority have even a portion of their ideas published in the media or in books. Confession in religion and psychiatry is strictly private. The study of the habits and mentalities of nations, classes and groups does not necessarily reveal what goes on in the mind of wayward individuals. Could there be some other way to bring thoughts out of hiding?

Private thoughts are among humanity's most important assets, containing the essence of its experiences. A large portion of them are not shared with others, for fear of offence or the damage they might cause, or in the name of privacy, or from an inability to make a personal experience relevant to others. What is recorded in history is only the tip of an iceberg. Too many people never really get to know their own parents, or never pass on their intimate thoughts to their children, and regret it. Too many governments set an example of secretiveness, claiming that chaos would follow if their motives or their incompetence were revealed. All the learned studies of lying are adamant that social relations would collapse if people stopped lying. Business and politics have been relying increasingly on half-truths, employing more and more experts to conceal as much as to reveal. Even sport has been contaminated. Even scientific research is plagued by assertions that are not evidence-based. Intimate relations in private life collapse when pretence replaces trust. Secrecy is the illegitimate child of fear. Who will have the courage to insist that we do not have to live in a world held together by lies?

Individuals have recently been crawling hesitatingly out of the burrows they call privacy, painting a portrait of themselves in words or music of many kinds, proclaiming on the internet that they exist and want to know what other existences there are in the vast unknown space around them. On the web's social networks they have mainly specialised in brief and superficial exchanges with hundreds of 'friends' they have never met. Of the over a hundred million bloggers who are effectively writing non-stop autobiographies of sorts, half say they feel misunderstood outside their own small community. Their monologues, like those of autobiographers,

A world held together by lies

Friends one has never met

cannot be the last word in self-expression. Self-expression cannot be the last child that freedom will bear. Introspection cannot be the only path to self-knowledge.

The last child of freedom

I think in response to the thoughts of others. Of the millions of thoughts that enter my mind, a few impregnate it and give birth to new thoughts. Ideas are never sure who exactly their parents are, since they are ceaselessly matchmaking, flirting and making love in search of congenial partners. I cherish the moments when other people's thoughts do not arrive simply asking for a quiet place to sit in my memory, but seem to press a button in my head that switches on the light, illuminating my beliefs on that particular subject, clarifying them by juxtaposing a contrasting view and stimulating a modification I had not previously imagined. I like them above all to forge a link to people or ideas that previously seemed irrelevant.

The birth of ideas

I give no time to the solitary pursuit of that age-old riddle, 'Who am I?' I find other people much more interesting than the repetitive or self-deceiving reflections I can have by scraping the barrel of my own memories, or the labels I stick on myself in my efforts to establish my so-called identity. 'If I knew myself, I would run away,' said Goethe. I feel even more strongly, I cannot know myself. Though self-knowledge has from the beginning of time been paraded as the indispensable tool for a successful life, it remains as elusive as ever. The self-portraits from which I have quoted in the previous chapter are examples of how blurred is the vision that people have of themselves when they rely on introspection. There must be many more ways of talking or writing about oneself still to be

Reinventing
self-portrait-
ure
tried, or of painting, sculpting, filming oneself, which are not narcissistic, self-indulgent, nostalgic or complaining. The art of portraiture and self-portraiture is waiting to be reinvented.

Instead of 'Who am I?' the question I prefer is 'Who are you?' That is how a conversation starts and how a self-portrait is born. Few people will or can just sit down and write an autobiography which they feel does them justice, and is not mere reminiscence and anecdote or an exercise in egoism. Many more enjoy a conversation, and in a conversation they sometimes find themselves trying to explain who they are, which is in effect the beginning of a rough sketch for a self-portrait.

I am interested in people who feel starved of the kind of conversation that is not just superficial chat, or gossip, or argument, or professional shop talk. I have no desire to revive the supposedly lost art of conversation, because so much of what passed for conversation in previous centuries was ruled by etiquette, where you said what you were expected to say, flattering the powerful and trying to show your superiority over those you despised. I do however want to discover how other people see the world and what is most important to them, as well as what is

When the
world
becomes a
different
place
important to myself. When two people converse with mutual respect and listen with a real interest in understanding another point of view, when they try to put themselves in the place of another, and to get inside their skin, the world becomes a different place, even if it is only by a minute amount. They lift the mask behind which almost every person hides, even if only partially, which is more effective in establishing equality between two people who have the courage to be open with each other

than any law can be. It is possible to confess one's sins to priests, but they will not confess their sins in return. One can pour out one's anxieties to psychiatrists, but they will not ask one for opinions about their own anxieties.

New kinds of conversation have in the past opened up new phases in human relations, as when parliaments were invented. When the word *parlement* was originally used, it meant conversation between two (and occasionally four) individuals meeting for a discussion, to parley. It took a long time for larger numbers to learn how to converse. So long as hierarchical status dominated all activities, people spoke in order of precedence. So long as violence was the usual method for settling disputes, discussions often ended in fights, as they still did in 1992, when some members of the Russian Duma started punching each other. Only gradually were rules introduced to dissuade people from all talking at the same time, cursing, cat-calling, breaking out into song or challenging opponents to a duel. The Protestant Reformation made a big difference because it regularly brought people from different social classes together. The American Revolution also reshaped conversation. Tocqueville in the 1840s wrote that 'to discuss [was the] biggest concern and . . . the only pleasure an American knows,' and that American women loved attending public meetings 'as a recreation from their household labours . . . Debating clubs are, to a certain extent, a substitute for theatrical entertainments. An American cannot converse, but he can discuss, and his talk falls into a dissertation. He speaks to you as if he were addressing a public meeting.' As literary, scientific, political and other associations were established in

New kinds of conversation

America reshapes conversation

many countries, they developed their own styles; battling variously with

aggressive, long-winded, arrogant, waffling and bee-in-bonnet orators. Then the 'meeting expert' appeared, skilled in controlling and reducing disagreement to innocuous compromise. But meetings can now occupy half of a business executive's time, often with little benefit, leaving participants wondering what is really going on in each other's heads and what sort of characters are concealed behind the public performance.

Could a new kind of conversation open up a new phase in human relations? That may sound too ambitious. But a series of experiments I have conducted, involving over two thousand people in a dozen different countries, have demonstrated that when conversations are carefully prepared and structured, the results are surprising. Guests are randomly seated in pairs so that they each face a stranger or someone they barely know, often drawn from a completely different background. Each is given a

Menu of Conversation, which looks like a restaurant menu, divided into Starters, Fish, Grills, Salads, etc., but instead of dishes, it lists about two dozen topics for discussion, in the form of questions. For example, 'What are the limits of your compassion?', or 'How have your priorities changed over the years?', or 'What moral, intellectual, aesthetic and social effects does the work you do have on others and on yourself?' The participants are invited to exchange their experiences, to reflect on how these could be of value to other people, to compare them with attitudes to the same problems in other civilisations, and to search for practical applications that might emerge from their conclusions. The range of topics discussed is widened with other Menus, sometimes composed at the request of specific organisations or occupations. The rules of the game ensure that the conversation does not lapse into a monologue by either party or into a regurgitation of pet obsessions.

The results, despite the big variations in the kind of people who participated, have been consistently similar. The guests welcome having questions that raise issues they habitually leave half-answered at the back of their minds, they remark that they particularly appreciate the questions being difficult and demanding a lot of thought, which gives the conversation unusual solidity, and they value having a structure, which prevents them from being distracted into aimless chat. They wonder why there are so few opportunities to talk honestly to one person for two hours or more without interruption. 'I'm amazed at the frankness with which people were saying things to each other within minutes,' said the CEO of a confederation of employers. A refugee living in a hostel for the homeless said, 'This is the first real conversation I have had in the five years of my exile.' 'While I learned much about my colleague, I learned even more about myself. She helped me reveal more about myself that can prove helpful for me,' said a man working for a mobile phone company. 'I thought things I haven't thought before and maybe realised things I didn't know,' said a science researcher. 'I do not remember when was the last time I had this kind of conversation with anyone,' said a social worker. A trade union leader paired with someone half his age said, 'I enjoyed meeting, talking and listening to my conversational partner and she has restored my faith in younger people.' 'I found it thought-provoking and inspiring,' said a chief superintendent of police. 'I sat next to a guy who is a work colleague.

What people say the morning after

I've known him for twenty years on and off but I found out more tonight from speaking to him than I did in twenty years of working near him and passing him by.' 'We talked about things we would never discuss with work mates, and rank did not play any part,' said a local government clerk. 'Fascinating and enjoyable; hidden depths uncovered,' wrote a doctor in charge of a national health system. 'I've lived in six countries and work in English, French and Chinese,' said a lawyer, 'and feel keenly the appropriateness of this project.' 'It opened up areas of dialogue that people in the work environment would be reluctant to open up,' said an accountant.

Surprisingly few, very few indeed, avoided the difficult questions to slip into gossiping about nothing in particular, or else lost their concentration and interest in their partner. The method has also been used by corporate bosses to improve collaboration in their organisations, and by heads of government ministries so that they could get to know their colleagues better. On the 22nd of August, an annual Feast of Strangers is held in public parks where tourists and natives can converse with the aid of the Menu to discover one another, the opposite of a carnival, with no need to pretend.

The Feast of Strangers

A hunger for more profound conversation can be a gnawing misery in all walks of life, in love, in the family, at work and in communities, but so far humans seem to have struggled largely in vain for both the right and the ability to speak freely. None of the declarations of human rights has proclaimed the right to be listened to. Even the First Amendment of the U.S. Constitution only protects the citizen from limitations on free speech imposed by the state; nothing protects against restrictions by employers and nothing obliges the free media to publish what it does not want to hear. The first duty of love is to listen, said the theologian Tillich, but how many people does each person love and how many lovers listen? How many people have mastered the art of talking about themselves without breaching modesty or honesty, and without being boring or misunderstood? If everyone weighed their words before speaking, and wrote only what they were sure they wanted to say, there would be long silences, and most would write nothing at all. But if a conversation is recorded and made the basis of a draft written self-portrait, it can be corrected and added to and gradually shaped into a coherent picture of what one wants others to understand about one.

What one wants others to understand

Enormous courage is needed for ordinary people to reject the tyranny of despots, and just as much courage is needed to escape from the worry that one might reveal oneself, by what one says, as being inadequate or despicable. If, ever since my youth, I had made a habit of having a conversation with one different stranger every week, a ritual like taking my clothes to the laundry, cleaning my mind of prejudices, I might eventually have been introduced to 15,000 individual visions of the world. That would be a small inroad into the seven billion people I would ideally need to know to feel that my visit to the planet earth has not been superficial. But if people made self-portraits, I could read and see and be puzzled by many more. A gallery of self-portraits is slowly being formed not as a collection of the gems of high art, but to give all human beings a place where they can have a conversation and then make and display a self-portrait combining any medium, film, photography, sculpture, painting,

A gallery of self-portraits

music and text, which says not simply 'This is who I am', nor 'I am not what I appear to be', but also 'This is what I can contribute, this is what I have not yet done'. Parents are often mysteries to their children and vice versa. A student who showed his self-portrait to his father found that it led to the first real conversation they had ever had. I wish my parents had left me self-portraits; there is so much more I wish I knew about them.

What I have not yet done

Diderot complained when an oil portrait was painted of him: 'I warn you it is not I. I had in one day a hundred different appearances, as determined by what was affecting me. I was serious, sad, pensive, tender, violent, passionate, enraptured. But I was never as you see me here.' In each of the chapters of this book, you see me from a different angle, confronted by a different puzzle and by the concerns of different individuals. Lucian Freud's gaze awoke sensitivities and sharpened ideas of which I may otherwise not have been aware. The distinction between a portrait and a self-portrait is misleading. There needs to be another word in between them.

A conversation and a portrait are not magic solutions for the enmities that regularly ruin the best-laid plans. I am not seeking solutions, only paths to explore.

[4]

What alternatives are there to being a rebel?

O NLY HUMAN BABIES CRY when they first see the world. Do they instantly realise that though they belong to a species that has defeated all others, subjugating nature to its whims, they do not like what they see? Some may spend their life protesting and rebelling, while others will eventually shut up and tell pollsters that they are quite or very happy with their lot, but what other options are there for crying babies, for bewildered adolescents, for frustrated adults, and the countless other categories who have reasons for rebelling?

A century ago, the cinema was heralded as the great technological innovation destined to transform the mind-sets of the masses by opening their eyes to worlds they had never seen. One of Russia's most gifted film directors, Sergei Eisenstein (1898 1948), believed he could use the cinema – which he hailed as a 'new Muse' – to 'shock the audience' and convert the 'ignorant peasants' so that they would abandon centuries of custom for a socialist utopia. Interpreting art as a revolutionary act, and putting his faith in the 'Army of Art', he developed brilliant techniques for producing 'collisions' between images, and extraordinary visual metaphors, at once poetic and disturbing, to stimulate new ideas. However, for all his inventiveness, he did not know how to escape being another classic rebel,

Opening eyes to worlds unseen

retreading the path of history's long line of frustrated original geniuses.

He had the traditional background of a rebel. He hated his 'tyrannical' and 'bourgeois' father while admiring his frustrated, rebellious mother, who divorced her husband to lead an independent life, travelling abroad alone: 'She was eccentric. I was eccentric. She was ridiculous. I was ridiculous.' (Nobody has yet counted the mothers, seemingly corseted in conventional roles, who have guided their children into unconventional paths.) Though trained as an engineer like his father, he abandoned that profession to become first a caricaturist – expressing his contempt for all authority – and then a reformer of the theatre. But he was a bit too rebellious and was expelled from his drama school for 'incompatibility'. Fascinated by revolution, violence and conflict, he rejected religion, though he con-tinued to be haunted by its rituals. Despite his extra-ordinarily wide culture, living 'knee-deep in books', absorbing the think-ing of all nations, making friends with the greatest artists of his time from all over the world, inheriting a mixture of Russian, Latvian, German and Jewish origins, speaking five languages, studying Japanese during his military service, he was nevertheless unable to get himself understood beyond a limited circle: the masses liked his films only when they saw them as reinforcing their traditional patriotism. France and England both banned the showing of his first masterpiece, *Battleship Potemkin*. Holly-wood rejected him for not being commercial enough. The Soviet govern-ment persecuted him and ordered him to remake his films to fit Stalinist ideology. So he banged his head against almost every possible obstacle. His oppressor Stalin also banged his head against the obstinacy of old habits, and killed many millions of people, terrified that he would never have enough power to defeat all his enemies.

Eisenstein ended up humiliated, forced to obey Stalin and listen politely to his pontificating about how films should make the masses happy workers: that was the only way he could continue to be allowed to film. He found himself in the same dilemma as Galileo, threatened with death by the Inquisition, forced to recant. 'In my personal, too personal history,' he wrote, 'I have had on several occasions to stoop to these levels of self-abasement.' He died at his desk, composing a letter which said: 'All my life I've wanted to be accepted with affection, yet I've felt compelled to with-draw . . . and thus remain forever a spectator.' He never pursued the insight he had into why this was so. In *The Glass House,* a film he planned but never had a chance to make, he had wanted to show how people do not see each other, because 'it never occurs to them to look', they do not have curiosity, they do not know how to look. He was a long way from the architect Frank Lloyd Wright (1867–1959) who, at around the same time, believed that modern houses with glass walls were enough to bring about 'the freedom of the individual' and a new way of life. How to look at others, and how to develop a curiosity in others so that they would enjoy looking at others, was something Eisenstein did not discover, mainly because there were limits to his own curiosity; he saw the peasantry as a class, not as individuals. He filled his films with types, not individuals, choosing as his actors people who looked like caricatures of the part they played. Not that he was unaware of the complexity of individuals – he once used three people to appear on stage simultaneously playing different sides of one

Compelled to remain a spectator

Limits to curiosity

person – but his ambition was to escape from the distraction of detail, to make generalisations about humanity as a whole, to reach the ultimate goal of the dissatisfied, 'to change the world'.

How could Eisenstein believe he could convince huge masses of people to think as he did himself, or make them have new thoughts, or even enjoy thinking? The history of his predecessors, who like him have wanted to make big changes, is discouraging. Humanity's brilliant triumphs of ingenuity are counterbalanced by revolutions that have seldom achieved the hoped-for results, or have created unforeseen problems. When despotisms have been overthrown, they have often been replaced by other kinds of dictatorship, concealed behind populist slogans. Peasant revolts, slave revolts, tax revolts, famine riots, strikes, revolutions, youth movements, women's movements, and protests against war or military conscription, even when they seem to be successful, can find their achievements disappearing in the mazes of bureaucracy or reversed by reactions which surreptitiously turn the clock back to where it was before. Despite the innumerable protests of the oppressed and the frustrated over many centuries, almost everyone still has a grievance or a regret of some kind. Hardly anyone can avoid having some elements of a troubled conscience, which neither prosperity nor hygiene have been able to wash away. Almost no-one can escape being disadvantaged because of their sex, their appearance, their background, their peculiarities or the stereotypes into which they fall.

'The distance that separates the rich from the rest increases daily, poverty is becoming more unbearable and hate is growing more bitter':

The history of failure

No-one can escape being disadvantaged

these words, written twenty years before the French Revolution by L. S. Mercier (1740–1814), remain largely true today – except perhaps for the phrase about hate, the privileged having become increasingly skilful masters of the alchemy that turns hate into acceptance of what is presumed to be inevitable. Mercier was the author of a utopia, *The Year 2440*, in which he foresaw the abolition of prostitutes, beggars, dancing masters, priests, pastry chefs, standing armies, slavery, arbitrary arrest, taxes, guilds, foreign trade, coffee, tea, tobacco and immoral literature. None of these predictions have been fulfilled.

Predictions never fulfilled

Rebels have not become more efficient at attaining their goals, because by their very nature they are prone to disagree amongst themselves and it is inconceivable that the rebels of the world should unite. Even when revolutions occasionally do succeed, it is frequently by betraying themselves, adopting the weapons of their opponents, becoming violent and repressing dissent. Moreover, everyone is taught obedience at school, whereas rebellion is an untutored instinct, rarely rewarded. No wonder that by middle age so many young men and women have packed their idealism away in a bottom drawer, like clothes that have gone out of fashion. But the fact that big revolutions occur only rarely, at most once or twice in a century, should not make one forget the many thousands of lesser, local uprisings not commemorated in school textbooks, which emphasise that discontent is a dormant volcano that can suddenly erupt as easily in prosperous times as in moments of depression. How can it avoid once again spewing no more than a greatcloud of smoke? That is the question that Eisenstein provokes.

The collapse of idealism

The rebellious and the artistic

Rebellion is not the only alternative to obedience or stagnation. Independence or eccentricity are not the only ways of not being totally nondescript. Just as there is a rebellious streak in most people, so there is also an artistic one, and art can be a subtle way of revealing one's attitude to reality. Westerners normally think of artists in the narrow context of paintings and objects collected in museums, or of geniuses setting standards of beauty that few can attain. But there is a very ancient tradition that everybody who wishes to live fully needs to be a practising artist. In China, the very act of writing, using a brush, made one aware that every brushstroke could be a thing of beauty. Literacy and artistry were one. All literate people were encouraged to be painters, poets, calligraphers and musicians. Bureaucrats in cities, imprisoned by office routines, were urged to nourish their spirit by going on 'imaginary journeys through landscape paintings'. Millions of Confucian officials became 'the largest group of art patrons the world has ever seen'.

Artists in ancient China

The first history of art ever written, *The Record of Famous Paintings of Successive Dynasties* (A.D. 847) insisted that art 'perfected civilisation' and 'supported human relationships'. To be an artist in China meant not just finding beauty in nature, but discovering one's place in it. Painting involved viewing nature from many different angles (rather than through the single perspective Westerners adopted) and illuminating the relationships between seemingly disparate elements. Relationships were at the heart of art. The passion for landscape was supplemented by an intense interest in portraits, seeking not a likeness but a revelation of where a person stood in relation to the world. Painting could also be a cooperative activity among friends, joining to improvise pictures together. There was room both for spontaneity (including throwing ink on paper, long before Jackson Pollock) and for the precise scientific observation of individual plants. Being an artist meant investigating life and developing aesthetic criteria to supplement moral ones.

In ancient India, people were likewise urged not to be just passive admirers of the arts but to be artists themselves. The *Kama Sutra* advised not only on how to be a good lover, but also on the need to supplement that by being a painter, sculptor, woodcarver and clay modeller, and to participate in the poetry parties which were one of the chief pleasures of the educated. The ideal woman was not only the dutiful and obedient housewife: there were also admired professional courtesans whose servile occupation was to satisfy men, but who were educated and talented and skilled in 'the sixty-four arts' which included not only music, dancing, singing and acting, but also logic and architecture, fencing, archery and gymnastics, carpentry, chemistry and gardening, teaching parrots to talk, writing in cipher, making artificial flowers, conjuring, and much more. The Indian *ganika*, the Japanese *geisha*, the Greek *hetaerae*, the Italian *cortigiana onesta* the Korean *kisaeng* and the Babylonian *naditu*, despite their differences, showed how women, though often abused, could introduce art into the prosaic lives of men.

The sixty-four arts

Though much art may appear to have been the opposite of rebellious, offering obedience to the taste of patrons or to academic rules or to tradition (Veronese said, 'I am obliged to do what my predecessors did'), it has also shown that there is more to the world than meets the ordinary eye. But too many artists, like Eisenstein, are still battling against being misunderstood, just as rebels are, which happens when art becomes a soliloquy of self-expression instead of a conversation between two imaginations. The celebration and commercialisation of a small number of outstanding artists, raised to the status of geniuses, diverts attention from this other function of art, to encourage a reciprocal exchange between people inhabiting different fragments of reality and having different sensibilities. But the traffic between imaginations seldom runs smoothly. How to pass through the ever more numerous barriers and checkpoints that divergent tastes and prejudices raise up is the question that demands an answer. Eisenstein was foxed by Russia's peasants because he was so absorbed in constructing his marvellously imaginative inventions that he never got round to discovering what each one could tell him that he did not know, what fantasies, personal to themselves, distinguished them from their superficially similar neighbours, and why they could find no room for his ideals.

Art as conversation between two imaginations

The dichotomies of politics, the calculations of economics, the promises of ideologies and the ingenuities of technologies do not suffice to teach people how to understand one another. Eisenstein could make no impact on the mentalities of the masses because people have always feared change, and when they have felt the need for it, they have usually looked back to the past, and demanded that the imaginary good old days should be restored. To be comfortable with a vision of the future they need it to be not strange but familiar. That is precisely what film is capable of doing, by creating imaginary alternatives to the world as it is, that can be

Creating imaginary alternatives

experienced safely in advance so that they cease to be intimidating. Science fiction has encouraged the acceptance of technology, but the cinema has yet to put on its screens visions of other, more intimate kinds of future, or its own prophesies of what humans could be.

The ancient Greeks provide a hint as to how strange ideas can enter into heads ruled by custom. They did not just build temples and shrines to beg favours from the mysterious divine beings hidden in the sky, who symbolised for them the forces that governed the universe. They also liked to look at their problems from the perspective of different arts and different branches of knowledge, which they personified in the Nine Muses, one for each of the arts, one for astronomy (which provides a sense of how all the detail fits into a big picture), and one for history, because they were ever conscious of past experience; they consulted the Muses for advice, and in the process were led to think about larger and more general issues than their own mundane problems.

How strange ideas enter heads

Ever since, poets have sought out a Muse for inspiration, to stimulate new ideas in them, but it has not been only poets who have owed their achievements to the equivalent of a Muse, the messenger of a different point of view. Scientists and innovators, famous or humble, of many kinds, have needed one too. Albert Einstein could not have done what he did on his own. 'I cannot do mathematical calculations easily,' he wrote. 'My particular ability lies in visualising the effects, consequences and possibilities, and the bearing on present thought, of the discoveries of others. I grasp things in a broad way easily.' He needed his friend Marcel Grossman to introduce him to the mathematical models which enabled

The Muse, messenger of a different point of view

him to develop the synthesis that became general relativity. Calling this 'creativity' is misleading if the word is taken to imply an inherent gift that mirrors the creativity of divinity, the ability to create something out of nothing. Einstein rightly emphasises what he owed to others. They were his Muses. What he did was to generate a new idea in a way that has more in common with parents generating a child who is an independent and different creature. When two beings glimpse something in each other that neither was aware of before, and when that recognition ignites a spark which enables them to do together what they could not have done separately, so that they cross the frontiers of their private imaginations, they have found a new door to freedom. Everybody is potentially a Muse, and *Many muses* everybody needs a Muse, or rather many Muses, to enable their talents to bear fruit.

But where can one go to find a Muse? It is not creativity, but sensitivity, that makes one recognise in someone else an idea that can combine with an idea of one's own to generate a novel opportunity. It is interest in others, an awareness that everybody is different and potentially surprising that *Encountering* opens the way to encountering a Muse. A spouse or a sexual partner can *a muse* be a Muse, but so can anyone else. The Greek Muses lived in the sky, but Muses can be found anywhere on earth; people of all sorts can seek inspiration from other people of all sorts, not least from those whom they are unlikely to encounter in the normal course of their existence and who are less liable to repeat what they have heard many times before. Hitherto most institutions have aimed to bring together individuals who resemble one another, or have something in common, and that has suited conventional ambitions, but boredom with *déjà vu* is revealing a hunger for adventure outside the frontiers of habit. It is 'more interesting' to meet people who might surprise one, and more satisfying to create a meeting place designed to encourage not superficial exchanges but more imaginative thinking, a better understanding of the past and a clearer vision of the future. The Muses of mythology were not teachers or law-makers but catalysts who aimed to bring excitement and sparks of meaning and beauty into everyday lives, refining the emotions through the practice of the arts, enabling people to see and to say what normally they dared not, asking not for worship but to be celebrated in festivity, banquets, song and dance. They provide an ideal that is an alternative to the romantic hero, and to the romantic rebel. Instead of encouraging obsession with an idealised passion, or confrontation with enemies whom one dreams of destroying, they incite one to explore and muse about the infinite variety of humankind.

An alternative to the romantic hero

Of course, many people have chosen to limit their curiosity, assuming that wearing coloured spectacles makes life more bearable. Family tradition has also shaped their choice as to whether they developed open or closed minds, and became curious or blinkered, conformists or non-conformists. An ingenious statistician has calculated that the most adventurous individuals in Western history were younger sons, and later younger daughters. The first-born members of a family were apparently seventeen times less likely to accept new scientific ideas than later-born ones. During the political revolutions of Western Europe, the champions of radicalism were eighteen times more likely to be later-borns, while in

Younger sons as rebels

the Protestant Reformation those who suffered martyrdom in the cause of the new doctrines were forty-eight times more often later-borns. The family, supposedly the guardian of normality, was in reality a furnace of rebellion, firing and extinguishing rebellion. But the family has changed. The privileges of the eldest, and of males, are no longer as stereotyped as they once were. Likewise, the different professions, which were in some ways a substitute or additional family, also limited curiosity through specialisation, but that heritage is being challenged too.

So now there are probably more rebels – of sorts – than ever before. The ideal of constant innovation is a recipe for a mild version of permanent rebellion. But since rebellions have such a chequered history of limited success and painful side effects, rebels may now want to redefine themselves as explorers. As such, instead of being simply angry, they have more freedom to view enemies from a variety of perspectives, penetrating behind the poses they adopt and uncovering hidden cravings or vulnerabilities; they can discover whether too many people have been wrongly classified as enemies, who may turn out to be so only in parts of themselves, in only some of their attitudes; they can expand the imaginations of bullies (in public or private life) who are interested only in themselves because they have not learned to be interested in others; and they can discover when the most effective response to dictators who derive their sense of achievement from defiance and cruelty is likely to be not rebellion but removing oneself from their clutches, escaping, emigrating, leaving them to fight their own kind and destroy one another.

Rebels redefined as explorers

A rebel and an oppressor are not thought of as being a couple, though they may be as obsessed with each other as a couple in love. To be locked in such a relationship is like living permanently in a cage. When in a group linked by mutual animosity, it becomes even harder to free oneself of hate.

What can the poor tell the rich?

WHEN ALL SHE EATS IN A whole day is just three handfuls of rice boiled with a little salt, what does a poor woman want, more than anything else? 'I am incapable of begging,' she answered. She did not want charity, which she considered humiliating. She preferred to pretend that it was her personal choice to cook but once a day. 'People concluded that my diet was strictly in accordance with the requirements of a spiritual life. I used to say: I am not hungry. But in truth I could not sleep the whole night because I was so hungry.' When she could no longer afford even one meal a day, she collected discarded scraps, and even ate clay. Once, she went without food for a whole week. She said she was willing to die. 'I had known nothing but misery all my life.'

'Nothing but misery all my life'

These are the words of Haimabati Sen, born in Bengal in 1866. At the age of nine she was married off to a man of forty-five who died within a year. Then her parents died. All alone, and shunned because Hindu custom saw widows as bearers of misfortune, she drifted from place to place, wherever she could find shelter with relatives or strangers, earning her keep doing domestic work. When she grew to be a handsome woman male predators tried to ensnare her, but she refused to be a mistress or a prostitute and escaped from several jobs that were not as innocent as they had seemed.

To be a poor person, in most civilisations until very recently, used to *What poverty*
mean to be one who had no family. Haimabati Sen sought help from a   *used to mean*
large number of close and distant relatives, but their compassion often
proved demanding, insulting or greedy. Respectability came only when
she married again at twenty-three, to a husband whose generous ideas she
respected. But he immediately abandoned his job to devote himself to a
'search for God', and she became the breadwinner. He expected to be
waited upon, and once beat her, causing serious injury. When he died she
had no money to pay for the funeral rites. Her five children, she complained,
harassed and oppressed her; all but one were ungrateful, lacking in
sympathy for her failing health and interested only in their own affairs;
their spouses were even worse.

'I cannot understand what I have gained by my suffering,' she said at
the end of her life. But it was very far from being a tragic life. On the
contrary, she demonstrated forcefully what can be achieved without   *What can be*
money, in three different domains. Though girls were told that no-one   *achieved*
                                                                          without
would marry them if they were educated, she learnt to read with the help *money*
of her brothers, and persisted in study, eventually winning a scholarship
to a medical school, and becoming a hospital physician. She did all this
while at the same time raising her children, getting up at four in the
morning to do the household chores and serve her husband – who helped
not at all. Being a doctor did not make her rich because she was paid
a small fraction of what her colonial British superiors earned, but she
found enormous satisfaction from helping patients. The shortage of money
never bothered her. 'I realised the human heart did not attain peace

through the performance of duty in return for pay . . . It is the duty of every human being to help others.' Though she had disdained receiving charity when she was on the brink of starvation, she now said 'Charity is the one tender impulse in our heart, nothing can soften our souls and teach us self-sacrifice as well as charity.' To sacrifice oneself for others was, for her, the purpose of life. She repaid society's cruelty towards her with infinite

Beyond the desire for material comfort

kindness. 'I do not see any need for fine clothes or quality shoes . . . nor excellent beds and mattresses. You fall asleep when you are sleepy, it does not matter where you lie down.' The desire for material comforts destroyed peace of mind. There was no point in 'living like a worm gorging on worldly things'.

Since families did not always function as ideally they were supposed to,

A substitute for a disappoint- ing family

she created a substitute for the family, based not on kin but on free choice, mutual affection and gratitude. She did not conceal that she needed not only to care for others but also to be cared for and to feel protected herself. 'You are my mother – or daughter or son – from today,' she would say when she encountered someone hungry for love or attention. 'I shall look after you.' Her compassion ignored all the limitations of prudence; she could not refuse help to anyone; eventually, thirty or forty orphans lived in her house at any one time, and in total she raised 485 children. All her meagre earnings were spent on them. Small families bred selfishness, she said. 'The more relations you have in this world, the better for you.' Her favourite daughter, who was most devoted to her, was an adopted one. 'When all my children come to me and call me Mother, my heart swells with joy.'

She got higher marks than anyone else in her medical examinations, but the male students went on strike to prevent her being awarded the gold medal, which they said had never been given to a woman. She did not protest, and agreed to settle for the silver medal. Nor did she refuse to be the typical obedient wife deferring to her husband without argument: she gave all her salary to him 'to use it as he thinks best'. The fear of being abandoned by him was like an ever-present noose that threatened to choke her: 'Who will then look after me?' And yet at the same time the cruel world that men seemed to delight in disgusted her, a world based on 'strength and money', callous towards children forced to 'do all the work', ravaged by extortionate moneylenders 'who take away by force all the cultivator owns and sells the same to dealers at double the price'. Her response was to build her own world side by side with the cruel one and to try to ignore the 'vanity and pettiness' of men.

Disgust with the cruel world

Haimabati Sen died in the year I was born, 1933, leaving a wonderful autobiography in manuscript, which lay forgotten for two generations until it was rescued and translated by the great historian of 'sensitivities', Tapan Raychaudhuri. It is one of the most detailed personal narratives of intimate life to be found anywhere, with the words and the voices of each character preserved in a way that novels can only imitate. Had she lived a century later, she would have been subject to much stronger temptations to become rich, perhaps to emigrate and be a fashionable doctor curing the neuroses or obesity of the overfed. But there are many times more poor people now than there were in her own day, because the world's population has grown so much, and the complaints about poverty expressed

'The vanity and pettiness of men'

The balance between the mighty and the lowly

Progress produces poverty as well as prosperity

centuries ago show how little has changed. Zhang Tao (1560–1620), a minor official writing when China was experiencing another of its economic booms, and expressing the views of many who were bewildered by shameless displays of luxury, wrote: 'One man in a hundred is rich while nine out of ten are impoverished. The lord of silver rules everything. Avarice is without limit, everything is for personal pleasure . . . In dealing with others, everything is recompensed down to the last hair . . . The balance between the mighty and the lowly was lost, as both competed for trifling amounts . . . Each exploited the other and everyone publicised himself. Deception sprouted and litigation arose.' Belief in the fairy tales of progress has continued to obscure repeated disappointment in every era of business expansion. Progress has always produced poverty as well as prosperity. When have most people not been poor? All attempts to abolish poverty have failed, even if some are less poor than they used to be. Ever since money was invented, there has never been enough for everyone to have as much as they want or need. There can never be enough money.

All the talk about human rights and democracy has done nothing to prevent 85 per cent of the world's wealth still being owned by a mere tenth of its population. The supposed end of colonialism has not stopped hundreds of billions of dollars being annually transferred from poor to rich countries. Even in the U.S.A., four-fifths of the population still own only 15 per cent of the wealth, while the richest 1 per cent own around one-third. Industrialisation, in its first stages, has regularly impoverished more people than it has enriched. Botswana, the model of African achievement by the criteria of finance – registering economic growth of

over 7 per cent for twenty years, and increasing GNP more than sixfold – still has half of its population with less than one dollar a day. After
even more impressive economic growth, 55 per cent of India's urban
population live in a space no bigger than 5.5 square metres, which is the   *Living in five*
                                                                             square metres
minimum specified for U.S. prisons.

It is well known that Adam Smith's *Theory of Moral Sentiments*, which
supplements his *Wealth of Nations,* insists that the creation of wealth
must be accompanied by the simultaneous creation of mutual benevolence, sympathy and gratitude. He was convinced that being selfish is not
in one's own interest, for humans need the approval, sympathy and affection of others, and find it beneficial to be concerned about 'the fortunes
of others, regardless of our own self-interest.' For him, there could be no
true prosperity if there was no increase in mutual understanding. But he   *The illusions*
                                                                            of prosperity
had no prescription for making people more benevolent. He just hoped
that their piety would lead them to recognise that God was benevolent,
and that they should therefore model themselves on Him; or else, they
should demonstrate their good taste by practising benevolence, because it
was 'pleasing' and 'bestows a beauty superior to all others'. Adam Smith
would be horrified by what has become of his theories. His prediction was
that someone who has only industrial or specialist skills becomes 'stupid   *Becoming*
                                                                             stupid and
and narrow minded. The torpor of his mind renders him not only in-   *narrow*
capable of relishing or bearing a part in any rational conversation, but   *minded*
of conceiving any generous, noble or tender sentiment, and consequently
of forming any just judgement concerning even the ordinary duties of
private life.'

A different direction might have been taken if more attention had been paid to a pupil of Socrates, Xenophon, known as the 'Attic Muse' (born *The economics* around 444 B.C.), the author of the first book ever written about econom-*of friendship* ics, which originally meant reflection on the best way of running a home and a family. Money was worthless, he said, if it did not lead to a good life. Socrates was wealthier than the wealthiest man in Athens, because though he went barefoot in ragged clothes, refusing to be paid for his teaching, he had all he needed from his stone-mason's craft and was content with his modest home; whereas the rich man whose properties were worth a hundred times more was burdened with so many obligations to maintain his reputation that he needed three times more than he owned to be sure that 'the gods and his fellow citizens might tolerate him'. You were only really wealthy if you knew how to use your wealth. Becoming rich meant learning what to do with life as well as with money, rather than just making money. So his book *The Economist* was about relationships and friendship, and character, and particularly the relations of man and wife, and how there was no point in a wife wearing high heels, enamelling her face with white lead, and colouring her cheeks with rouge from the alkanet plant to win her husband's admiration any more than he would win hers by smothering himself with cosmetics made for men. *Couples and* The goal of a couple should be to become 'true helpmates', a counterpoise *helpmates* and counterpart to each other. They would be truly rich if they were honest, kind and hard-working, enjoying nature and homely pleasures, because 'the cadence of sweet music dwells even in pots and pans set out in neat array.' Xenophon takes one back to the most basic form of human interaction, which is communication. But conversations between people who want to understand one another well have still to overcome huge barriers.

When, more than two millennia after Xenophon, 20,000 poor people from every continent were invited by the World Bank, whose mission it is to end poverty, to explain what they needed more than anything else, they made clear that 'money was not the answer.' Isolation mattered more. 'It is neither leprosy nor poverty that kills the leper, but loneliness,' said a Ghanaian. 'When you are poor, no-one wants to speak to you, everyone is sorry for you, no-one wants to drink with you,' complained a Bulgarian. The stigma of poverty brought shame, so that one was unable to participate fully in social life, and one dared not attend weddings or feasts. 'Everyone is on their own; we do not visit friends as we used to; people are hostile and alone,' said a Russian. 'Poverty is like living in a jail, waiting to be free,' said a Jamaican. Emerging from the obscurity of destitution, said an Egyptian, risked 'endangering one's honour or safety or future'. The police, said a Brazilian, only make one's loneliness worse, robbing and humiliating those who call for help. Widows, in some places, suffered even worse as outcasts. Governments were corrupt. The 'bottom poor', least touched by aid programmes, complained of being regarded with 'a mixture of pity, fear, disgust and hatred'.

'No-one wants to speak with you'

'Pity, fear, disgust and hatred'

The World Bank concluded that ending corruption, violence, ineffective government and powerlessness was the answer. But these are scourges as ancient and as resistant as poverty itself, and not likely to be eliminated in any foreseeable future. So the Bank adopted a different solution, proposing that instead of trying to change the world, it would try to change people: the poor should be given the 'capabilities' to lead a decent life, through education, skills training and job creation, enabling them to make their own choices, 'control and consciously direct their living conditions' and 'participate in the social and economic life of their communities'. But this solution is still one imposed from above.

Those who are mindful of the surprises of history and the unpredictability of individuals may be tempted to explore another option at a more *The isolation* intimate level. Since governments cannot propagate benevolence, and *of both poor* since education does not necessarily produce people capable of making *and rich* sensible choices, or even agreement as to what is sensible, they may prefer to listen more closely to what the poor told the World Bank about isolation, which afflicts not just the poor but in varying degrees the vast majority of humanity. Each escape from isolation, whether by the poor or not, involves the forging of a relationship of two people appreciating and valuing each other, which neither laws nor money can bring about. Without such intimate bonds, finding homes for the homeless and jobs for the jobless only goes halfway towards making them resilient enough against the knocks of life. Haimabati Sen's relationships were reciprocal, between an adult and a child, a mother and an orphan, who each had something to give that the other did not have. But when two people begin to appreciate each other and together create something out of their friendship that did not exist before, the result can no more be foreseen than the *Love in big* character of a new baby. Individuals are used to taking the risk of loving *organisa-* a stranger, which powerful international organisations are not. Only they *tions* see that it is not only those who receive the fewest monetary rewards who need to be rescued from isolation; people loaded with wealth or the accolades of fame can be even more isolated.

A beggar holding out his hand in a Paris street, ignored by the crowds hurrying past him, said the worst part of his ordeal was that it made him wonder whether he really was alive, since no-one seemed able to see him. *Are you alive if no-one notices you?*

Most people, and not just the destitute, might also say that the world is unaware of their existence. The humanitarian response to the homeless is that they should not be seen, that no-one should be homeless on the streets. But what the destitute have to say is infinitely precious because it is about life stripped of hypocrisy, the truth about the fragility of the foundations of civilisation. Nothing is more arbitrary than the value placed on different forms of experience and knowledge.

The spontaneous human response to the suffering of others used to be more personal, when the poor were not as segregated as they are today. More recently, many charities have come to be run like corporations by professionals on business principles, paralleling and complementing what governments do, aiming to increase prosperity and justice, and justifying themselves by demonstrating tangible results, efficiently attained. Meanwhile, the poor donate a larger proportion of their wealth to good causes *Experimental philanthropy* than the rich, and the homeless are sometimes the most generous of all. So there is room for new experiments in philanthropy, to respond to isolation, to introduce more reciprocity in giving and receiving, and to invent original ways of living rather than merely patching the holes in existing ones.

Haimabati Sen is a muse to me because she reveals how it is possible

Beyond the 'culture of poverty'
to advance beyond the long debate about the so-called culture of poverty and the supposed resignation of the poor, their acceptance of their destiny and their sense of helplessness. She was certainly frequently overcome by a feeling of helplessness and resignation – 'I must accept my fate,' she kept on saying – but she was also an indomitable fighter against all the traditions that oppressed her as a poor person and as a woman. Joining the Brahmo religion (a reformed version of Hinduism that rejected the subordination of women) did not satisfy her; she recognised that even its enlightened leaders could not succeed in entirely eliminating old habits. No institution could live up to her demands. Her message was not 'women unite', because she accepted that many women, for different reasons, made other choices. Instead, her achievement was to show how building one-to-one relationships of sympathy, understanding, trust and gratitude

Non-material wealth
could gradually create a life that was rich in non-material terms, and how this could spread beyond family and neighbours to embrace a wider circle of affections. Far from being a distraction from the struggle for the improvement of material conditions and social justice, it is the source of the courage needed to persevere, because human warmth can often melt helplessness away.

[6]

What could the rich tell the poor?

O F ALL THE RICH PEOPLE WHOSE money-making exploits make
them heroes to MBA students as theologians once nourished
themselves on the lives of saints, one captain of industry stands out as
having seemingly done most to implement the precepts of Adam Smith.
While Haimabati Sen was on the brink of starvation, Andrew Carnegie
(1835–1919) was in the process of becoming one of the richest men who
ever lived. He began even poorer than she, and left school at the age of
twelve. But instead of relying on his poor relatives, he used his wit, charm,
geniality, memory and energy to rise rapidly from being an errand boy
to enter each of the new industries that were transforming the world:
telegraph, railways, bridge building, iron and steel, quickly proving to his
employers that he was as clever as they, and a little bit quicker. In each
case, he spotted the most promising opportunities at just the right moment
and formed partnerships with people who could best help him achieve
highly ambitious goals. By the age of thirty-three, he was worth seventy-
five million dollars in today's money.

He then made a resolution: 'Beyond this, never earn, make no effort to
increase fortune, but spend the surplus each year for benevolent purposes.'
Until then, he said, he had had only one 'idol', to amass wealth. But this

*A philosophy
for plutocrats*

was 'one of the worst species of idolatry. No idol is more debasing than the worship of money.' 'To continue much longer overwhelmed by business cares and with most of my thoughts wholly upon the way to make more money in the shortest time, must degrade me beyond hope of permanent recovery.' He resolved to make money only in the mornings, and devote the rest of the day to 'instruction and reading systematically'. At the age of thirty-five he would retire, 'settle in Oxford and get a thorough education, making the acquaintance of literary men', and then devote himself to writing, public affairs and the 'improvement of the poorer classes'. To a business acquaintance who prided himself on always being in his office at seven in the morning, he said, 'You must be a lazy man if it takes you ten hours to do a day's work. What I do is to get good men, and I never give them orders. My directions seldom go beyond suggestions. Here in the morning I get reports from them. Within an hour I have disposed of everything, sent out all my suggestions, the day's work is done and I am ready to go out and enjoy myself.' He never went to Oxford, which would doubtless have disappointed him, but instead he travelled all over the world. He meditated on Indians 'on the verge of starvation' and found it 'pitiable' that a wealthy Chinese man should be 'driving in his carriage alone' unaccompanied by a woman, for women were 'the fountain of all that is best in life. In life, without her, there is nothing.' The work ethic was ruining life. 'I hope Americans will find some day more time for play.'

But play and socialising were not enough. 'In company, Mr Carnegie indulges in music and delights in humorous stories and when solicited by friends he sings a good song, or gives a recitation with dramatic effect.'

'Make money only in the mornings'

He showered his guests with 'every variety of wholesome entertainment', including dancing, cards and parlour games. But he never became a playboy. 'At this period of my life I was all at sea. No creed, no system reached me. All was chaos. I had outgrown the old and had found no substitute.' Then he read Herbert Spencer, and progress became his religion. From Spencer he acquired the conviction that progress was a law of nature, not an accident but a necessity, and that moral and material progress went hand in hand: industrialisation was a higher state of civilisation that would make humanity not only wealthier but also more moral. It was sad that many workers earned starvation wages, but that was inevitable in the period of 'transition' towards universal well-being. 'All is well since all grows better became my motto, my true source of comfort.' There was no conceivable end to 'man's march to perfection'. Spencer became his master, 'the great thinker of our age', providing him with a justification for his wealth and the assurance that his success was leading inexorably to the improvement of all humans. He wrote a book explaining how *Triumphant Democracy* (1886) had made America the best place on earth. He presented himself as the 'workers' friend', a millionaire socialist, preaching cooperation and profit-sharing between employers and employed; he claimed to understand both, because he had been a worker himself in his youth.

The religion of progress

   The Gospel of Wealth (1901) summarised his thinking and was designed to establish his reputation as the philosopher of a new age led by business achievement. The gap between rich and poor was 'inevitable'. But individuals with a 'talent for organisation and management' who accumulated vast fortunes must realise that this wealth was not the product of their

The gospel of wealth

efforts; it was the joint product of the community. So they must adminis-
ter their wealth for the good of the community. He resolved to give away

The duty of a millionaire

all his money in his own lifetime. 'The man who dies rich dies disgraced.'
Becoming extremely rich required no apology, because it enabled him to
use his vast resources, and his 'wisdom, experience and ability to adminis-
ter' in the service of his 'poorer brethren', 'doing for them better than they
would or could do for themselves'. He would not leave anything to his
heirs, because poverty had been the spur to his own energy: 'Poverty is
the only school capable of producing the supremely great, the genius.'
The more millionaires there were, the more society would advance,
and the trouble with countries like China and India which were poorer
than America was that they had too few millionaires. It was the duty of a
millionaire 'to increase his revenues', so that he could continue to use
them for the benefit of the poor.

Giving money away

Carnegie devoted most of the second half of his life to making dazzling
philanthropic gifts. He built or helped 1,689 public libraries in the U.S.,
660 in the U.K., 607 elsewhere, seeing self-education as the key to
progress, because that was how he had become what he was, able to recite
from memory whole pages of Shakespeare and Burns. He spurned the
elite universities and gave donations instead to small technical colleges
that could help poor workers acquire practical skills, and to the Scottish
universities that were traditionally open to people from modest backgrounds. The Carnegie Institution in Washington, dedicated to scientific
research, expressed his faith in technical progress. A Hero Fund rewarded
civilians, instead of soldiers, for bravery in ordinary life, and a pension

fund expressed appreciation of modest teachers. Carnegie's home towns, Pittsburgh and Dumfermline, were glorified with public buildings and parks. And finally the Carnegie Endowment for Peace was set up to stop what he hated most, which was war.

Optimism was one of Carnegie's greatest strengths. But when the Great War of 1914 broke out, he was shattered. His appearance was transformed, he suddenly seemed ten years older and he stopped talking. Had the 350 million dollars he had given away, the equivalent of hundreds of billions today, been in vain? He was plagued by the feeling that his business achievements did not quite give him what he most wanted. It was not a feeling of guilt.

The sudden collapse of optimism

His autobiography showed that he was not troubled by the contradictions in his career. His mastery of every business and financial skill enabled him to create the most technically advanced steelworks in the world, but he had not shared the profits as fairly as he pretended. In the years 1892–9, for example, the value of what he manufactured increased by 226 per cent but the workers' wages fell by 67 per cent. Repeatedly rejecting the workers' demand for an eight-hour day, he had insisted on a twelve-hour day, seven days a week, at less than one and a half dollars a day for many. But he defended this on the ground that what the workers wanted more than higher wages was steady employment. 'There are higher uses for surplus wealth than adding petty sums to the earnings of the masses. Trifling sums given to each every week or every month – and the sums would be trifling indeed – would be frittered away, nine times out of ten, in things which pertain to the body and not to the spirit, upon

Reasons for low wages

richer food and drink, better clothing, more extravagant living, which are beneficial neither to rich or poor. These are things external and of the flesh, they do not minister to the higher divine part of man.' He claimed to know better than they did what to do with money; he had his own interpretation of what cooperation and sharing with the workers meant. In public he claimed not to be personally responsible for the veritable war his company waged to annihilate the trade unions, a war in which it brought in a gun-carrying private army to physically fight them. His instructions to *War against* his subordinates were always ruthless: unions and strikers should be met *trade unions* by a simple tactic: no negotiation, close the factory down, let the strikers starve and then take back only those who accepted his terms. Despite his tact and brilliance at putting a favourable gloss on his actions, he did not escape blame. The nationwide outcry at the deaths of several workers in his battle against the unions destroyed his reputation in the working class. To replace recalcitrant workers who resisted him, he brought in poor East European immigrants ready to accept any wage at all. He modernised by substituting cheap for skilled labour. Homestead, the town in which his main steelworks was situated, henceforth carried the same sinister meaning as Peterloo. Nowhere in America, said the novelist Theodore Dreiser after a visit, is the vast gap dividing the rich and the poor so evident, with Carnegie's splendid white library in the affluent suburb, far from the grey, sordid, sad slums.

Carnegie, the son of a Chartist rebel who had fought the rich in Scotland, liked to portray himself as just an ordinary worker made good, but as the principal owner of a huge company he had quickly lost touch with the ordinary worker, who became an abstract entity, and no longer a particular individual whom he personally knew. His bonhomie, his cheerful, conciliatory, tactful or manipulative manner concealed the fact that the managers who helped him grow his empire were also only super- ficially his friends, friends when he needed them, with business ultimately triumphing over friendship in a crisis. Only rarely did they tell him what they thought to his face. His most senior collaborator, however, losing his temper, did once write to him: 'I had become tired of your business methods, your absurd newspaper interviews and personal remarks and unwarranted interference in matters you knew nothing about. It has been your custom for years when any of your partners disagreed with you to say they were unwell and needed a change . . . I warn you . . .'

What is missing from success?

Carnegie pined for friendship, or more accurately for friends who would appreciate him as he thought he deserved to be appreciated, not as a business success, but as a wise man of experience to whose advice all those in power, in every domain, should listen. He did not marry till he was over fifty, after the death of his mother, with whom he lived till then, and from whom he received adoration, but he also hungered for praise from the powerful and the famous. Making friends in high places was an art in which he excelled, for he knew how to flatter to the extremes of sycophancy, entertain guests with lavish luxury, but also with excellent conversation, because he was unusually knowledgeable, personally amus- ing and good company. Almost everybody of note in literature, politics and the arts, in America and Europe, was invited to endless parties in his many palatial residences. He was constantly writing to newspapers, giving

Hunger for praise

interviews and making speeches to every kind of meeting. Six successive presidents of the U.S., whom he prided himself on 'knowing intimately', were bombarded with advice from him. They treated him as an equal, and not just because he was a contributor to Republican election funds. All these powerful people wanted the same thing as he did, which was appreciation and flattery from those who mattered. It did not mean that they listened to one another on subjects on which they disagreed. President Theodore Roosevelt treated his advice on foreign policy with apparent respect, and they exchanged much correspondence with many assurances of friendship and high esteem, but privately Roosevelt said that he thought Carnegie's ideas were 'absurd' and 'washy'. He 'had tried to like Carnegie,' he was reported as saying, 'but it is pretty difficult. There is no type of man for whom I feel a more contemptuous abhorrence than for the one who makes a God of mere money-making and at the same time is always yelling out that kind of utterly stupid condemnation of war . . . [from] hopelessly twisted ideals . . . Unrighteous war is a hideous evil, but I am not sure that it is worse evil than business unrighteousness.' President Taft was equally hypocritical, publicly attentive but privately mocking Carnegie's philanthropy as 'the plans he had for making himself poor'.

Hypocrites and sycophants

Mark Twain, who was another of Carnegie's 'dear friends', wrote this of him: 'He is himself his one darling subject, the only subject . . . he seems stupendously interested in.' It was not his capitalist achievements that he bragged about, but the famous people who had paid him compliments. 'He talks forever and ever and ever and untiringly of the attentions which have been shown him.' He needed to tell people how important other people believed him to be. He would escort his visitors from room to room, pointing out mementoes, autographed books and photographs, 'buzzing over each like a happy hummingbird, for each represented a compliment to Mr Carnegie'. His letters, which he wrote to vast numbers of famous people (from whom he received obsequious replies), were sprinkled with news that this or that great man had 'sent for him'. 'If you let Carnegie tell it, he never seeks the great – the great always seek him.' Mark Twain's conclusion was that Carnegie was incapable of self-knowledge: 'He thinks he is a rude, bluff, independent spirit, who writes his mind and thinks his mind with an almost extravagant Fourth of July independence, whereas he is really the counterpart of the rest of the human race in that he does not boldly speak his mind except when there isn't any danger in it. He thinks he is a scorner of kings and emperors and dukes, whereas he is like the rest of the human race, a slight attention from one of these can make him drunk for a week and keep his happy tongue wagging for seven years.'

Self-deception

He was once briefly visited at his grand Scottish estate by King Edward VII: 'Mr Carnegie cannot leave the King's visit alone; he has told me about it at least four times, in detail; he certainly knew that it was the second, third or fourth time, for he has an excellent memory . . . He has likable qualities, and I like him, but I don't believe I can stand the King Edward visit again.'

There is nothing unusual about this. The powerful have very often been as hungry as the poor, starved of appreciation, recognition, applause or admiration of a convincing kind, causing as much distress as the shortage

The powerful as hungry as the poor

of money. The hunger for love, in many varieties, has not been satisfied by the modern synthetic substitute – 'Love yourself' – on which some rely to generate self-confidence, though it can also produce hallucinations of grandeur and sad self-deception, and become a sort of mental masturbation. The stories of Haimabati Sen and Andrew Carnegie end up agreeing that, even though they may have enjoyed very different degrees of material comfort, what hurt them most, and what they missed above all else, was the lack of emotional sustenance. All the calculations about who is rich and who is poor are incomplete; they do not go far enough; they do not weigh the quality of the personal relationships that determine the effect of wealth and poverty. The Industrial Revolution made that more difficult to see, by changing the meaning of the word 'comfort', which used to signify personal support, on the moral level, until it was simplified into a physical sensation that could be acquired by the purchase of material goods. The change can be dated almost precisely: the French imported the English word, in its new meaning, in 1815.

The stultifying effects of physical deprivation, of the lack of the basic needs for survival, food and shelter, are all too real, and are not diminished by such consolations. But one of the reasons why poverty has been regarded as a problem that can be palliated by alms or economic growth is that hunger for food has been isolated from these other kinds of hunger. If it were not so, this wider notion of poverty would be recognised as a suffering that afflicts the vast majority. The skills that people on low incomes use to cope with shortage by finding value in every scrap of natural resource and by exchanging generosity have never had a price put on

A synthetic substitute for love

Calculating who is really rich

them, or been included in any national accounts. Can one imagine a new kind of accountancy that distinguishes between wealth that is superficial and wealth that is profound, that goes beyond self-satisfaction?

Carnegie did not find a satisfying way of responding to the resentment of those who have never been rich. In a work entitled *Occupational Pursuits of Certain Wealthy Persons*, Han Shu wrote in A.D. 25 complaining that wealth was seldom won by wholly admirable means, saying of one magnate: 'What others gave away, he grasped. What they undertook, he abandoned. As he earned, he saved . . . disregarding the law . . . monopolising mineral resources.' Of a leading businesswoman, Ching, widow of Pa (246–210 B.C.), who inherited the monopoly of China's mercury ore, he wrote, 'She used much of her wealth to protect herself, so that people did not dare turn against her', and so that the emperor treated her 'with ceremonies equal to those of the ruler'. Han Shu concludes: 'Was this not because of their wealth?' Carnegie's privileges and methods aroused as much scorn as admiration. *Responding to resentment*

To be financially rich has always been just a beginning, a challenge to find ways of spending money. Carnegie had great difficulty in deciding whom to give his money to; the only one of his benefactions he thought of himself, he confessed, was his Hero prize. His donations were distributed by managers in a business-like, impersonal way; he hardly ever responded to the avalanche of begging letters he received, so his wealth did not draw him any closer to the rest of humanity. Poor Haimabati Sen, with her much more modest resources, was more generous than he. *Answering begging letters*

So instead of banging my head against the same brick wall, as so many experts have done and are still doing, trying to make the poor richer, with alas very limited success, instead of waiting I do not know how many centuries for wealth to be distributed more widely or more fairly, or loaned out in little doses, without wanting to discourage those who persist in their generous quest, I prefer to explore in a different direction. How to relieve the hunger that one is not properly appreciated, and how to

Appreciating uncongenial people

appreciate others, uncongenial though they may seem? How to escape the misconceptions that both the possession and the lack of money create? Every time Haimabati Sen was on the brink of despair, she reassured herself that God was looking after her, however grim her suffering – as innumerable rich and poor alike have done – but she still yearned for more human understanding and more human kindness. The dream of becoming very rich appeals to those who have never witnessed the traumas of

The dream of becoming middle class

very rich people. The dream of becoming middle class makes sense for those desperate to escape from the suffering that penury brings, but being middle class is a long way from paradise. So what else is there to aim for?

A different attitude to wealth was shown by the Indian industrialist G. D. Birla (1884–1983), who established the largest private foundation in India, on the basis of his huge interests in jute, sugar, paper, cars, banking, cement, chemicals and textiles. Birla's enemies accused him of being interested only in personal enrichment, whose benefactions to religion and education were made to avoid taxes. But in his autobiography, *In the Shadow of the Mahatma*, Birla explained why despite believing in large-scale industrialisation – whereas Gandhi was the apostle of the small-scale village artisan – he became the principal financial backer of Gandhi's campaign for national independence. It was not just because he had been humiliated by the British and their 'racial arrogance', which meant that 'I was not allowed to use the lift to go up their offices, nor their benches when waiting to see them . . . I smarted under these insults.' He was fascinated by Gandhi's life of simplicity: 'a saintly person who had renounced all comforts. Though I did not agree with him on many problems, I never refused to obey his wishes. He not only tolerated my independence but loved me all the more for it, as a father would his child. Our attachment became one in the nature of a family attachment, of a father for a son.' Though Birla did not scorn luxury himself, he preached Gandhi's doctrines to his children. 'All pleasures should be shunned. Spend the bare minimum on yourself. Those who eat food only for the taste die prematurely. Take food as you would medicine.'

Smarting under insults

The basic difference between the Indian and the American tycoon was Birla's open acknowledgement of the role that friendship and family played in business life. He highlighted 'the importance of knowing people, the value of personal contact'. Whereas Carnegie was desperate to win either the approval or the obedience of others, Birla was concerned with the emotional bond with his fellow humans. 'In India, we are emotional,' he wrote. 'We respond to friendship; we are moved by love and sympathy, we feel pity. We are also capable of strong hatreds but these are generally against aggregates and systems, and if they are against individuals, they are as often as not against those whom we have not met or seen . . . Contact reveals truths. The good we discover in others far outweighs the evil.'

Hatred against those we have never met

So what appealed to him in Gandhi was his 'sincerity in the search for truth'. That search was what mattered most. Gandhi summed up his own life as a series of 'Experiments with Truth'. Birla wrote: 'Often I could not follow his reasoning . . . but always there was the belief that he must somehow be right in a sense that I could not grasp. There was nothing I could refuse him. But he was never a dictator and was essentially humble. He took criticism without the slightest anger.'

Criticism
without
anger

Birla is no more an ideal model for MBA students than Carnegie. He was no less ruthless in business, and no more successful in his private life, which was darkened by a discordant family. But the financial wizardry of both men makes it clear that there is an alternative to the profit and loss accounts that hold the business world together. The criteria of business success are too narrow so long as they ignore the sacrifices in the quality of life that it often entails. Accountants were invented (not all that long ago, in the middle of the nineteenth century) to guard the public against dishonesty and corruption in business, but they have become so intertwined with business, and often placed at the helm of business to make decisions on essentially financial grounds, that the hope that they might evolve to have a status comparable to an independent judiciary has not been fulfilled. To ignore what cannot be measured in precise numbers is like counting the stems in a bouquet of flowers while ignoring the indescribable perfume and beauty of each bud.

Accountants
as an
independent
judiciary

A currency that would be adequate to assess the quality of a life would resemble honey rather than money. Honey has long symbolised what makes life sweet, which is what humans value most of all, more than money. In virtually every mythology, honey is the food of the gods, the emblem of love, the source of energy, the bactericide magic in which pharaohs were embalmed so that they would triumph over death. Only very recently has it divulged the immemorial secret of its healing power, which is the protein that each bee places in it from its own immune system. Honey is impossible to sum up in a formula, to fabricate or forge; it is neither animal nor vegetable, it contains over 200 different ingredients and comes in innumerable varieties.

What makes honey sweet

What people do with their money, and what they do without money, is what accountancy has yet to weigh up and reflect on. What rich and poor people absorb not just in knowledge but also in wisdom and compassion and taste from their contact with others, and what others absorb from them, what insights are generated from each encounter and not just how many pennies have been exchanged, what price is paid in lies and crimes, in sacrifices and betrayals in the course of amassing more possessions than others, these are all items that need to figure in a statement of profit and loss. Making lots of money remains a fascinating mirage because so very few people have tasted the pleasures and pains it offers. The seventy-five million individuals who own half the world's wealth are the most secretive and least understood of all human beings, as distant and elusive as those half-divine half-animal gods of ancient civilisations: a study of their zoology would doubtless reveal many unknown species and unsuspected variations of habit. Only if the reality of their lives were to be revealed would it be possible to judge more impartially the merits of an economy dedicated to prosperity and the accumulation and expenditure

The price of wealth

of wealth. So far, only rarely have the very rich spoken about what wealth has done to them, though their children need to know the truth about their parents, for nothing is more dangerous than to be the offspring of a millionaire. Though they may not wish even to think about the menace of a redistribution of wealth, every class in society would benefit from a redistribution of envy and pity.

Children of wealthy parents

7

How many ways of committing suicide are there?

SUICIDE IS TODAY A MUCH MORE frequent answer to life's torments than it was in the past. Every forty seconds somebody in the world chooses to escape. There are many more who contemplate doing so, or make unsuccessful attempts. But an even larger number, without actually killing themselves, amputate parts of their spirit in a way that leaves them only partially alive. A suicide occurs every time an individual's world becomes smaller by cutting off concern for other people, places or ideas. A slow, long-drawn-out suicide occurs in all who earn their living in work which leaves them feeling less than alive. Some people give the impression of engaging voluntarily in self-mutilation but it is very often the institutions they belong to that drive them to it.

Voluntary self-mutilation

The artist Benjamin Haydon (1789–1846) was so determined to die that when he shot himself in the head and the bullet failed to penetrate more than a few inches into his skull, he persevered and slashed his throat with his razor again and again until he collapsed. What kind of suicide was this? He had filled twenty-six folio volumes recording his many difficulties in participating fully in life. He was always seriously short of money. His friends Keats, Shelley and Wordsworth made fun of his confidence in the promise of the Book of Isaiah that 'the Lord God will hold thy right hand, saying unto thee, Fear not, I will help thee.' Haydon was adamant that without his faith, 'I should have gone mad.' Why then did he kill himself, begging for God's forgiveness with an allusion to *King Lear*: 'Stretch me no longer in this tough world'?

Skill in borrowing and lending

Never having enough money, and constantly having to borrow it to achieve unattainable ambitions was a dilemma that Haydon struggled with all his life. And three-quarters of the population of the U.S.A. now define success as the ability to pay off their credit card debts. Between the art of being poor and the science of becoming rich there lies the skill of borrowing and lending, the ability to distinguish between a debt that is a surrender of part of one's life to another, and a debt that draws people together.

Benjamin Haydon's life shows the co-existence of two contrasting civilisations. Loans could be testimonies of friendship, compassion or encouragement. Or else they could be purely commercial. When the arrears of Haydon's rent reached £100, roughly the equivalent of £10,000 today, his landlord did not throw him out: 'I should not like ye to go,' he said. 'You always paid me when you could, and why should you not again when you are able?' Haydon said he needed two more years to finish the huge painting on which he was working, and the landlord agreed to wait two years. At the John o' Groats chop house nearby, when he confessed after a meal that he had no money and asked if he could pay the next day, the proprietor called him into the back room and volunteered long-term credit: 'For two years did Mr Seabrook, Rupert Street, receive me with a smiling face and an open hand, without one complaint, one surly air, and one shade of disrespect, as if I had paid like a nobleman.' Another landlord, a carpenter by trade, became an admirer and amassed a collection of Haydon's paintings in lieu of rent. A journalist meeting Haydon in the street, hearing that he was 'dreadfully anxious', because 'I have got fifty-eight pounds to pay today and have only got fifty,' replied, 'My dear Haydon, stop a moment', disappeared round the corner, pawned his watch and returned to give him the eight pounds he needed. Even the banker Coutts lent him money knowing he would never get it back. Even the sheriff's officer who came to take him to jail for debt was so awed by the huge painting of Christ on which Haydon was working that he said he would come back later when it was more convenient. These people were treating Haydon as they would their own family, recognising him as a man with a vision that others could not quite understand, but whose strong convictions so impressed them that they felt pleasure in assisting him in realising what could possibly turn out to be amazing.

Lending without expecting repayment

In his day, most ordinary shopping was done on credit, on the basis of the seller's personal knowledge of each customer's character, idiosyncrasies and opinions on politics and religion. It meant entering into a personal relationship of trust, mixing business with mutual hospitality, at a pace structured around the demands of neighbourly conviviality. Customers might be invited to dinner after a purchase, and they often came to shops to chat rather than to buy. London shopkeepers living above or beside their shop outnumbered those who worked away from home. Itinerant pedlars were constant visitors. The links between buyer and

Shopping, politics and religion

seller were emotional and not just commercial, and Haydon once refused to pay off his tailor completely because that would end their relationship and he would henceforth be 'treated as a stranger'. As late as 1895 a trade magazine could write: 'No well-thought-of firm ever demanded or expected more than a yearly payment of their debts', and there are cases of debts not being repaid for as long as sixteen years. Tradesmen allowed the rich to postpone settling their bills because the connection with them could be valuable outside commerce. There are instances of individuals dying with debts to more than a hundred different people, almost a sign of popularity in one's community, even if at the same time others were reduced to pawning a child's boot for a loaf of bread and a small piece

Forgiveness of debts versus donations to charity

of butter. Forgiveness of debts was common, and more was spent on writing them off than on donations to charity. Society was held together by multiple webs of debt; 'Every man is to his neighbour a debtor', with most debts being oral and informal. Sometimes even commercial debts could represent mutual esteem between two individuals more than a business transaction for profit. The best example is the financing of the early years of English settlement in America, much of which was done by merchants who made only the vaguest references to when they expected to be repaid.

Painting to change the world

Haydon was an artist not so much because he painted pictures as because he saw art as changing the shape of the world, and borrowing money meant changing the speed of time, forcing people to hurry up and achieve quickly what they only dream about. Painting for him was not a pleasure or a profession, but a mission. To win appreciation for his talent was only a beginning: his ultimate goal was to transform the taste of the British people, to teach everyone to draw, so that even 'the merest door-painter might paint the human figure'. The result, he was convinced, would be to 'lift the soul above this world', to give 'strength of mind' and to stimulate 'heroism or repentance or virtue'. His pictures were not intended to copy objects and make them look delightful, nor to appeal just to the senses, but rather to have a moral effect and convey inspiring ideas. Though he had an exceptional talent for capturing likenesses, he despised conventional portraiture, still life and Dutch interiors, preferring to devote himself to grand, world-shattering historical subjects, on huge canvases, ten-foot high, which conveyed a powerful message from the Bible or the classics and made the great events of the past more real than those of ordinary life. Applying the techniques of church painting to the ideologies of his time – patriotism and political reform – he wanted all public buildings to be decorated with edifying images of the victories and hopes of the masses. Two centuries later he might have made historical blockbuster films: he loved enhancing his paintings with what he called 'poetical invention' and 'a feminine touch', saying 'nothing is beautiful which is not feminine'.

Art which gives strength of mind

Painting the hopes of the masses

By borrowing money he was able to pursue his ambition to educate 'respectable labourers' to appreciate art, shattering the barrier between 'high art' and industrial production. 'Art must cease to be a mystery for humble mechanics, artisans and journeymen.' The same principle, he said, should apply to 'the milk jug as to the heroic limb', meaning that artistic appreciation of the curves of the human body could enable one to make more beautiful practical objects. Just when artisans were losing their autonomy and being forced to accept factory routines, he toured the country making rousing speeches, urging that all workers should receive the same training as artists, learn to draw the human figure and apply inspiration, originality and aesthetics to manufacturing. But the manufacturers were more interested in discipline, perseverance and profit. So though Haydon helped to establish a School of Design (which fifty years later became the Royal College of Art) with the objective of turning industrial production into creative art, he shocked conservatives by hiring female as well as male models for the students to draw, and his dream of an educational revolution which would 'elevate the artisan' came to nothing. Already in the 1840s, practical people were mocking 'a widespread mania of becoming artists' and relegating art to third place behind science or technology.

'A widespread mania of becoming artists'

Choosing to become an artist, and to be idealistic beyond what most practical people aspired to, was Haydon's first foray into the dangerous territory that lies between adventure and suicide, between maintaining a bridge to normal society and migrating into a land where the only food was imagination and hope. He complained that he was an 'outcast' and a 'victim', an outsider in a world ruled by people with influence and money unable to appreciate him. He was so scathing about every other kind of art except his own that the Royal Academy refused him membership again and again. Whereas fashionable artists with less talent but more willingness to produce the kind of art most people wanted could make a comfortable living, he could not, being obstinately reluctant to

The artist as victim and outsider

become a bread-and-butter painter of portraits of self-satisfied wealthy men and pretty women, just for the money. He tortured himself searching for ways to deal with those whose taste he abhorred though they were the ones who might have given him lucrative public commissions. He remained short of cash not only because he could not ingratiate himself with them, but because there were limits to his own imagination: he did not know how to cope with people who disagreed with him, how to benefit from their incomprehension, how to derive not just a reinforcement of his own determination, but also inspiration that could have broadened and enriched his ambitions, how to be part of a couple at loggerheads but fruitful all the same. Instead he got angry and saw himself surrounded by 'adversaries'. Dramatising the disagreements, exacerbating them by hurling sharp insults all around him, accusing his opponents of deliberately promoting 'mediocrity', deriding them as 'despots', he could never understand why the Royal Academy preferred a banal crowd-pleasing portrait of a little girl with a pink sash to his giant moralising painting of an ancient Roman hero. Sniping at institutions that resist and punish dissidence is rarely effective when practised with only anger for ammunition.

Coping with people who disagree

Crowd-pleasing art

So convinced was Haydon that he was 'destined for a great purpose' that he painted relentlessly, often for twelve or sixteen hours a day, never stinting expenditure on canvases, models and colours whether he could afford them or not. He left enormous debts when he died. Dickens was one of many who were irritated by this apparent contempt for the rules of money and in *Bleak House* used his character Mr Skimpole to denounce the selfishness of people, however charming they might be, who fell regard-less into debt. But on hearing of Haydon's death, Dickens sent five pounds to his widow.

Being out of tune with the masses

Haydon finally realised how hopelessly he was out of tune with the masses he wanted to educate when he was publicly humiliated at his last exhibition, held in the same hall as the dwarf General Tom Thumb of Barnum's Circus, one metre in height, who attracted 12,000 paying visitors, while only 133 came to see his huge painting, *The Blessings of Justice,* showing King Alfred instructing the first English jury. And then a friend, at least one whom he believed to be a friend, refused to lend him some money again. That was when he finally felt the world had no place for him. If friendship could not be relied on, what was there left?

He has been dismissed as having had 'a genius for failure'. However, when his journals were published after his death he was revealed as an astute analyst of his time and a talented writer. Dickens said he should have been a novelist. Perhaps anyone who wants to change the world should start by being a novelist and practise moulding reality, not in utopian schemes, but out of fragile emotions and unpredictable accidents.

The most cowardly form of suicide

Besides, there was as much courage as despair in Haydon's suicide: most people commit a more cowardly form of suicide when they abandon their ideals, but he did not do that.

Haydon lived in a country that hesitated between two civilisations, one of neighbourliness and one that rejoiced in the power that money could exert. It was not just that neighbourliness could metamorphose into indifference under the pressure of urbanisation, industrialisation and overpopulation, or that the more society was commercialised, the less were loans and mutual help likely to be inspired by personal sympathy. Haydon was made aware that moneylenders had other priorities by being arrested seven times, and jailed four times, always for not paying his debts to creditors untouched by sentiment, with bailiffs selling all his worldly goods, even his brushes, to pay them off.

The place of money in life had already begun to change in the thirteenth and fourteenth centuries. Academia, which today complains about being diverted from its disinterested search for truth by ignoble fundraising, in fact played a decisive role in the monetisation that was to transform large portions of life. It provided the intellectual foundations for a new vision of what was important by developing a new concept of nature, no longer seeing it as static and perfect but as dynamic, needing to be constantly measured. The dons of Merton College, Oxford (founded by the Lord Chancellor of England), who were bureaucrats as well as scholars, became known as the 'Oxford Calculators' because of their passion to measure and quantify almost every human activity, even the strength of the quantity of grace in each soul and the strength of Christian charity, as well as the price of every examination, continually repeating that money measures all things.

A new place for money in life

A new concept of nature

That coincided with a vast increase in the supply of money: in England in 1170 the Mint produced 1,300,000 pennies; in 1250 fifteen million. Half of the king's income came from debasing the coinage, calling it in and reissuing it with a lower silver content. Lords who used to regard their forests as giving them status and pleasure increasingly valued them as sources of income to be exploited for profit. But it was only gradually that the strict fulfilment of contracts eliminated emotion from accountancy. Eventually, fixed prices and exact repayments put an end to the theatrical pleasures of bargaining.

A new idea of equality

What completed the transformation was the new ideal of equality. Customers increasingly wanted to assert their independence, 'for he who is in debt is owned by others'. They preferred hire-purchase loans to come from invisible companies that would not interfere in their private lives. Instead of searching for patronage, they felt resentment at being patronised. Freedom came to mean having no obligations. Paying in cash meant 'my money is as good as yours'. These changes were welcomed because the old world of close encounters, in which everybody knew everybody, far from being universally warm and cosy, was often asphyxiating, humiliating and cruel, torn by jealousies and bickering, and fomenting a

Escaping the judgement of neighbours

desperatedesire to escape the scrutiny and judgements of one's neighbours.

Haydon's contemporary, the Chinese poet and philosopher Gong Zizhen (1792–1841), complained that humans were becoming more selfish than animals, with no appetite for the personal generosity that comes from intimate contact. But it was in England that a new path leading to another kind of suicide was opened up. When Lord Vestey (1859–1940) revolutionised eating habits in innumerable countries by importing refrigerated meat from Argentina, Russia, China, Australia and elsewhere, he created

Severing the umbilical cord between rich and poor

an offshore multinational corporation which was virtually exempt from taxation. He reduced the tax on the profits of his butcher's shops to 0.0004 per cent. In doing so, he severed the umbilical cord between rich and poor and whatever emotional ties had once existed between them. He had no outside interests beyond his total dedication to business, six days a week, living in modest houses, basing every decision on how much tax it would save, spending only one-fortieth of his income on raising four children, investing the rest, priding himself even when he owned the wealthiest private company in the world, that 'I never spend any of my profits, I live on what I earned twenty years ago.'

In the twentieth century, the British colonial empire was replaced with a less visible but even more powerful financial empire composed of an archipelago of some sixty offshore tax havens presided over by the City of London. A new virtual nation-without-borders was born, armed not with guns but with money, defying democracies and tyrannies alike. It became so omnipotent that it was able to force humble taxpayers to pay off its gambling debts. It revealed itself capable of ignoring with impunity the wishes of whole electorates. When it sold off loans to anonymous firms who had absolutely no personal care for the borrower, it became clear that the rich were cutting their own veins, embarking on a slow suicide by rupturing their emotional links with the rest of humanity. The poor might still dream of becoming rich, but rich and poor were henceforth divorced. There was no sympathy left between them. Money ceased to be a social cement.

The invisible British financial empire

Rupturing emotional links

The taste for suicide continues regardless. People with power commit suicide when they cease to believe in themselves, when they feel that nobody believes in them, and when they cannot keep their promises. Experts commit suicide by making predictions which do not come true.

The taste for suicide

Specialists commit suicide when they become incapable of understanding what other specialists say. Kind people commit suicide when they enter professions where there is no room for kindness. The most frequent form of suicide is to lose hope.

The suicide of gratitude

But the saddest suicide of all is the suicide of gratitude. Envy, greed and arrogance are chronic diseases that are unlikely ever to disappear, but they used to be held in check by gratitude. That was the bond that once held society together, or at least dampened its resentments: gratitude to gods, ancestors, parents, teachers, neighbours, nature. But the more equal a society aspires to be, and the more it is based on rights, and the more it is commercialised, the less place there is for gratitude, which is perceived as an insult to independence and a denial of self-esteem. 'Gratitude is expensive,' said Gibbon. 'Gratitude is a burden,' said Diderot. 'Gratitude is a sickness suffered by dogs,' said Stalin.

However, that need not be the end of the story. I shall return to the question of suicide in my last chapter: it holds the key to understanding what being alive can mean.

8

How can an unbeliever understand a believer?

W HAT IS THE RELIGION of a person who can identify the conductor of a Beethoven symphony simply by listening to a recording? And who is a lover of jazz as well as classical music, and French movies, and a wide range of European and American literature, while also having a passion for football, to the point of illustrating alternative strategies for economic development by comparing the different styles of German football teams?

How to discover a person's religion

Abdurrahman Wahid (1940–2009), who for three years was president of Indonesia, inherited from his grandfather and father the leadership of the largest Muslim organisation in the world, the Indonesian Renaissance of Religious Scholars (*Nahdatul Ulama*), which provided forty million members with education and medicine; while his maternal grandfather was a pioneer of Muslim schools for girls. Born in Java, educated abroad at Karachi Grammar School, and then in Islamic studies at Cairo's Al-Azhar religious university and in Arabic literature in Baghdad, he could quote from the major Arabic religious and philosophical classics, as well as from the works of the Egyptian founders of modern 'Islamism', Qutb and al-Banna. But tears came into his eyes when he saw an Arabic translation of Aristotle's *Ethics* on display in an exhibition in Morocco, because

Surprise in religion

it made him recall how near he had been to becoming an enemy of the West: 'If I had not read Aristotle and his great book as a young man,' he said, 'I might have become a Muslim fundamentalist myself': Aristotle had shown him that it was possible to 'arrive at the truth without the aid of religion simply by using his reason and understanding the human soul'. Wahid also studied Hindu philosophy, and on being elected president of the largest Muslim country in the world, one of his first acts was to pray at a Hindu temple. He ended the persecution of Indonesia's Chinese minority, came to the defence of Salman Rushdie's *Satanic Verses* and visited Israel six times, declaring that 'Those who say I am not Islamic enough should read their Quran. Islam is about inclusion, tolerance and community . . . The essence of Islam is encapsulated in the words of the Quran, For you, your religion, for me, my religion.' And more than that, 'democracy is not only not *haram* [forbidden] in Islam, but it is a compulsory element of Islam.' Irrepressibly witty, he translated a book of Soviet humour into Indonesian to teach his compatriots to laugh at themselves, and when he lost power he said he regretted it much less than losing the twenty-seven recordings he had collected of Beethoven's Ninth Symphony.

Democracy 'a compulsory element of Islam'

The Quran, said Wahid, refers to God as the Truth, and each person may apprehend the truth in a different way. 'Islam honours and values that difference, recognising that each human being comprehends God according to his or her own native abilities and propensities, as explained in the Hadith Qudsi (the Words of God as repeated by Muhammad): *I am as my servant thinks I am* . . . Those who presume to fully grasp God's will

'Islam honours difference'

and dare to impose their own understanding upon others are essentially equating themselves with God and unwittingly engaged in blasphemy.' The famous saying in the Quran, 'Let there be no compulsion in religion,' he said proudly, 'anticipates the Universal Declaration of Human Rights.' For him, sharia laws offered a 'path to God', but they were man-made not God-given laws, formulated in the centuries following the prophet's death, and needing to be revised constantly as society evolved. 'The severe blasphemy and apostasy laws . . . prevent Muslims from thinking outside the box not only about religion but about vast spheres of life, literature, science and culture in general.' The search for the truth, he concluded, 'should be allowed free and broad range, whether employing the intellect, emotions or various forms of spiritual practice'. Islam had reached its 'intellectual and spiritual maturity' in the Middle Ages by incorporating a 'humanistic and cosmopolitan universalism' based on the amalgamation of Arab, Greek, Jewish, Christian and Persian influences. Its 'long decline' was the result of scholastic and government constraints which paralysed it. Wahid married a leading pioneer of women's rights. He asked that these words should be engraved on his tombstone: HERE LIES A HUMANIST.

Maturity and paralysis

Why was there such a contrast between Wahid's religion and that of Hassan al-Banna (1906–1949), the founder of the Muslim Brotherhood, by whom Wahid was initially attracted but whose ideas he eventually rejected? Wahid valued freedom above all else and expressed that desire through a boundless curiosity. Al-Banna wanted certainty, 'to do away with the wavering mind and restlessness and shake off perplexity and fluctuation of opinion'. That was a different idea of freedom. Rejecting all

Two different ideas of freedom

frivolous distractions, al-Banna derived his nourishment entirely from the Quran, guided by humble local teachers in his village, and by his father, who was at once an imam, a smallholder, a watch repairer and a seller of religious gramophone records.

Freedom from disagreement

While he was still a schoolboy, he started a Society for the Prevention of the Forbidden to reprove all those who missed prayers or ate when they should be fasting, sending them letters warning them to mend their ways on pain of forfeiting their place in Heaven. A few years later he started another Benevolent Society to eliminate alcohol, gambling, pagan customs and Christian missionaries. He never hesitated to correct people, however eminent, who deviated from Islamic morals, even telling government ministers to remove the gold ring from their finger, because Islam forbade men to wear gold jewellery. Waitresses who served him bareheaded he sent away to cover themselves with a scarf.

When he went to Cairo to train as a teacher, he was disgusted by his fellow students, whom he described as 'nihilists and libertarians'. He was horrified too by the debauchery of the Europeans, their addiction to liquor and frivolous entertainments, their talk about the liberation of women, casting doubts on tradition, and treating everything Western, American or British as sacred. The theatres, concerts and cinemas of the city did

A passion for certainty

not interest him, nor learning foreign languages. He abhorred the 'conflicting debates' within Islam, 'the tangles of terminology and scholastic labyrinths' of its theologians and their 'petty squabbles', and so started preaching to the public in coffee houses. He proved to be extremely persuasive, charismatic and a brilliant organiser. A group formed around him swearing to follow him, 'to live and die for Islam'. He wanted them to 'hold identical views with me' and to be people who 'love the upholders of such views', rejecting 'the hotch-potch of confused . . . non-Islamic ideas'.

Then he added nationalism to his creed. As a primary school teacher in Ismailia, Britain's principal military base in Egypt, a sense of 'humiliation and captivity' in the face of foreign occupation inflamed his fervent patriotism. 'I wish to train the nation for an honourable and dignified place in the world . . . It is incumbent on every Muslim that he must become the leader of the world', excelling in every field, while avoiding materialism or self-promotion. Soon he was attracting huge crowds in mosques and establishing branches of the Muslim Brotherhood all over Egypt. His followers gave the Brotherhood as much as half their earnings; they established businesses to support its work, and a welfare organisation that provided friendly help for the needy, the sick, the unemployed and the very young – cheap medicine, vocational training, financial assistance. He himself lived in a rented room very modestly, constantly affable, saluting everyone, enquiring about their children by name, the progress of their education and even the welfare of their animals; his memory was prodigious.

Nationalism in religion

These two versions of the Muslim ideal were diametrically opposed. They expressed a clash of imaginations. Indonesia contains 17,508 islands, 300 different ethnicities, and speaks 742 languages and dialects, and it has had to adapt its original animist religion successively to Muslim conversion, Hindu rulers, Dutch colonisation, Japanese occupation, the world's third largest communist party, nationalism and capitalism. Variations of

Belonging to several religions

each of these ideologies survived in different places in different degrees. Change was often resisted, to the extent of some communities maintaining their refusal to pay tribute for two centuries, but innumerable Indonesians learned to live with others of seemingly opposed philosophies, ignoring each other's beliefs, valuing not theoretical adherence to a dogma but practical good sense and experience. They treasured their village feasts which brought them together, including every nuance of opinion. Children moved between different households, choosing a favourite aunt or uncle from outside the family, so that families unconnected by blood were common, for it was considered improper to refuse if another family asked to foster or 'borrow' your child. 'For weddings and funerals, people needed Islam, for earthly blessings, they appealed to ancestors, and for magical protection they contacted the village guardian spirit.' The care-taker of the mosque who led prayers at weddings and funerals did not always bother to fast during Ramadan or pray five times a day; one of them said that those who did were 'just showing off', and the only hell he person-ally feared was the police station. A village headman summed up this doctrine of live-and-let-live thus: 'Islam means welfare and prosperity, which all people seek, so everyone is Muslim.' A pious puritan condemned three-quarters of the inhabitants as being Muslims only in name, seldom praying or performing their religious duties. For a long time those who ignored religion were, on the whole, not harassed.

Live-and-let-live religion

But at the end of the twentieth century that suddenly changed. What the locals called 'Arab Islam' arrived, different from the Indian version that had converted Indonesia many centuries before and had been more individualist, internalised, tolerant, shaped by a kind of Sufism that placed less emphasis on public worship. The new preachers became more threatening: 'People are ignorant and it is our duty to teach them; a Muslim must behave like one; ignorant people cannot decide these things for themselves, they need to be told; and if they do not comply, they must be punished.' Schoolchildren were taught to memorise the Quran in Arabic; though they did not speak the language; as one of them said, 'God never said anything I could understand.' Women began wearing head-scarves. Arab Islam became the new face of modernity, replacing both nationalism and communism as a response to humiliation, poverty or disappointment. A born-again Muslim said: 'For the first time in my life I feel awake . . . I feel my faith getting stronger by the day, almost like a force . . . Did you notice how full the mosque was on Friday? After five hundred years, Islam is finally making progress.' Of course there were many who resented being told what to believe and what to do. But others said, 'Nowadays, people have too many wishes and a thousand ways of satisfying them; they are ruled by their passions. Islam saves you from yourself.'

The rebellion against too many choices

There is not a clash of civilisations between Christianity and Islam, but a clash of imaginations within each of them. Both have endlessly clashed inside their own ranks about how to interpret their ideals, because they harbour such a huge variety of temperaments. Most civilisations and most religions have clashed internally between two visions, between on the one hand civilisation as a city-fortress, surrounded by walls, protecting itself against barbarians and rejecting the vices of the external world, and on the other hand the city–port, always hungry for what it does not possess,

The fortress versus the open port

searching for a better life by trading with strangers and importing novelties without too many worries about where they might lead. It is a division between those who want life simplified and those who accept that it is a

Accepting contradictions

muddle of contradictions and complexities, between those who like to know what is expected of them and those who prefer to invent their own solutions, between those who value having basic laws and texts that need to be obeyed and those who question, argue and resist. However, because individuals have inconsistent attitudes in different situations and few have been either puritan or worldly in everything they do and say and think, the clashes between them are not collisions but more like bells rung together out of sequence.

Varieties of puritanism

Al-Banna was part of a long tradition found intermittently in most religions, protesting against greed and lechery, demanding stricter morality and a renunciation of frivolous pleasures, aiming for ecstatic experiences of the divine through abstinence or asceticism or even martyrdom. Puritanism has alternated between trying to impose its ideas on everyone else so as to eliminate sin from the world, and withdrawing from its wickedness to pursue a self-contained existence isolated from pernicious influences. The founders of America's Southern Baptists rejected modern morality in much the same way as al-Banna.

Wahid's universalism, by contrast, represented an equally widespread tradition, which flourished with exceptional brilliance during Islam's golden age, as well as in periods of renaissance in other regions. After conquering large portions of the earth, Muslims had the confidence to be curious about all previous wisdoms, to absorb them, to synthesise them, to advance beyond them, innovating not only in many branches of know-ledge, but also in the arts, with a vast multiplication of heterodox ideas and a free flowering of passionate love poetry unrestrained by convention. The inventor of the World Wide Web, Tim Berners-Lee, is in this tradition, and calls himself a Universalist Unitarian, a member of a religion which has no fixed creed, giving each member freedom to search for truth and to incorporate elements of other faiths. He draws a parallel between this religion and the internet, which facilitates interest in all cultures. Though Unitarians began as a Christian nonconformist minority, they are almost as open to other faiths as Eastern religions which reject the idea that to follow one religion must necessarily be to exclude all others. An extraordinary number of pioneers have links with the Unitarians: Susan B. Anthony, the pioneer of feminism, John Locke, the pioneer of toleration, Florence Nightingale, the nursing pioneer, Albert Schweitzer, possibly the first *Médecin sans frontières*, Josiah Wedgwood, who not only industrialised pottery making but may have also been the inventor of modern marketing (using direct mail, money-back guarantees, and buy one and get one free); Frank Lloyd Wright, Charles Dickens, Thomas Jefferson, four other U.S. presidents and a whole variety of adventurous minds.

Religion without borders

Does this mean that puritans of different religions can appreciate each other and realise what they have in common? No, religions which make proselytising an important part of their creed are rivals in the race to capture hearts and minds. Though interfaith dialogue is increasingly fashionable, competition between religions is in many places intense. Nobody knows how many converts each religion makes each day, or the

Religions as rivals

*Proselytisa-
tion across
national
boundaries*

exact effect that has, but the passion for proselytisation across national boundaries has never been so widespread. The Brazilian Universal Church of the Kingdom of God, for example, established in a poor suburb of Rio de Janeiro in 1977, has over a thousand churches in eighty countries, with an international organisation that 'would be the envy of many a CEO'; able for example to convert a Pakistani in Russia who then starts a Brazilian church in his home country. The international arm of Japan's Nicheren Buddhists, the Soka Gakkai, claims twelve million followers in eighty-two countries. Turks are opening Muslim schools in the southern parts of the old Soviet empire, training the new elites, while Koreans are advancing into its Asian domains, as well as Africa. Formerly colonised countries are now sending missionaries to convert their colonisers. There are perhaps half a million professional missionaries travelling the world, and innumerable amateurs who go abroad for short periods of proselytis-ing, in addition to the constant duty to convert compatriots. This is the spiritual counterpart to globalisation. Pentecostalism has in less than half a century made about 500 million converts, but there is an enormous variety of options to choose from. The use of every kind of media and every kind of marketing method is making competition between religions almost as vigorous as between business brands.

*The
alternative
to rivalry*

However, humanity's inability to agree on what it wants to believe does not inevitably condemn it to permanent conflict or mistrust. Past experi-ence suggests that when people feel appreciated rather than threatened, they can become more curious about the world outside their own. One of the greatest compliments one can pay another is to show interest in them.

One of the best ways of enriching oneself is to learn what others think. Humans do not always have to imitate the snail which retreats into its shell at the slightest sign of danger.

I once had a meeting with an eminent Iranian ayatollah. He fulminated angrily for an hour against the misdeeds of the West. When he had finished, his anger vanished, he smiled, he put his arm round me and said, 'I should like to come again.'

'Why?' I asked.

'Because you listened to me.'

That gesture, that one remark, opened up a human side that usually remains hidden in the confrontations of doctrine. It immediately turned disagreement into curiosity. But I know that curiosity by itself is only a beginning, an opening of a door, which leads nowhere unless it is accompanied by knowledge. To listen is not enough, to understand requires a preparation with information, reading and enquiry so that one is not just an uncomprehending stranger. To be understood involves being able to offer ideas that illuminate the concerns and resonate with the thoughts of those whose stance one does not share. Understanding does not eliminate disagreement, but it transforms disagreement into an enriching experience, a feeling that one is being allowed to enter into the mysteries of human variability and to escape from being only partly alive. Despite all the bitter quarrels between and within religions, I value the memory of this ayatollah insisting that one essential feature of the Shi'a tradition is that it respects individual judgement. Ideals seldom become reality, but this is a clue not to be missed.

Turning disagreement into curiosity

The mysteries of human variability

9

How can a religion change?

THE MORE EDUCATED PEOPLE ARE, the more doubts they have. By the twentieth century, a Catholic monk, having studied at Cambridge and Columbia universities, was praying in these words:

'My Lord God, I have no idea where I am going
I do not see the road ahead of me.
I cannot know for certain where it will end.
Nor do I really know myself,
And the fact that I think I am following your will does not mean
  that I am actually doing so.
But I believe that the desire to please you does in fact please you.
And I hope that I have that desire in all that I am doing.
I hope I will never do anything apart from that desire.
And I know that if I do this you will lead me by the right road
  though I may know nothing about it.
Therefore I will trust you always though I may seem to be lost and
  in the shadow of death.
I will not fear, for you are ever with me, and you will never leave me
  to face my perils alone.

Thomas Merton (1915–1968), who wrote this now much repeated prayer, spent many years trying to discover what he should do with his life. Opening the Bible at random in search of guidance he put his finger on the phrase 'Thou shalt be silent', so he withdrew from the world and became a Trappist monk. Nonetheless, neither his faith nor his activism for peace and social justice could wholly satisfy him and he devoted much energy to conversations with leaders of Eastern religions. His autobiography was a bestseller because he openly expressed widely shared doubts, and these show no signs of disappearing. The more religions, ideologies and distractions there are to choose from, the fewer the escape routes out of doubt.

Escape routes out of doubt

'We all worship the same God.' Is that true? And what about those who say they have no god? Is a single religion that would please and unite everybody a possible goal? At the age of twenty-four, a handsome and charismatic native of Babylon called Mani (A.D. 213–276) decided it was. He invented what for over three centuries was one of the most widespread religions on earth. It expanded rapidly, from France and Spain and North Africa (where St Augustine was a follower for nine years before becoming a Christian) as far as India and China. The Uighur empire, which once extended over large parts of Central Asia and was remarkable for its passion for theological debate, adopted it as its state religion. It flourished, with ups and downs, for nearly a thousand years in China, where Mani came to be regarded as a reincarnation of Lao-tzu and his religion virtually amalgamated with Taoism. In one wave of persecution, 4,600 of its monasteries and 40,000 temples and shrines were said to

A religion to please everybody

have been destroyed, but it recovered and revived, and metamorphosed into a Chinese secret society.

'At once global and local'

Other religions, said Mani, were linked with one country, and presented in one language; but he was offering a faith that would combine all faiths, for every country in every language, adapted to local traditions and even local beliefs, however discordant. He wove Christian, Buddhist, Gnostic and Zoroastrian thoughts into a dramatic mythology about how the world came to be in the mess it was. In the Middle East, he presented himself as an apostle of Christ. After visiting India, he adopted the doctrine of transmigration of souls. In Iran, he incorporated Iranian divinities. He travelled everywhere for many years, personally enrolling kings and communities of all kinds to his cause. No religion has ever been so flexible. It was as though the executives of the Hong Kong and Shanghai Bank, which today claims to be at once global and local, were to change their clothing as they fly around the world, exchanging their pin-striped business suits for the flowing robes of the bazaar or kimonos or saris.

Combining pessimism and optimism

Mani knew how to appeal to both pessimism and optimism. God, he said, was not omnipotent, he could not solve the conflict between good and evil, though his angels might try to contain it. Evil came from Greed. It was no use fighting it. He prophesied that there would be war, strife and poverty till the end of time. But he offered a refuge: the creation of beauty, gentleness, non-violence, vegetarianism, and simple living. His religion grew rich as it expanded, despite its belief in simplicity. The way Mani won adherents reveals that his converts were not necessarily won over just by his teachings, let alone by such rituals as a whole month of fasting each year. He was an aesthete. He devoted himself not only to proclaiming his gospel, but to literature and the fine arts. The trouble with previous religious reformers, he said, was that they only talked, but never wrote books. So he wrote seven. He illustrated them himself, and indeed his seventh volume was composed entirely of pictures. He also wrote an autobiography, devised a splendid calligraphy, and made his books into complete works of art with amazing bindings covered in gold leaf – and this passion for beauty became a tradition in all the subsequent literature of his religion. He is remembered as a great artist in his native country today, overshadowing his ancient reputation as a heretic. He was also a devoted musician and pictures have been found showing a full orchestra accompanying his religious services.

The role of art in religion

He was more interested in bringing light into the world than in battling with dark devils. The methods of his disciples are revealed in a manuscript about one of them, Julia of Antioch, who migrated around A.D. 400 to Gaza in Palestine, accompanied by two younger women and two young men, described as particularly beautiful, of humble disposition and gentle character. She went door to door, visiting people in their homes and inviting them to hers, making converts by offering social services to the poor. That only annoyed rival churches, who accused her of holding orgies at which lavish meals were served.

A world religion is a challenge to all existing religions. Mani's readiness to form loose alliances with almost any faith aroused the hostility of all those for whom religion was a community with finite boundaries and a vision of the truth that outsiders could not fully appreciate. His

The challenge of a world religion

enemies had him arrested and he died in prison, flayed alive according to one legend. For centuries after his death, Manicheanism continued to be regarded as a serious rival by the leaders of all the established religions – Zoroastrian, Muslim, Christian and Confucian – who gradually succeeded in wiping virtually all trace of it from the face of the earth, with unusual thoroughness. Only very recently have astonishing archeological finds in Egypt and Turkestan, exhuming its vanished monuments and scriptures, begun to reveal what the insults of his detractors had concealed.

Valuing other religions

Mani's idea that all religions are, if not completely the same, at least capable of living together like suburban neighbours who do not interfere with each other, is almost what many in the U.S.A. have come to believe. In 1920, 94 per cent of American Christians said their religion was the only true religion; today, only 25 per cent do, and the rest believe that there is some truth in all religions. 'Our government', said President Eisenhower, 'makes no sense unless it is founded on a deeply held religious faith – and I don't care what it is.' But that attitude infuriates many others. 'My religion offers the only true path to God' is what (according to a poll) 79 per cent of Saudi Arabians think, and 65 per cent of South Korean Christians, and 49 per cent of Indian Muslims, 42 per cent of born-again Americans, 37 per cent of Indian Hindus, 33 per cent of Israeli Jews, 31 per cent of Korean Buddhists, 25 per cent of Peruvian Catholics, 24 per cent of Orthodox Russians, 16 per cent of American mainstream Protestants and 15 per

Interfaith marriages

cent of American Catholics. On a more down-to-earth level, about two-thirds of Muslims, Hindus and Jews assert that they disapprove of interfaith marriage. So consensus is not just around the corner.

When the Bahai (founded 1844) attempted to create one world reli- *The prospect*
gion, even recognising most existing religions as valid, and incorporating *of endless*
a modern programme against discrimination and inequality, other reli- *religious*
gions rejected it as a rival, because it presented itself as a separate religion, *wars*
based on a prophet's divine revelation; and since it had a Shi'a origin, it
was apostasy to Muslims. It is better to stop talking about religion as
though it is a single, uniform force. Each religion has a separate voice, and
usually many voices. Even UNESCO announced that it did not know
what 'religion' meant, listing forty-eight different definitions. The World
Parliament of Religions, inaugurated in 1893, is, like the United Nations,
a confirmation of the independence of each.

This may suggest that all one can look forward to is yet more religious
wars and disagreements, even though religion's aim is to offer certainties
amid the anxieties and chaos of life. However, when I delve into the history
of certainty and doubt, I get a glimpse of other possibilities. In their early *How*
years, religions did not expect or win complete acceptance of strictly *religions*
defined beliefs. After Jesus' death, some Christians believed in one God, *have changed*
but some in two gods and some in thirty or 365 gods. The very notion of
belief used to be much looser, implying not conviction and certainty
but an emotional attachment rather than an intellectual assent. *Creed*
originally meant *cor do*, I give my heart, I love. The Bible was originally
valued as a collection of tales about heroes, allegories open to many interpretations, without a necessarily consistent message. The early Jewish
rabbis established a tradition that the scriptures should be an invitation
to continuous discussion and development, a tradition perpetuated in

the saying that when two Jews meet, there are at least three opinions. Medieval Christian preachers used sacred stories as launching pads for individual spiritual journeys. The *Compendium of All Speculations*, written by Madhava Acharya in the fourteenth century, describing every known theology and atheism with dispassionate impartiality, illustrated the capacity of Indians, in some periods, to find harmony between apparently irreconcilable ideas, while believing that none contained all the truth. The idea of heresy developed slowly. 'Heresy' originally meant choice, and there was nothing pejorative about it. Only gradually did theologians turn disputations into condemnations. Only slowly was disagreement seen not as an opportunity for intellectual and spiritual vitality but as a threat to harmony, and it was then that churches became increasingly censorious, often proclaiming new doctrines not because they had discovered a new truth, but to repress dissonant voices within their fold. Sometimes, in imitation of absolute monarchs intent on eliminating all rival warlords, they tried to impose absolute obedience to their orthodoxy, on pain of excommunication. Sometimes, in response to the questioning of science, they tried to match its precision by envisaging God differently, no longer as indescribable and unfathomable, about whom nothing certain could be said, but as a leader larger than life speaking with precise commands. Religion used to be poetry. But under attack, it became prose. It thought it was entering the same boxing ring as science, and became unrecognisable.

The origins of heresy

The rise of dogmatism

Of course the sacred texts have always been the bedrock of belief. But they had to be interpreted, and scholars who interpreted often disagreed.

So there has been an enormous amount of uncertainty in religions through most of their history. In medieval Islam, for example, the differences between the 'five schools', each interpreting the law with its own methodology, and each dominating different territories of the Islamic world, were accepted as instructive rather than antagonistic, nurtured by an 'ethics of disagreement' (*adab al-ikhtilaf*). Scholarship meant argument, ingenuity, and independent reasoning (*ijtihad*). One of the most famous of all Islamic theologians, Imam al-Haramayn al-Juwayn (1028–1085) said, 'The purpose of shariah enquiry is not to reach the right result but the enquiry itself.' That is what scientists say today.

An 'ethics of disagreement'

The Christian Bishop Gregory of Nyasa in Turkish Cappadocia (A.D. 335–394) was not shocked by lapses from orthodoxy, when there was much less orthodoxy than there would be centuries later. He refused to give his followers exemplars of the good life drawn from the past, telling them instead to choose people known to themselves. He wrote books that were deliberately ambiguous, believing as he did that the Bible contained fruitful ambiguities to make its readers think for themselves. Religious doctrines had not hardened yet. His biography of his sister Macrima gives her masculine as well as feminine virtues, and he argued that when humans are resurrected, 'there will be no males or females'. And Bishop Demophilus of Constantinople (d. 386) responded to objections to his opinions by quoting the gospel of Matthew: When you are persecuted in one city, flee to another. Recent research has shown how in the early years of Christianity, most worship was organised locally, independently of any central lead or regulation, dominated instead by families or clans with

Fruitful ambiguities

wildly different emphases, and resisting the efforts of bishops to impose uniformity upon them.

So the boundaries between different religions used to be less clear-cut, even though furious religious disputes persisted. Confucianism, Taoism and Buddhism were, for a time, given official recognition in China *Three* as being not rivals but Three Teachings to be valued simultaneously, each *Teachings in* in a different sphere, the first to guide public administration, the second *China* to comfort private anxieties and the third to offer hope of ultimate individual salvation while also bringing all classes together in great festivals. The collaboration appealed to the first Ming emperor Taizu (1328–1398), who started life as an illiterate orphan peasant, an outsider to the philosophies of the learned elite, and so open to the idea that all three teachings could contribute to the maintenance of peace and to his own glory. In medieval Spain, Christians, Muslims and Jews lived side by side, also for a time, in more or less peaceful '*convivencia*', with some brilliant results in agriculture, poetry, singing and scholarship, bilingual in Latin and Arabic, though with some persecution mixed with the toleration.

In the eighteenth century, the Church of England abandoned enquiring into the private beliefs of its members, and became a 'broad church', *Behaviour* maintaining that the exact details of liturgy, doctrine and ecclesiastical *more valued* organisation were 'things indifferent' in the eyes of God, who cared only *than belief* about moral behaviour. In the U.S.A., Henry Ward Beecher (1833–1887), the most famous preacher of his day, argued that charity was more important than belief, and that ostracising unorthodoxy was unchristian. Humanity may imagine that it is becoming more 'tolerant' but it is losing an old tradition of finding the sacred wherever it could. Many dogmas are denser and harder than they once were.

The most widespread religion of all, 'popular religion', has never bothered much with metaphysical distinctions, and has throughout the ages focused principally on obtaining practical relief from the anxieties of life, sickness, misfortune, poverty and hunger. Its unchanging concerns through three thousand years are revealed in China, where the ancient God of Wealth Tsai Shen continued to be worshipped irrespective of ideological fashions and his effigy, which attracts prosperity, is still to be found at the entrance of many homes and buildings. Numerous Chinese temples are being rebuilt today, not to preach new or old theologies, but to aid in the struggle for survival, to bring folk customs out of hibernation, to reassert peasant ideals of mutual help, to organise festivals, build schools, facilitate the bribing of local officials, fight for positions of leadership, and provide services such as fortune telling and exorcism, which are paid for, since religion is also business. That is why in just one northern province of five million inhabitants (Shaanbei) over 10,000 temples have recently been revived. It is in the same spirit that one half of Americans have changed their religious affiliation, and half of these have changed it at least twice, not because they have changed their theological opinions (only 18 per cent give that reason), but more commonly because they marry someone of a different faith (37 per cent), or because they move to another city and make new friends (25 per cent). A church is to many essentially a community of mutual support. When young Americans are asked what their religion means to them, most reply that it provides someone to ask

'Popular religion'

Reviving ancient temples

for help when things go wrong; and they add that a religion is true when it makes one happy. However, even popular religion becomes sectarian as expectations rise, and inequalities lose their justification, and frustration reaches boiling point, because even moderate prosperity and respect seem unattainable, and it is then that religion turns into an angry political movement.

Manipulation

The battles between believers and unbelievers have been in great part due to religion being transformed into an instrument of power and control. Much of the hostility to religions has been not a quarrel about supernatural mysteries but a protest against the arrogance or corruption or hypocrisy of the pious telling everyone else how to behave. Governments have used religion to increase obedience and business leaders to make their employees work harder. Religion has even allied with patriotism to turn nation against nation. But this manipulation has also encouraged people to seek refuge in religion, to seek from it what earthly powers do not provide; in India, for example, there are two and a half million places of worship but only 75,000 hospitals.

Corruption

The world's religions began as revolutions. The prophets have all been rebels protesting about the morals of the masses and the corruption of the rich and powerful. They have all wanted to change the world. But when a message is encapsulated in an institution, it metamorphoses into shapes that would surprise its founders. As religions grow rich and powerful, they can progress from enthusiasm to complacency, from courage to compromise, from idealism to corruption. Most of them, at one time or another, have made deals with aristocrats and plutocrats, while preaching equality and humility. Success is not the ideal partner of spirituality. That is why new sects, schisms, heresies, interpretations are born almost every day, privately or publicly; each is a mini-revolution, a reminder of what has not been achieved.

It is impossible to predict how people may behave from the beliefs they nominally profess. In Northern Ireland, Catholics and Protestants, after fighting each other in one of the most merciless of religious wars, revealed themselves, in the first enquiry ever made into what they actually know about religion, to be unable to say what the First Commandment is (only 17 per cent of young people aged between sixteen and twenty-four know it, and only 46 per cent of the older generation); only 21 per cent of the youngsters and only 54 per cent of those aged over sixty-five know that there are four gospels. Only half of Americans can name even one of the gospels; and about a quarter call themselves Christians while believing in reincarnation and astrology. After a half century of atheist education, very few Chinese (only 8 per cent) say they belong to a religion, but they still have religious practices and beliefs; 44 per cent think that life and death are controlled by the Will of Heaven or by the God of Fortune; 56 per cent have had a 'religious, spiritual or visionary experience', which is more than Americans (49 per cent). Only 4 per cent identify themselves as Buddhists but 27 per cent pray to Buddha and three-quarters affirm beliefs which were once Buddhist but no longer carry that label. *Ignorance*

I am not sure that I, who never received any religious guidance from parents or teachers, and who only began interesting myself as an adult in what religion meant, am more disadvantaged than those who have had *Children's religion* the elementary religious education that is normally given to children and that usually dissuades them from paying attention to any but their own prophets.

Reinventing tradition

Though religions have always tried to be havens of stability, protecting against the confusions of daily life, they succumb to trends and fashions nonetheless. Established creeds are being supplemented by new therapies and spiritual techniques from bizarre sources. Counter-cultures are unobtrusively being absorbed by conventional churches. Even denominations that aim to preserve ancient traditions are creating new ways of doing so. People who have lost their self-confidence are once again seeking reassurance from exotic beliefs, just as the Greeks and Romans became adepts of numerous Oriental and mystical sects when their empires crumbled. The Japanese turned to a succession of new religious movements in the Middle Ages when they felt their world was, as they put it, 'turning upside down', and they are doing the same again today. 'All human efforts are stupid and vain,' said one of their poet-musicians in the twelfth century, withdrawing from the city to worship nature, while demoralised warriors transformed tea drinking into a spiritual ceremony, and merchants making fortunes exporting arms to the world (Japan was once supreme in that trade) re-

Quick-fix salvation

engineered Buddhism into a simplified, quick-fix guarantee of personal salvation, freed from any worries of conscience or any need for ascetic privations. Japan today is a major manufacturer of new religions, as much as of electronics and cars.

New religions are being invented almost every year, winning millions of adherents and spreading to distant continents far from their local roots.

The world now counts 4,200 different religious denominations, but within each there is a multitude of nuances. To say that one is a Roman Catholic in Brazil, Mexico or the Philippines glosses over the practices each country is re-appropriating from its African, Aztec-Mayan or Malayo-Polynesian past. Nigerians, who now almost outnumber the English in the Anglican Church, are resurrecting the stricter morals of the Pilgrim Fathers. Many African Christians are finding inspiration in the Old Testament through the conviction that their society resembles that of the ancient Hebrews. Like many African Muslims, equally devoted to a memorised Holy Book, they are reviving radical aspirations for social justice. The Methodists of Fiji are not content to maintain Wesley's rituals: they teach their children not just 'the way of the church' but also 'the way of the land'. The converted natives of Peru often forget what the missionaries taught them and claim to 'have always been Christians'. The victims of colonisation are revealing that their conversion left a less permanent impression than the colonisers believed. Women are finding that their struggle for recognition is increasingly being ambushed by revived misogyny. The fall in religious observance in Europe is counterbalanced by fervent concern for the environment, which is of course the oldest religion of all. At the same time, the motivation of adherents varies as denominations pass through phases of being dynamic or static, aggressive or defensive.

Mergers and acquisitions in religion

The oldest religion of all

Religions build walls around themselves to maintain their coherence and to keep out strangers, but they have demonstrated over the centuries that they are capable of changing; even on subjects on which some are so adamantly uncompromising now, like marriage and abortion and homosexuality, their attitudes used to be quite different. However, they have not applied the Quran's famous injunction – 'We have created you male and female and have made you nations and tribes so that you may know one another' – because they know one another only as monolithic organisations, not as a collection of individuals with a whole variety of opinions and temperaments. The more they interest themselves in others, and not just themselves, the more there is a possibility that they will use less of their energies in mutual hostility.

Superficially bizarre beliefs in ancient Egypt

The more they recognise their debt to each other, the better they can appreciate what individuals seek through religion. The superficially bizarre beliefs of the ancient Egyptians cease to be irrelevant to me when they come to the conclusion that immortality is not just for pharaohs, but for everybody: that is an invitation to consider what immortality can mean apart from survival, what gift each individual should leave to benefit humanity after death. The realisation that seven of the Ten Commandments are taken from ancient Egyptian texts makes me reflect on how beliefs can be transformed by seemingly slight modifications. When I hear the Jewish sage Hillel (a near-contemporary of Christ) sum up his faith in one sentence: 'That which is hateful to you, do not do to your fellow. That is the whole Torah; the rest is the explanation' – words that exactly echo the Golden Rule of Confucius, I meditate on why all attempts to create a universally accepted common world ethic have failed. When the story of the adoption of monotheism by the Israelites is told – one of the most momentous events in history – the unexpected consequence emerges, that they gave up on having a female consort for their God, which they used to have, and which the polytheistic ancient Greeks also had, with priestesses holding respected public positions and exercising important influence. It is fruitful to reflect on how the whole of history would have been different if the Prophet Muhammad's efforts to get Jews and Christians to agree to a united reformed religion had not been rebuffed.

Women in religion

Not mutual toleration but mutual knowledge is one answer to the supposed clash of civilisations, but only half or a third of an answer. Knowledge is always limited by doubt and uncertainty, and doubting has not yet been raised into a satisfying art. And knowledge, like food, tastes and looks different depending on who cooks it and how it is served and what meals the diner has eaten before. Knowledge is never raw. Cooking and eating knowledge is perhaps the most difficult of all the arts.

I shall not ask you what your religion is. I prefer to ask instead: How do you put into practice whatever beliefs you have?

I shall not ask you what you religion is

10

How can prejudices be overcome?

SINCE THE BEGINNING OF TIME, humans have been proud of what distinguishes them from others, but also uncertain about how best to deal with the disagreements that bring havoc to their lives.

'What is your religion?'
'The religion of every sensible person.'
'And what is that?'
'A sensible person never tells.'

The Earl of Shaftesbury (1621–1683), who advocated this strategy of silence, was not afraid of rebelling against his king and beheading him, nor of colonising unexplored Carolina, nor of being a risk-taking politician, which ended in him being tried for high treason; but only on his death-bed did he have the courage to confess that he believed Christ was not God. It was dangerous to reveal one's opinions when religious wars were devastating Europe, killing as much as half of the population in some areas, all in God's name; and when the Catholic Inquisition was harassing about 150,000 'heretics' – the terrorists of that time – and when opposing varieties of Christians imagined each other to be messengers of the devil, while preaching the need to love thy neighbour.

Terrorists in other times

Leaving individuals to decide and profess their own religion seemed to be the only way to avoid the continued persecution of disagreement. The American Constitution enshrined this idea, and other countries followed, but it has not proved to be a complete solution. Mass murder inspired not just by religion but by passions of many kinds has continued to plague the world. Toleration has not sufficed to remove mutual ignorance or contempt. Even when people of differing opinions are not physically attacked, they resent not being understood. Each epoch and each group has taboos that it is unwise to question or mention. Relief from persecution is only a beginning, because to be surrounded by indifference can be too much like solitary confinement.

The tradition of mass murder

Solitary confinement outside prison

Replacing physical by verbal disagreement, substituting talking for fighting, was a great breakthrough. But the war of words between opposing parties that democracy has institutionalised perpetuates the military tradition of a victor defeating an enemy; it has not achieved the ideals that its Athenian inventors held most dear, that no-one should feel defeated, that past injuries should be forgotten and forgiven, that the victory of some over others was a sign of an inability to resolve conflict in a way that created harmony. Despite a proliferation of democratically approved laws, greed and arrogance still flourish and wars are still used to distract from domestic conflicts. Democracy has not advanced much beyond the sad conclusion of Solon (638–558 B.C.) that conflict was an unavoidable evil that enters every house, jumps over the highest walls, and that no door can stop it.

No-one should feel defeated

At a more personal level, politeness has been developed to cushion the

Politeness versus sincerity

collisions of discordant minds. It added elegance to social relations and provided new avenues for the expression of kindness. But there has always been uncertainty as to how to combine it with sincerity, how to avoid it being just a game in which lies are exchanged, not always to deceive – only the naïve are duped – but rather to conceal the harshness of reality. Bismarck's advice to be polite even when declaring war shows the limitations of politeness; it has not diminished admiration for aggressiveness, which continues to be rewarded in public and business life.

Disagreement is not a disease

Nevertheless, despite all these efforts to tame disagreement, it continues to grow as education spreads and critical faculties sharpen. But disagreement is not a disease. It is not just conflict; it is also the source of what distinguishes humans above all else. Humans think and reason. Disagreement forces us to clarify our thoughts, to put thoughts into words, and to discover new questions. Without disagreement, there would be no reflection, no search for truth, no enlivening conversation; humans would have nothing to dissuade them from constantly repeating the same platitudes, nothing to expand their tastes and their sense of wonder. Can at least some kinds of disagreement be more frequently a source of energy?

Anxiety the cruellest kind of imprisonment

It may be that personal differences cause more havoc than public disagreements. Public life breeds enemies and wars and quarrels about power and privilege, but private life is rampant with mistaken first impressions that abort friendship before it can start, petty disputes that leave a lingering poison in the heart, hurt pride which becomes a wound refusing to heal, as well as jealousies and anxieties that can be the cruellest kind of imprisonment. Should all this be treated as unavoidable?

One of the oldest disagreements that have kept humans apart has been between East and West, the archetype of a couple seemingly unable to escape from mutual misinterpretation and mistrust. One of the most courageous attempts to span the divide was made by Rabindranath Tagore (1861–1941), the first non-European to win the Nobel Prize for Literature. Why, he asked, could there not be a 'fusion of diverse races and religions and sciences'? All human beings, he said, have the divine in them, and only selfishness and narcissism prevented them from realising what they could do for each other. Their love of nature and literature, poetry and song could free them from petty obsessions. He wanted the East to expand the imagination of the West, and for the West to share its technological skills with the East. India was ideally suited to be the intermediary. 'To establish a personal relationship between man and man has been India's constant endeavour.' Its people called everyone close to them father, brother, auntie, even if they were not related; they delighted in maintaining contact with distant relatives and childhood friends irrespective of wealth and caste. 'These ties were prescribed not by the scriptures but by the heart . . . The moment we come into contact with a person, we strike up a relationship with him. So we do not slip into the habit of looking on man as a machine or a tool for the furtherance of some interest. There may be a bad as well as a good side to this, but at any rate, it has been the way of our country, more, it has been the way of the East.' If only the East would assimilate what was best in the West, 'what a full character will be formed from a synthesis between these two.' Why did the world not listen to Tagore?

Tagore's dream

The marriage of East and West

When he travelled in the West, he discovered that those who dominated its thinking had deep reservations about his attitudes. For them, poetry, song and imagination were quite separate from real life. They dismissed his ideas as mysticism. Beatrice Webb wrote: 'He has perfect manners and he is a person of great intellect, distinction and outstanding personal charm. He is beautiful to look at. He clothes himself exquisitely.' But when he said 'the intellect solves no problems', or 'all governments are evil', she became indignant, resenting his criticisms of the West and also his resentment at her criticisms of Hindu tradition. Her conclusion was that 'this all-embracing consciousness of his own supreme righteousness compared to men of action is due to the atmosphere of adulation in which the mystic genius lives and has his being.' Bertrand Russell wrote after talking with him: 'It was unmitigated rubbish – cut and dried conventional stuff about the river becoming one with the ocean . . . His mystic act did not attract me and I recall wishing he would be more direct. He had a soft rather elusive manner, which led me to feel that straightforward exchange or connection was something from which he would shy away. Naturally, his mystic views were by way of dicta and it was not possible to reason about them . . . His talk about the Infinite is vague nonsense.' And Tagore, emerging from one of Russell's Cambridge lectures, wrote: 'I listened, and yet afterwards I do not remember a word of what the professor said, though my ears listened intently and appreciated the facility of his method. But it was all entirely irrelevant to the important matters of life and devoid of scientific discernments of demonstrably accessible facts.' The Westerners who admired his poetry often saw what they were

What Great Minds could not understand

'I do not remember a word of what the professor said'

already familiar with, for example Christian humanism. Darwin's daughter said, 'I can now imagine a powerful and gentle Christ, which I never
could before.' Despite his fame, for many people he remained 'not one of
us', and often nothing more emerged from a meeting with him than a re-
iteration of pre-existing convictions.

*Reiterating
pre-existing
convictions*

In Germany, which in the nineteenth century had led the Western
world in the scholarly study of Indian religion, his poems were at first read
as illuminating Eastern faiths, rather than as a contribution to world literature; and for long it was religious, not literary, publishers, who chose to
translate him. In the U.S.A., when he tried to fund-raise from Dorothy
Whitney, heiress to one of America's greatest fortunes, she said she was
put off by 'the woolliness of the poet's ideas and the phoney business of his
dress and play-acting'. She overcame her first impressions only after her
husband went to work for him and opened her eyes to his extraordinary
and immensely varied talents.

Westerners placed him in the pigeon-hole of 'Indian culture', though he
devoted his life to trying to change it. He said, 'I love India but my India
is an idea and not a geographical expression', and he poured scorn on its
corruption, greed and 'barbarous inner discord'. When he spoke about the
'world's soul', it was assumed that he was preaching an archaic religion,
though he was an advocate of scientific knowledge and agricultural innovation, sent his son to study technology in Germany, and was even a pioneer
of environmentalism, initiating the Festival of Tree Planting in 1928. To
foreigners his appearance suggested a prophet from ancient times, but to
Bengalis he was a man of the future, the apostle of their Renaissance, and

*The pigeon-
hole of
'Indian
culture'*

hearing him in their own language, they were exhilarated by his 'verbal zest' and his fervent songs that set their emotions on fire.

Which art is best understood?

Few men have laid bare so openly, unashamedly and thoughtfully their emotions, their hopes and the full range of their mental processes as Tagore did, and few have done so through so many forms of expression, music (over two thousand songs), drama (more than thirty plays), opera, novels, short stories, essays, poetry, philosophy, history, autobiography, travelogues, and lectures all over the world. But self-expression – which has for long been worshipped as the supreme blessing of individual emancipation – does not automatically engender receptivity, the capacity to absorb what others say and understand what others mean; it concentrates attention on the assertion of individual identity.

Tagore is probably unique in having tried to transcend human divisions by so many different routes. He appealed to reason, writing highly intelligent books for intelligent readers, who of course did not all agree with him. At the same time he appealed separately to the emotions, and first of all through poetry and music. If people wanted to understand him,

Is music the universal language?

he said, they should look not in his biography but in his songs. He believed that his greatest gift was for music, and that it was the best way to 'communicate with the outside world'. He was inspired by the folk songs of the 'Baul' – wandering minstrels who for many centuries combined Sufi, Vaishnava, Tantric and Buddhist ideas to express the deepest yearnings of Hindus and Muslims alike, ignoring religious and political disputes. India and Bangladesh each adopted one of Tagore's songs as their national anthem, and pop stars still set his lyrics to new tunes. 'No poet or composer other than Tagore was able to produce so endlessly and effortlessly words and music at the same time, so spontaneously that he relied on associates to write them down quickly before he forgot them.' In his songs, the world ceased to be 'broken up into fragments by narrow domestic walls'. The line 'My buds are secretly fragrant with your scent' encapsulates his idea of a whiff of inspiration sufficing to create a relationship. He sang about a future 'Where the Mind is without Fear'; and in the face of rejection, he offered this encouragement: 'If they answer Not to Thy Call, Walk alone.' However, he gradually came to the conclusion that 'it is nonsense that music is a universal language'; even his own compatriots, he lamented, did not fully understand his songs; and the West could not be expected to without a serious deepening of its knowledge of the whole of Indian music. *Understanding songs* He finally decided that neither his music nor his words could transmit his international message, and that pictorial art was a better medium for cross-cultural communication.

Neither his admirers nor his detractors realised that in later middle life he discovered that he was colour-blind, the victim of a genetically *Colour-blind paintings* caused confusion between red and green and a defective perception of red. He suddenly became aware that he saw people imperfectly; it was not only others who saw him imperfectly. At the age of sixty, painting became one of his principal occupations, through which he struggled 'to blend my colours with everyone else's colours'. In his poetry, he had never been able to describe the beauty of red flowers or of autumn foliage. Now, visiting the museums of the world, he studied every form of art – ranging from Egyptian monuments and Japanese woodcuts to English watercolours, but with particular sympathy for primitivism wherever he found it – 'not to fall back on tradition but to enlarge it, not to be bound by one's lineage but to increase one's power of receptivity and to transform outside models so they became one's own' with a 'rhythm that would make them dance'.

Imposing new meanings on old objects

But his painting did not change opinions. It became an experiment to make sense of what he could not see, a way of imposing new meanings on old objects. Instead of treating his ailment as a curse from which he must free himself, he preferred to regard it as symbolising the possibility of 'touching the sacred'. The contrast between the seen and the unseen fascinated him. His conclusion was to 'glorify the invisible'.

Glorifying the invisible may define Tagore either as an idealist or as a spiritualist, which means rejecting the world as it is. So too does being a practical entrepreneur who wants to replace the present by the future, which Tagore also devoted enormous effort to doing. Having detested his schooling and never having bothered to go to university, he founded his own school and his own alternative to a university, which he named Visva-Bharati, evoking the goddess of learning and the arts, the equivalent of the Greek Muses. He wanted to introduce pupils to all the different cultures of India, and then all the cultures of Asia, and then those of the West; to offer them not just 'fullness of knowledge' but also 'to establish a bond of love and friendship . . . and a sense of kinship with all mankind and nature', enlivened by aesthetic appreciation of all their different arts. Classes were held in the open in the tradition of the forest schools of ancient India; but they also had elements of the most modern Western educational theories; there was no common syllabus but each individual was to have their own

An alternative to a university

programme of study with an individual teacher. Memorising and moral instruction were replaced by the encouragement of 'freshness of mind'; instead of relying just on books, he provided practical agricultural and social work with neighbouring villagers: 'There is education in the mere effort of knowing a living person directly.' Many of his students became famous world figures, like Indira Gandhi, who became prime minister, the Nobel prize-winning economist Amartya Sen and the film-maker Satyajit Ray, who said his three years there were the most fruitful in his life, liberating him from his exclusive obsession with Western civilisation by 'opening my eyes for the first time to the splendours of Indian and Far Eastern art', making him 'the combined product of East and West that I am'. However, Tagore came to believe that to attain his goal he would first have to bring all the regional and spiritual traditions of India together, and then get the whole of Asia to 'know itself': 'the Mind of Asia is not yet fixed . . . Before Asia can cooperate with the culture of the West she must synthesise all the different cultures which she has.'

Education through face-to-face encounter

'The Mind of Asia'

There was profound disagreement between Tagore and the other towering figure in the struggle for Indian independence, Gandhi, though their relations were respectful and even friendly. Nehru said no two people could be more different. It was not just the Brahmin confronting the Vaishya merchant caste, the reserved aristocrat in expensive robes against the man in the loin-cloth who could rouse massive crowds, Bengali against Gujarati, internationalist against nationalist, openness to modernity against withdrawal to the village. Tagore rejected Gandhi's idea that Indians should go back to the spinning wheel, protesting that 'the spinning

Tagore and Gandhi at odds

wheel does not require anyone to think.' When Gandhi, for whom time moved slowly, said that the people needed an idol, and had to go through nationalism in order to reach internationalism, in the same way that they needed to experience war in order to want peace, Tagore said he 'could *Treating the* not bear to see the masses treated as children', having their irrationality *masses as* or credulity exploited, 'which may have quick results in creating a super-*children* structure, but sapping its foundations'. He lamented that his idealised vision of what India could be was far from the reality: 'Divisiveness reigns supreme and innumerable petty barriers separate us from one another.' He complained, 'I have always been attacked by political groups, religious groups, literary groups, social groups.' He concluded that 'only when our different religious communities and castes have been schooled together can you hope to overcome the violent feelings which exist today.' But educa-tion has not succeeded in making everyone wise and gentle; the quarrels of highly educated people are as relentless and often as futile as ever. And European and American students did not flock to his school, as he had hoped, with a desire to incorporate the full richness of Indian think-ing into a grand universal synthesis.

The Tagore insisted that 'the history of the growth of freedom is the history *perfection of* of the perfection of human relationships', but in private he confessed that *human* *relationships* personally he could not reach that goal. 'It would be difficult for you fully to realise what an immense burden of loneliness I carry about with me ... I am by nature unsocial – human intimacy is almost unbearable to me. Unless I have a lot of space around me in all directions, I cannot unpack my mind, mentally stretch out my arms and legs ... I have lost most of my friends because they asked me for themselves, and when I said I was not free to offer myself away, they thought I was proud. I have suffered from this over and over again, and therefore always feel nervous whenever a new gift of friendship comes my way.' The solace he sought though 'communion with nature' never sufficed. He married a ten-year-old bride, without seeing her, and years later wrote to her: 'If you and I could be comrades in all our work and in all our thoughts, it would be splendid, but we cannot attain all that we desire.' 'My connection with my family has turned into a shadow. If anyone belongs to my so-called family, that does not mean he is favourable to me.' 'I am a vagabond at heart . . . No-one will be able to put a chain on my feet.' Fame only increased his loneliness. 'My market price has risen high but my personal value has been obscured. This value I seek to realise with an aching desire which constantly pursues me. This can only be had from a woman's love and I have been hoping for a long time that I do deserve it.' But he kept his distance from the woman who offered him her love because he feared he would become her possession.

Does fame increase loneliness?

However, he did establish a lasting bond with his British assistant, Leonard Elmhirst (1893–1974), half his age, who was instantly attracted by what he saw lurking behind Tagore's dignified presence. 'The eyes perpetually lit up with gleams of humour, almost of mischief. This was no mystic sage. This was no gatherer of disciples, but a very human, human being . . . There was no aspect of human existence which did not exercise some fascination for him.' And Tagore wrote: 'I think you are the only one who closely came to know me when I was young and old at the same time.'

A lasting bond between Indian and English

Elmhirst said: 'I have sometimes found myself describing you as the most lonely of men. This seemed to be the inevitable penalty of true greatness.' Nevertheless, 'So often you cared for me like a father, so often we laughed together like children.' Tagore responded: 'I shall always remember you not merely as a friend but as a sharer in the intimacy of a joint creation.' Elmhirst had come to work for Tagore, paying his own fare, and with no prospect of a salary, inspired by a brief meeting to apply his agricultural training to the revitalisation of an impoverished Indian village; and he then set up the Dartington educational and agricultural experiment in England, combining the ideals of the two men, a monument to optimism that radiates Tagore's influence to this day, and one as significant as the utopian factory created in New Lanark by Robert Owen (1771–1858). It was a partnership that transcended time: Tagore wrote, 'The old is old and the young is young, and it is very seldom that the twain truly meet. But I am sure that we did meet.' They were a 'couple of the mind', who demonstrated how practical collaboration between quite different person-alities could bear fruit of a kind neither could have imagined on their own. It was also a partnership that illuminates the role of private sensitivities in the shaping of public events.

'The intimacy of a joint creation'

A 'couple of the mind'

There has been an important change in how these sensitivities have been expressed. Traditionally, 'honour' was of supreme importance. Aris-tocrats wanted public recognition of their superiority, and devoted most of their energy to proving it by practical demonstrations of military prowess, ostentatious displays of wealth, generosity or hospitality. Less privileged people struggled to win the accolade of respectability, independence and honesty. The fragility of public reputation still haunts most lives, but a revolt against submission to the opinions of others has made people worry more about their own self. The less confident they become, the easier it is for them to misinterpret their experiences.

When a male and a female produce a child, they bring someone into the world who mixes their characteristics in unpredictable ways and with whom neither parent can be in total agreement. It is the same with ideas, which are born of mixed and sometimes unknown parentage. Humans have never yet created something out of nothing. The best they can do is to procreate, which requires a partner, an inspiration, a meeting with another, at the very least. They are alive so long as they are acquiring knowledge, which is a process of disagreeing with oneself. That is a preparation for going beyond the ambition to love everybody, and the problem of disagreeing with most people. Compatibility can keep couples warm, but their incompatibilities can also make them sparkle and glow.

Fruitful incompatibilities

Tagore said, 'I am proud of my humanity when I can acknowledge the poets and artists of other countries as my own.' I am grateful to him for making it possible for me to imbibe some of his experience, and through him to have been given a privileged glimpse of India's unique but multiple traditions, and the subtlety of the answers it offers. If I had met him in person, as Bertrand Russell did, I might have been put off, as he was, by a feeling that there was a barrier between us, as happens in most brief encounters, but Tagore's books and letters are such intimate self-portraits of his many personalities in contact with a huge variety of characters and situations, showering me with new questions and making me think afresh

Tagore is not dead

about familiar ones, that I feel I have established a memorable relationship with him. He will never know it but he is not dead to me.

Nations have equipped their citizens with birth certificates and passports to prove that they are alive, but without giving any hint as to what life means to each one in terms of suffering and joy. Bertrand Russell reacted almost allergically to a fraction of Tagore's peculiarities, which distracted him from discovering many other qualities. It is in this way that small events produce big results. Tagore and Elmhirst put aside their different backgrounds and discovered what each could give the other.

Instinctive
repulsions

Instinctive repulsions are the main reason why so many people fail to appreciate one another; they jump to conclusions from the first piece of evidence they encounter. This is a universal human response, and many pride themselves on being able to make accurate, intuitive, instant judgements. But there is another reaction that is slower, based on the belief that it is possible to discover something new each time two beings meet in situations, moods, conversations or challenges which reveal a different voice

The willing-
ness to be
proved
wrong

or mask. Receptivity is an openness to surprise and a willingness to be proved wrong. It can be dangerous, which is why reading history is a safe way of practising: it reminds me that I do not know everything and never will; it warns me that I do not need to take disagreement as a personal insult, and it rewards me sometimes with droplets of the detachment that unfamiliar encounters demand.

I am uncomfortable on the see-saw of routine exchanges, which carefully avoid anything controversial. Dictators protect themselves from controversy by trying to annihilate disagreement, though it then festers underground and grows more bitter. Libertarians respect disagreement and coddle it, which may allow new thoughts to sprout, but also the same disagreements to survive, and the same themes to be endlessly debated, When Tagore described an ancient monument – the Taj Mahal, built by the emperor Shah Jahan (1592–1666) in memory of a deeply loved wife, prematurely deceased – as 'a tear drop on the face of eternity', he showed how poetry can shift the perspective and liberate the imagination. Thinking that involves inventing hypotheses and chasing and unravelling evidence likewise channels the imagination away from old disputes towards unexpected targets. 'Thinking is the hardest work there is,' said Henry Ford, 'which is probably why so few engage in it'. But it can be as intensely absorbing, as exhilarating and as relaxing as play.

Thoughtfulness as exhilarating as play

Tagore was able to achieve what he did to a considerable extent because he was born into one of India's most broadly cultured families, interested in everything that was normally out of bounds – pioneers of women's education and of religious reform, founders of the first theatre in Calcutta, introducers of the orchestra into Indian music, combining Hindu, Muslim and European civilisations, and speaking half a dozen Eastern and Western languages. He imbibed courage from the originality of almost every relative. His exposure to the literatures of the whole world enabled him to separate the indigestible husk of Britain's colonial oppression from the inner nourishment of its culture, drama, poetry and what he called its 'large-hearted liberalism'. Most people without such a background have to grow their own surrogate family to inspire them, and they can continue to grow it all their lives. But the Britons who governed India very rarely had

A 'family of the mind'

any idea of the breadth and depth of the culture of the sub-continent's elites, who had the advantage that their minds were stocked not with one culture, but with both Indian and British memories, and indeed with several historical and regional cultures too. Few Britons could understand how Tagore coupled the inspiration he got from his Vedic ancestors with modern thinking, so that he was able to say that 'in religion as in the arts what is common for a group is of no importance'. The coupling of civilisations has never had predictable results. What the East has borrowed from the West has included as many rotten as fruitful ideas, while in plundering the East the West has distorted or oversimplified the spiritual messages it brought back. What is distinctive about Tagore is that when he spoke of unity he accepted that it would and should contain contradictory opinions: his ideal was an 'eternal symphony played on innumerable instruments', but with no room for 'the pomp and pedantry of pontiffs and pundits'. His spirituality was based not on rigid beliefs but on individual experience, and yet, at the same time, 'separateness' was unbearable to him because it produced 'a fearful loneliness'.

In 1913, almost unknown outside his own country, Tagore was suddenly and passionately embraced by the taste-makers of Western literature as a kindred soul and awarded the Nobel Prize just six months after the publication of the English translation of his Bengali poems. Then, only a few years later, when the traumas of the First World War gave birth to new preoccupations, his most fervent admirer dismissed him as a pedlar of 'sentimental rubbish'. The ebb and flow of his reputation, between fame and near oblivion, is a good illustration of how memories are reinvented

Collecting other people's memories

Making a symphony out of contradictions

The ebb and flow of reputation

to suit transient moods. But disagreements are born not only from changing memories but also from memories that refuse to go away: Tagore *Memories*
was flummoxed by the Indian peasants who were his contemporaries and *that refuse to*
go away
whom he tried to cajole into collective grass-roots experiments and greater
efficiency: he asked why they resisted, why they 'do so little for themselves'; and they replied: Why should they change? The landlord would
benefit, not them. They lived in a different time zone, while he, the glory
of the Bengali Renaissance of the nineteenth and twentieth centuries,
suffered from the same sense of isolation as the artists of the Italian
Renaissance. In the next chapter, I shall investigate whether a new understanding of the passing of time might make it more likely that disputes
could be turned into enlightenment.

11

How else can one think about the future, apart from trying to predict it or worrying about it?

THE TWO NOBEL PRIZE-WINNERS Albert Einstein (1879–1955) and Rabindranath Tagore once had a much publicised conversation, but it was 'a complete non-meeting of minds'. Einstein was as dedicated as Tagore to the idea of the reconciliation of civilisations, and of humans too. He joined with thirty-three of the world's most eminent scientists in a manifesto proposing that scholars of all branches of knowledge should combine to 'bring forth a comprehensive world view'. He supported the One World Movement, declared himself (during the First World War) to be a European; and in 1935 urged Arabs and Jews to 'peaceable and friendly cooperation'. The *Collected Papers of Albert Einstein*, containing his writings, correspondence, speeches and interviews, which are still in the process of being published and will fill twenty-five large volumes, reveal an individual with an encyclopaedic curiosity. But in matters of daily life he was no better than anyone else when it came to making predictions about the future. He acknowledged as much: when invited to become president of Israel he declined, saying that he had 'neither the natural ability nor the experience to deal with human beings'.

What Einstein did not know

He was far from certain that there would be more mutual understanding in the future: 'Specialisation in every sphere of intellectual work', he said, 'is producing an ever-widening gulf between the intellectual worker and the non-specialist', and he half-jokingly added: 'Since the mathematicians have invaded the theory of relativity, I do not understand it myself anymore.' And very few imagined that his calculations could ever make a difference to their own future. The London *Times* denounced his ideas as 'an affront to common sense'. The Archbishop of Canterbury said that he could make 'neither head nor tail of his theories' and that 'the more he listens and reads on the subject, the less he understands'. *Why misunderstanding is increasing*

It took a long time for anyone to realise that Einstein was creating a totally new understanding of the future, partly because he suggested that he was really more interested in the past. 'What really interests me,' he said, 'is whether God had any choice in the creation of the world.' In other words, was there a disagreement at the origin of the universe, two or more incompatible options? When Cardinal O'Connor of Boston attacked the theory of relativity as atheistic, Rabbi Goldstein of New York sent Einstein a telegram: 'Do you believe in God? Stop. Answer paid 50 words.' Einstein replied, 'I believe in Spinoza's God, who reveals himself in the lawful harmony of the world, not in a God who concerns himself with the fate and the doings of mankind.' It was not too reassuring, either to the Rabbi or the Cardinal, to find Einstein attached to seventeenth-century ideas: Spinoza had been excommunicated from his synagogue in 1656 for being sceptical about organised religion and for being obstinately independent in rejecting all dogma and all idea of God as being distinct *Einstein and God* from nature; Spinoza even preferred to live in poverty rather than accept the constraints of a professorship offered to him by Heidelberg University. Einstein wrote a lot about Spinoza, and indeed composed a poem about him: Spinoza's *Ethics*, he said, 'will have a permanent effect on me'. He called himself 'a deeply religious unbeliever' – neither on one side nor on the other. Einstein lived neither in the past nor in the future, but outside time. Total absorption in scientific study gave him an 'inner freedom and security' from the aspects of ordinary life that he found uninteresting or unacceptable, nourishing in him 'a state of feeling similar to that of a religious person or a lover', with 'a simplified and lucid image of the world'. Others saw him as 'a queer mixture of great warmth and great aloofness'. He himself said that 'at the threshold of life I felt like a pariah kept on the side-line, disliked and abandoned by everybody.' When he made his first great discoveries he was very much a young man rejecting the ideas of his elders. Even when he was in his forties and world-famous, a journalist wrote: 'The impression is one of disconcerting youth, strongly romantic, and at certain moments evoking in me the irrepressible idea of a young Beethoven . . . and then suddenly laughter breaks out and one sees a student.' Einstein was irreverently witty and a 'kindly twinkle . . . never ceased to shine in his eye even through the sternest run of the argument.' He liked his own room to be in a complete mess, and refused to allow any cleaner or even his wife to tidy it: 'If a cluttered desk is the sign of a cluttered mind, of what then is an empty desk?' 'To punish me for my contempt for authority, Fate has made me an authority myself.' 'It is a strange thing to be so widely known and yet to be so lonely.'

'A deeply religious unbeliever'

Irreverent wit

'Why is it that nobody understands me, yet everybody likes me?'

He did not try to fulfil the expectations of others. 'To make a goal of comfort or happiness has never appealed to me. Such an ethical basis I call the ideal of a pigsty.' 'I have never belonged wholeheartedly to country or state, or my circle of friends, or even to my own family.' Marriage he defined as 'the unsuccessful attempt to make something lasting out of an incident', and he said he was 'scared away from marriage by fear of becoming a contented bourgeois'. Competition was 'an awful kind of slavery no less evil than the passion for money or power'. He did not drink alcohol and was a vegetarian 'in principle', eating meat 'with a guilty conscience'. 'I like neither new clothes nor new kinds of food.' He did not like his face either: 'If it weren't for this moustache, I'd look like a woman.' When he said 'Very few women are creative', he revealed not only that he was born in 1879, but that his brain was an archaeological site for very ancient prejudices as well as a fountain of bright new ideas.

'An awful kind of slavery'

'I am happy,' he said, 'because I want nothing from anyone. I do not crave praise. The only thing that gives me pleasure, apart from my work, my violin and my sail boat, is the appreciation of my fellow workers.' But while maintaining cordial relations with them, he expressed strong doubts about the place being given to randomness and the subjectivity of truth in quantum physics. 'I am firmly convinced of the harmony of the universe . . . Everything is determined. Human beings, vegetables, or cosmic dust, we all dance to a mysterious tune, intoned in the distance by an invisible piper.' Alternative explanations were a 'tranquillising philosophy,' comparable to religion; Niels Bohr (1885–1962) – who believed in

'A tranquilising philosophy'

complementarity rather than unity and whose motto was 'opposites are complementary' – was 'a talmudic philosopher [who] doesn't give a hoot for the "reality" which he regards as a hobgoblin of the naïve'. Einstein insisted that randomness would eventually be explained by a deeper level of determinism; it was 'unbearable' that space and time, electric and magnetic forces, energy and mass could not be unified in a single picture; and he devoted his later years, in vain, to unifying quantum physics and gravity.

Liberation from past, present and future

Tagore and Einstein had this in common, that they both felt isolated and misunderstood, with their ultimate ambitions unfulfilled, and this was partly due to their attitude to time. Tagore, who deliberately derived inspiration from many different epochs, was 'out of sync' with contemporaries who preferred to stay put with their habits in their own time zones. The most relevant idea produced by Einstein for the conduct of daily life is that 'the distinction between past, present and future is only a stubbornly persistent illusion', which placed him outside the frontiers of what most people believe to be common sense. If you or I were conversing with them, we would have to respond by explaining our own attitude to time, which is ultimately our most precious possession, life itself. I shall do this, in the hope that it will provoke you to explain the time frame within which you place your own existence, in effect your philosophy of history. There are plenty of ready-made philosophies of history to choose from, based for example on progress, exploitation, happiness, immortality, individuality or sexuality, and they often imply that a human is thrown into a stormy sea at birth, and spends years clambering onto a succession of leaky lifeboats, carried along uncontrollably towards an unknown seashore, or sometimes with no shore ever in sight, knowing only that one is doomed eventually to drown. I am not myself attracted to any of these philosophies, because they look forward to a future that is much like the present: more prosperity, more gadgets, more holidays, more catastrophes, more ailments, more therapies.

For me, the majority of disagreements are about either the past or the future, about what did or did not happen or what could or should happen. History shuffles the cards of what humans remember, forget and anticipate, and in doing so it can change the way they hope, argue or despair. The twentieth century, because it was in the throes of a revolution against parental power, focused attention on childhood memories as the most valuable pointer to the future. My aim is to discover how I can confront the future with other kinds of memories, and not just my own memories. Memories can no longer be treated as heirlooms to be hoarded or treasured. Recent science has transformed them into an Aladdin's cave containing many fakes and illusions. Since the pioneering experiments of Frederic Bartlett (1886–1969), remembering has been revealed as involving not the retrieval of an event as a complete entity but its reconstruction from innumerable dispersed fragments, which are almost inevitably mixed with more recent feelings and beliefs. We are constantly reinventing the past. One of the most significant discoveries of the twenty-first century is that our memories are formed in the same part of the brain where we think about the future. Our view of the future is determined by what we know of the past.

A revolution in the understanding of memory

*Living
outside time*

In this and in my previous books I have assumed that there is no good reason why the flow of time should always be presented in classical style and chronological order, and why history should not enjoy the same freedom as the pictorial arts. I juxtapose people and ideas from different centuries and backgrounds so as to find new answers to the questions that perplex the earth's present inhabitants. Einstein put aside the distinction between past, present and future for quite different reasons, asking himself when only sixteen years old, 'If I were to travel with a ray of light, what would I see?' His journey through time, and the somewhat different one by Tagore, offer contrasting visions of humans as time travellers. They impel me to explain what my alternative is to predicting or fearing the future.

*No-one lives
only in the
present*

No-one lives only in the present. We store not just memories of personal experiences in our minds but also beliefs and behaviour derived from different epochs, long before we were born, from people we never met. We construct our lives by borrowing broken-off fragments from what is labelled ancient, mediaeval or modern. No historical period is ever permanently replaced by its successor. Even those who are most up-to-date in following fashion have some fossilised beliefs and dinosaur dreams. We cannot predict which acquired tastes and lingering distastes will blight our lives or give birth to ingenious inventions. Our quarrels are often battles between clashing recollections of times past. Disagreement is more common than ever because people live in two worlds at the same time – the visible world, where they eat, work and raise families, and the invisible one, inhabited by yearnings and fears, convictions and doubts, music and myth, spirituality and idealism, the supernatural and the divine, and thoughts that cannot be put into words. The second world is becoming more crowded with ancient superstitions that refuse to die, reproducing themselves in mongrel shapes, and is being invaded by new and contradictory obsessions. When we combine memories in new ways there is a chance that they could change the taste of the future.

The Romans had almost a premonition of the implications that might follow. Janus, their god of time, of beginnings and endings, had two faces, one looking backwards to the past and the other to the future. He was also the god of conflict, travel, trade and shipping, the first to mint coins, a reminder that business is ultimately about buying and selling time. It has recently been discovered that patients with damaged memories have difficulty in thinking about the future; the more dementia sinks them into the darkness of forgetfulness, the emptier the future becomes; the more people fantasise about the past, the more their ideas about the future are fantasies too; the sharper their visual memories, the more the future has a visual shape. Memory is therefore not only about the past; it provides the building blocks from which the future is constructed. The narrower the range of memories one has, the less one is likely to have broad and original ideas about the future. How to feed one's memory becomes as important as how to feed one's body. Personal experiences are an inadequate diet, but they can be supplemented by vicarious memories we acquire from others, indeed from all humanity, alive and dead. With poor memories, we cannot imagine where we could be going next, apart from places we have been to before.

Dementia and forgetfulness

Constructing the future

Battles against the passing of time

When I converse with you, I hear not only what you say, but also echoes of what people of previous eras have said in a similar vein, as well as their protests against your statements. There is nothing unusual about this. Originally most civilisations did not separate the past from the present: constant and attentive discussion with dead ancestors was the basis on which they planned their future and how they tried to avoid disagreement. For them, the dead were as alive as the living. When people become modern, determined to do better than their ancestors, they cut many of their ties to the past, and became orphans of time. Knowing what to do next becomes more difficult. Machines have mitigated the insecurity this generates by creating regularity, a world constructed to produce predictable results, with clocks that allow every hour to be planned in advance and every duty to be given a fixed place in the day. But anxiously watching the minutes go by, never to return, can transform life into a perpetual war against time and into an endless dispute about how best to spend and savour one's precious moments. Punctuality and efficiency have often become slave-masters, whipping people to cram more activities and achievements into every day, forcing them to surrender their personal rhythms to fixed, anonymous timetables. Humanity is increasingly split not just by privilege, but also by temperament, between those who

The taste for regularity versus surprise

appreciate regularity and an ordered life, content to fit in to what society has arranged for them, so that they do not have to constantly make decisions for themselves, and those who want to be in control of what they do and when they do it, to perform each activity at their own speed, to obtain a good part of their pleasure from surprises, variety and improvisation.

This is the great division about what people would like the future to be.

Now time is being insistently revealed as more precious than money, not for everybody, far from it, and not at all stages of life, but enough to question whether existing ways of buying and selling time, which is what earning a living now involves, are the only ones that humans can invent. Technology has yet to tackle this problem. It has hitherto tried to conquer time, liberate humans from its constraints, make everything happen faster. In the internet it has created a gigantic freezer stuffed with memory, in which the past, the present and the future are stored, potentially an archive of all that has ever happened, as well as being the instantaneous messenger of every thought sparked by the present and the theatre where visions of the future are played out. This is organised to give you what you want, or what other people want you to want, but not to remind you of what you prefer to forget.

Buying, selling, conquering and freezing time

The French mathematician Henri Poincaré (1854–1912), who almost beat Einstein to the discovery of the theory of relativity, proposed that chaos was an integral part of the world and that inside order there was hidden disorder. Islands of turbulence in the midst of well-behaved regularity made it impossible to make long-term predictions because minute variations in initial conditions could ultimately produce enormous consequences at a later stage. He is at the origin of the idea which has now become familiar and which could only be fully understood when computers were developed much later, that the flapping of a butterfly's wings could create huge storms thousands of miles away.

Long-term prediction

He lauded intuition, by which he meant not guesswork, but the ability

Making sense of confusion

'to unite elements long since known but till then scattered and seemingly foreign to each other ... The value of an observation comes from its giving new value to the old facts it unites.' Einstein said that the goal of science was to discover 'the unity of a complex of appearances which to direct sense experience appear to be quite separate things'. Poincaré said the goal is to make sense out of confusion and to do so by reshaping it with elegance, and that one's guide should be to search for beauty. 'If nature was not beautiful, it would not be worth studying, and life would not be worth living. A scientist does not study nature because it is useful, but because he derives pleasure from it, because it is beautiful.' For Poincaré, beauty meant simplicity. It could be recognised because it economised thought, just as machines economised effort. He did not search for certainty. 'All certainty is a lie,' he said. A command of the facts was only half the

What makes a fact important?

journey. What mattered more was the relationships between facts. So he took an interest in almost every branch of knowledge, because nothing was necessarily irrelevant. His friends commented on how 'his imagination was almost poetic in its intensity and scope.' 'His religious feeling takes the form of a rapturous amazement' in the face of nature. He argued that the best training for a scientist was in the humanities. His favourite reading was stories of exploration and travel. In conversation, or in telling an anecdote, 'he hardly ever began at the beginning, his mind did not work in a straight line, but radiated from the centre to the periphery.' He was always searching for practical applications which would make good use of what in a short-sighted view would appear to be mere incongruities.

I value incompatibilities, disagreements and uncertainties that break up reality into fragments of truth and illusion and open the door to invention. When Humpty Dumpty falls off a wall and smashes his eggshell into little pieces, there is an alternative to just gluing those pieces together again. It is also possible to make an omelette out of the mess, combined with many other ingredients, and not only with ones to which one is accustomed. The future is an endless series of experiments. Disagreement is a challenge to the imagination. Detachment is the reward of conflicting memories. As knowledge expands and fragments, fractures appear between what is predetermined and what is not. Facts mutate into mysteries and questions breed more questions than answers. A more adventurous idea of freedom emerges. Freedom is not merely a right, but a skill to be acquired, the skill to view the world through different lenses, through lenses other than one's own, the skill to imagine what no-one has imagined before, to find beauty or meaning or inspiration. Each life is a fable about freedom.

A more adventurous idea of freedom

Freedom as a skill

Each life is a fable about freedom

Is ridicule the most effective form of non-violent protest?

'TAKE THAT SMILE OFF your face.' 'Stop playing the clown.' Those are the only pearls of advice about humour that I remember from my schooldays, when I was even given six strokes of the cane because my housemaster was worried that I was laughing at him. People in authority take care to conceal how vulnerable they are and how fearful of any hint that they may be thought ridiculous. The Indians, a very long time ago, believed that the gods created the world as a playground where they could amuse themselves like children building sandcastles and then knocking them down, but too many people find nothing very funny about the petty

Why there are no professors of humour

tyrannies that make havoc of daily life. Of course, no professor of humour could survive being told: 'From the moment I picked up your book until I laid it down, I was convulsed with laughter. Someday, I intend to read it.' No prophet has yet urged the jesters of the world to unite, so that humour could puncture arrogance or hypocrisy and rescue the powerless from contempt. Why is humour treated as a marginal amusement? Could it be an alternative to violent resistance or replace indignant street demonstrations? When so many people have to obey governments they despise as stupid or corrupt and have their lives poisoned by megalomaniac bosses, is mockery an art that could be developed to do more than protect them from despair?

While Eisenstein was experimenting with the new art of the cinema to relieve his suffering in a world that obstinately rejected him, his contemporary Lao She (1899–1966) was seeing what humour could achieve. He introduced the word into the Chinese language, *youmou*, winning fame as one of his country's best-loved modern novelists and dramatists, and becoming that rare phenomenon, a Chinese writer who was also a bestselling author in the U.S.A.

How one becomes a humorist

Lao She grew up in great poverty, to the extent of sometimes not having enough to eat. His family were all illiterate; his mother was a washerwoman and cleaner. With enormous difficulty, he managed to get a free place in a primary school and eventually qualify as a teacher. That would normally have meant success and a job for life, particularly as he was quickly promoted. But he resigned. He wanted to be independent. He refused to have to pretend to be friends with corrupt officials, whom he damned as 'hobgoblins and devils'. Poverty seemed preferable, even if, in mid-winter, he had to sell his fur coat to provide his mother with clothing and food. Being poor, he said, it was natural that he should malign the world, and being strong-headed, that he should judge others by the criterion of his own feelings. Humour enabled him to detach himself and to raise himself above suffering. At school he never once cried, however hard his teacher beat him, and never asked for pardon, just as his mother said she would prefer to die rather than ask for help. His alternative to rebellion was to assert his own dignity, and that of all poor people, whose company he always preferred to that of the famous and successful, even when he became one of the most famous people in China, proclaimed 'People's Artist', 'Great Master of Language', a member of parliament and much else. He did not just meet poor people in a tea house to 'secretly record their actions and their conversations. I have never done that. I only want to make friends. They help me and I help them. They come to wish me happiness on my birthday and I do the same when there is a marriage or a birth in their homes.'

Making fun of those with no sense of humour

At the age of twenty-five he left for England, part of the huge emigration of the Chinese that is the forgotten counterpart of European escape to the New World. Somehow he got a job teaching Chinese at the London School of Oriental and African Studies, where he spent five years, from 1924 to 1929. However, confronted by Londoners who seemed to assume that all Chinese were smokers of opium, smugglers of ammunition, or cruel barbarians, how could he defend himself, and how could he respond to condescending businessmen making money out of trade with China while ignoring the country's magnificent ancient culture? How could he be polite to patronising missionaries convinced of their own superiority? 'The English are prejudiced and boring,' he wrote, 'but they are not as mean as they appear to be; they have no humour; and I can only write about them in a humorous vein, for otherwise they would sound like a band of miserable, half-mad fools.'

His answer was to make fun of his humiliations and those of his fellow immigrants. Instead of reacting to cruelty and injustice through revolutionary protest, he preferred to soothe the pain of ordinary people by squeezing joy out of their minor, everyday triumphs over adversity, and by revealing the absurdities that surrounded them. He wrote novels in which he created laughable characters out of manipulative politicians, pompous policemen, prejudiced judges, educational experts constantly introducing new methods, 'superficially modern students . . . split into 327 parties' and incapable of deciding what to put in the place of the evils they denounced, bewildered bourgeois in search of values to justify their ambitions, clerks commuting between an office which is 'the monster which waits with its big mouth wide open' and a home where the wife is 'the female devil' waiting to swallow the husband up. He ridiculed 'official business', producing 'documents without conclusions', bureaucracy that 'eats money and vomits documents', and naïve importers of foreign habits. Above all, he denounced 'the sound and smell of money' as poisoning personal and family relationships.

Unmasking absurdities

At the same time, he created charming characters who could be loved despite their failings. The most cherished of them is Hsiang-Tzu, a poor rickshaw puller, trying to scrape a living and save enough to buy his own rickshaw, so that he could at last be free and independent, but who is repeatedly foiled by all sorts of disagreeable cheats and thugs, until he is driven to becoming a thief himself and betraying his colleagues, learning to smoke, drink and gamble, because a little temporary enjoyment is all he can dream of as a relief from the misery of his existence. 'Life was so cheerless, so painful and without hope. The pain of the poisonous wheel of life would be dulled briefly by the poisonous medication of wine and prostitutes, poison to kill poison. Who has a better plan?'

The ridiculous and the lovable

Lao She did not have a better plan. Humour, for him was 'an attitude of mind' that needed to be cultivated to make life tolerable. It meant watching people like a tourist finding everything interesting. His aim was to maintain joyfulness and generosity despite all the horrors that human-

Satire, wit and farce

ity perpetrates. Satire was not enough for him, its sarcasm was too cold, and its ambition to inspire antipathy towards its victims he considered unjust: 'I hate a bad person, but he also has good points; I love a good man, but he also had his bad points.' Wit did not satisfy him fully either, because it did not appeal enough to gut feelings. Farce, laughter for its own sake, was fine, but again there was something missing from it – sympathy, which was what he cherished most. His response to suffering was to show that everyone was fascinating and everyone was ridiculous,

Eccentricity

even the author who pointed that out. 'All humans are brothers and all have defects', and there was joy to be had from the recognition of 'the little eccentricities' of each individual. What delighted him was observing character, portraying its contradictions, the conflict of dreams and disappointments, and resilience in the face of almost inevitable failure. 'The art of the humorist consists in showing the ridiculous aspect of things . . . but he is not content to point this out; he recognises that it is the common lot of humanity.' He quoted Thackeray saying that 'the humorous writer professes to awake and direct your love, your pity, your kindness – your scorn for untruth, pretention, imposture – your tenderness for the weak,

The Chinese cousin

the poor, the oppressed, the unhappy'. Lao She has been called 'the Chinese cousin of Dickens and Mark Twain', whose writings he loved: they would not just have loved him if they had survived into the twentieth century, but also been shaken by the predicament of humour that he struggled with, the limits of what humour could achieve.

The problem with humorists is that they have usually been as vulnerable as those they mocked. Dickens used his enormous popularity to propagate his ideals as a social reformer, but his praise for the delights of family life concealed the collapse of his own marriage and an illicit love life he had to keep secret; he remained a prisoner of his unquenchable need for public applause and 'the vague unhappiness which tracks a life of constant aim and ever impels to some new aim in which it may be lost'. Mark Twain has retained his reputation as the ideal American, but he insisted that his autobiography should remain unpublished for a hundred years because he knew that Americans would not accept what he really thought – which has recently been at last revealed – that American soldiers were 'uniformed assassins' and that patriotism was 'humbug'; he could not speak with absolute frankness, and even though he could turn almost anything into a joke, he had to confess: 'I have not profoundly dealt in truth.'

The vulnerability of humorists

Like them and so many others, Lao She found it difficult to establish an ideal relationship between humour and serious reality. Swept away by feelings that overwhelmed his capacity for detachment, he could not resist being thrilled by Mao's promise to revitalise China, and he offered his help, until he realised he would lose all his freedom and have to say only what the leader demanded. The deep desire to be of use to his country struggled against the humorist's scepticism. He wanted both to criticise and defend his country. 'If I reveal the faults of the [Chinese], it is because

Idealism versus scepticism

I love them . . . Their misfortunes are also my own . . . their intelligence is equalled only by their stupidity.'

All his art rejected superficial generalisations about national characteristics, and he hated the way 'the savage was identified by the colour of his skin and the civilised by the waviness of his hair.' But humour could not entirely eliminate the resentment he felt against English people's 'narrow patriotism which is the origin of all their crimes'. That resentment provoked a contrary patriotism in him. He concluded that 'the people of a strong country are people and those of a weak country are dogs'. Until China became a strong power, its citizens would always be treated like dogs. Throughout his life, he repeatedly found himself torn between maintaining a smiling detachment and getting passionately involved on issues that he could not make fun of.

People and dogs

His self-mockery originated in something deeper than modesty. Far from being proud of his books, he was highly critical of them and pointed out their weaknesses with apparently total detachment. 'If I have any gifts, they are certainly not for intellectual reflection. I can write a warm letter to a friend, but am quite unable to make an intelligent proposition.' Writing about women frightened him too, and as for love, 'I am condemned to being superficial, unable to make any heart beat faster.' Though occasionally conceding that he might have some talent, he could find no trace of genius. 'The art of literature is really not easy,' he lamented, 'and I say this partly from disgust at my own mediocrity, and partly from a desire to give myself some courage.' He thought of himself as no more than a rickshaw puller: 'Is that not laying one's life down for others?' He hated himself

Self-mockery

Condemned to being superficial

for not being able to be a hero, but he was not willing to be an imitation hero, to play the game others played. He ended up becoming nostalgic about the old Confucian traditions, forgetting how he had made fun of the absurd results to which they could lead. He could not formulate a message for the next generation, simply telling it to try to do better than he had.

Nostalgic despite oneself

In one of his plays, *Teahouse*, a character commits suicide because he had lost everything that mattered to him and he no longer had faith in any of the solutions of government or society. In another play, *The Problem of Face*, another character is so humiliated that he chooses to commit suicide, 'and move to another world where his shame could be washed away' and 'where he could have cool, clean, happy freedom'. Not long afterwards, tragically, Lao She, aged sixty-nine, was arrested by the Red Guards of the Cultural Revolution for having the wrong opinions, beaten and publicly humiliated. When he was allowed to go home he found it looted, and his papers, paintings and possessions strewn all over the courtyard. He did not enter the house, but walked away to the nearby canal and drowned himself. The list of humorists who have committed suicide is terrifyingly long. But before concluding that humour is therefore ultimately a form of despair, I must add that it is not certain that Lao She did commit suicide. He may have been murdered by the Red Guards. We cannot be certain.

When humorists commit suicide

Humour may often seem to be just another form of opium for the people, a pain-killer for suffering and cynicism, a harmless riposte to disappointment, or a return to childhood. If that is all it is, it would not

Laughter in Egypt

be surprising that it has made so little headway against the stupidities it denounces or the suffering it consoles. The Egyptians, for example, have been famous for their joviality since at least 2200 B.C., when the *Tale of the Shipwrecked Sailor* declared that 'in the eyes of the gods, the strong and the weak are a joke'; the Romans issued decrees against Egyptian lawyers notorious for making too many wisecracks at their expense; in the fourteenth century Ibn Khaldun found the Egyptians 'unusually mirthful and irreverent'; and most recently the star of the classical Egyptian cinema Kamal El-Shenawy (1922–2011) nominated the joke as 'the devastating weapon which the Egyptians used against invaders and occupiers'. But however much the Egyptians made fun of their rulers, and even though jokes remain indispensable conversation starters for them, humour has not been enough to dislodge any tyrant. They may have mocked President Mubarak by giving him the nickname *La Vache qui rit* to express their contempt for him as a grinning peasant buffoon, and they may have laughed at the story that when President Nasser was searching for a vice president, his only criterion was that he wanted someone more stupid than himself, and so he chose Sadat, who also wanted a vice president more stupid than himself and so chose Mubarak, but Mubarak did not choose a vice president when he became president, and that was because he could not find anyone in the whole of Egypt more stupid than himself. But Mubarak survived for thirty years unscathed by all the jokes, as many other ridiculous tyrants have, as though protected by the armour of medals they have awarded themselves. Encircled by admirers, careerists, bureaucracies and armies, all who wield power can ignore what they do not want to hear; but that is not the only reason why mockery does not touch them.

Humour may be guilty of reinforcing conformity by being its safety valve. Though carnivals have throughout history made fun of authority, and turned hierarchy upside down, they did so only for a few days. Though privileged clergymen put on masks, or women's clothes, or vestments back to front, and sang bawdy songs, celebrated mock weddings with animals, and cursed instead of blessing their congregations, their aim was to strengthen their authority, as a group of them explained in 1444: 'We do these things in jest and not in earnest – as the ancient custom is – so that once a year the foolishness innate in us can come out and evaporate.' A contemporary judgement on Machiavelli, who called himself a 'comic and tragic historian' was: 'He laughs at human errors, because he cannot correct them.' Just as revolutionaries enjoy the conviviality and thrill of conspiracy, so those who laugh enjoy laughing too much to ask where else humour could lead, beyond relaxation and amusement.

The occasional smile

Humour, moreover, has repeatedly been assailed by formidable enemies. The powerful have relentlessly punished those who mocked them. The Christian Church for long declared laughter to be the work of the devil, though it did not succeed in eliminating it any more than all the other sins it condemned. St Jean-Baptiste de la Salle (1651–1719), one of the most influential educational entrepreneurs, the first to establish Catholic schools with lay teachers instead of priests, warned his pupils against smiling in his *Rules of Christian Decorum* (1703): 'Some people allow their teeth to be almost entirely visible. This is completely contrary to decorum, which forbids you to allow your teeth to be uncovered, since

The war against laughter

nature gave us lips to conceal them.' Even the French Revolution disapproved of laughter, its Code of Conduct for parliamentary debates prescribed that 'absolutely no sign of applause or approval will be allowed; insults and displays of individual character are forbidden, as too are outbursts of laughter.' In the hope that 'reason' would prevail in their decisions, the inventors of the Declaration of the Rights of Man restrained themselves, in twenty-eight months of debate, to only 408 outbursts of laughter, one every other day on average, rejecting the proud claim of the supposedly irrational masses that they were the most joyful people in the world, who liked to 'begin and end every activity with singing and buffoonery'. Even the land of freedom that is the U.S.A. expelled Charlie Chaplin.

The French Revolution's ban on laughter

A silent conspiracy by people in search of respectability has spread the myth that assuming airs of gravity is the best way to prove that one is wise and reliable, and that loud laughter is a sign of peasant vulgarity, to be looked down upon by the 'well brought up'. It may be that there is now less loud and uncontrolled laughter or sheepish grinning in the world than there once was. Theatres no longer have breaks in their performances to allow people in paroxysms of laughter to regain their composure, which used to happen in Feydeau farces. In the nineteenth century laughter may well have become more restrained as the middle classes evolved new ways of behaving, turning their laughter into a 'mere spasm'. Only children were allowed to laugh freely, whether in fear, or bewilderment or playfulness, but they were also taught that their survival depended on taking the world more seriously than it seemed to deserve. Politicians responded by trying to please everybody by demonstrating that while remaining serious,

Only children allowed to laugh freely

they could also appreciate a joke of the right sort: Theodore Roosevelt, the twenty-sixth president of the U.S.A. (1858–1919), was probably the first politician to allow himself to be seen smiling broadly instead of looking stern.

So there are many reasons why the extraordinary number of pathetic people who have been raised to high office have proved to be impervious to ridicule. They are not there to tell the truth, and certainly not the whole truth; they would have to resign in shame if they did; and besides their lies often make people feel better, give courage or hope; they are humorists in their own way too, in that they invent tall stories about their achievements. There can be no winners in this game of tennis balls that explode in the receiver's face. Lao She tried to make it less painful and, like a physician, remains one of humanity's venerable benefactors. But mockery by itself has only limited strength, it merely translates physical violence into verbal cruelty. So in the next chapter I shall explore what else can be achieved by humour, not in public but in private life.

People in high office impervious to mockery

I know humour needs to be approached with great caution and delicacy; it hates to be explained and repels all theories about it with deadly salvoes of wit; it would lose its charm if it ceased to be a puzzling and slippery art that disconcertingly paints with ideas and dances with words. But one can search for other possibilities in humour, so that it is more than a distraction and more than a weapon, and so that sarcasm, compassion and fantasy can play together in a grand, overpowering symphony that encourages ordinary people in their daily lives to put aside their pretences and discover the truth about one another.

Humour uncovers truth

My teacher who told me to wipe the smile off my face was an admirable, widely read and sad man, but we never spoke about anything except our lessons. He used to read philosophy books in French, and punished me by making me cut open their pages, for French books in those days were still bound in the old-fashioned way, with uncut edges; but he was too absorbed in his own philosophising, or too shy, to get to know his young pupils; so he never discovered what I was smiling about, and perhaps he would have been a happier teacher if he had found out that there was affection, not venom in my grin.

Why I was
smiling

How does one acquire a sense of humour?

S ir Thomas More (1478–1535) was one of the wittiest men of his time, though he is now remembered mainly as the inventor of Utopia or as a Catholic saint. His serious image as Lord Chancellor of England, Speaker of the House of Commons, a successful lawyer and a Renaissance scholar contrasts with an unusually jovial manner. 'From boyhood he was always so pleased with a joke, that it might seem that jesting was the main object of his life . . . When quite a youth, he wrote farces and acted them. If a thing was facetiously said, even though it was aimed at himself, he was charmed with it, so much did he enjoy any witticism that had a flavour of subtlety or genius.' He urged his friend Erasmus, 'prince of the Renaissance humanists', to write *In Praise of Folly*, 'which was much the same thing as setting a camel to dance'. Everyone in his house, including the servants, was encouraged to play a musical instrument of some kind, and participate in games and play-acting, inventing imaginary scenes and characters, and given lines to speak in the first person as in a play. 'A merry talk cometh never amiss to me.' He even employed a jester, who was treated with such respect that he was included in Holbein's portrait of the More family, a now famous painting which emphasised the importance More accorded to the intimate pleasures of private life and the education

In Praise of Folly

of his children, to bantering repartee with his wife, and above all to his almost daily very personal 'mutual conversation' with his most beloved daughter Margaret, whose talents he believed would one day equal his own.

Utopia, a young man's protest against absurdity

The imaginative quality of his wit showed itself in his book *Utopia*, which expresses the bewilderment that seizes young people capable of thinking for themselves when they are confronted by the bizarre expectations that the world has of them. On entering adulthood, Thomas More was so horrified by the vanity and greed of people in power, who think their 'own fart smells sweet' because they are so in love with their own opinions, that he withdrew into a monastery for two years to hide from them. He learnt Greek to seek inspiration from a vanished world, but used that knowledge to translate one of the sharpest comic and sarcastic critics of the Hellenic civilisation, the Syrian Lucian of Samosata (A.D. 125–c. 180). *Utopia* is a young man's book of revulsion against the society of his day, dismissing its most fundamental institutions and practices as absurd, condemning governments as 'a conspiracy of the rich who on pretence of managing the public, only pursue their private ends . . . and engage the poor to toil and labour for them at as low rates as possible', demanding the abolition of property, and of money too, which produces 'much anxiety and great occasions of mischief', and pleading that 'every man might be of what religion he pleased'. But all this was fantasy; he thought such dreams would never become reality, and he wrote his story

Objecting to one's own proposals

as a conversation in which he is one of the characters supplying objections to his own radical proposals.

That contradiction within himself tormented his whole life, wanting to give up on the world, but also to improve it. He accepted a post in the royal service 'much against my will', all the more so because he had watched a reformer he admired failing and escaping into exile. He thought he had a solution, not to expect too much, and to be as practical as he could: 'What you cannot make wholly good, you may at least make as little bad as possible.' He combined this with a determination that rulers should be honestly told the truth, even if it might lead to punishment. He struggled to discover how he could avoid the common fate of public servants, 'good, honest, innocent men' who were corrupted by 'the serpent of ambition'. *The common fate of public servants* Past experience seemed to say that honesty would not pay; but he persisted in thinking that rulers should be told the truth, and he refused to lie about his religious beliefs when his king changed his own. So he chose to submit to execution, which he could easily have avoided; it was in fact a virtual suicide, like the suicides of all the humorists who came after him. Though his idea of the afterlife was slightly different from Lao She's, he told his family: 'We will merrily meet in heaven.' His disapproval of the world around him was so strong that he was willing to leave it, despite all the pleasure he obtained from his family; but he kept his private and public life in separate compartments; in public office, far from ever smiling at those he judged to be delinquents, he treated them with remarkable ferocity. His sense of humour served only as a temporary escape from reality rather than as an instrument for understanding and reshaping it.

Since his day, despite all that has been done to make life more agreeable, many different kinds of anxieties have emerged, adding themselves *The need for new jokes* to long established ones, to make it more difficult to see the world dispassionately. Constant change stimulates fears of an uncertain future; big cities harbour loneliness; medicine not only cures but also generates an ever-growing list of threats that nourish hypochondria; invisible germs and viruses replace the demons and hobgoblins of the past; sharpened intelligence and increasing wealth do not protect from worry; self-esteem becomes more elusive as traditional hierarchies collapse; competitiveness increases stress; pressures at work damage relations between colleagues; fear of failure nourishes a sense of inadequacy; and neither more leisure nor more alcohol suffice to compensate. So it becomes necessary to think afresh about how to respond to these challenges.

Court jesters as pioneers

Court jesters do not normally appear as decisive influences on human evolution, but they are to be found from the earliest times, employed by kings, pharaohs, emperors, sultans and even popes to say what obsequious subjects dared not say. Only occasionally did a ruler, like Karl Ludwig, Elector of the Palatinate of the Rhine (1617–1680), say he 'did not feel the need to keep a court jester, for when he wanted to laugh he would summon two professors from the university, set them debating, then sit back and enjoy the folly of the scene'. Jesters were certainly valued as entertainers or antidotes to melancholy, but their importance comes from their having the right to say anything 'without offence', with immunity from punishment for slander, a privilege that no-one else has had. The actor-clown Richard Tarlton was allowed to criticise Queen Elizabeth I to her face

Freedom from flattery and intrigue

and to denounce her favourites as 'knaves'. The isolation and loneliness of kings, surrounded by flattery and intrigue, made humble jesters, who could never aspire to high office, indispensable in connecting rulers with reality, and unmasking hypocrisy and deceit. In their clownish garb, when they stood on their heads, they seemed to be seeing the world the right way up. 'They are the only ones who speak frankly and tell the truth,' wrote Erasmus, and the French court jester Marais told Louis XIII (1601–1643): 'There are two things about your job I do not like; to eat alone and to shit in public.' Abu Nawas, jester to Caliph Harun al-Rashid, used to take his master out in disguise at night into the streets of Baghdad to see what life in the city was really like. The relationship between king and jester could become quite intimate and the emperor Akbar wept when his jester died. The jester was 'an approved man of veracity' (and occasionally a woman – there are records of Queen Mary I rewarding her female jester with 'twelve pairs of new shoes').

Court jesters were called Wise Fools, and the function they fulfilled can be judged from the names of Chinese ones: Assisting Uprightness, Newly Polished Mirror, Adding Clarity. The most famous Chinese jester, Tung-Fang Shuo (160–93 B.C.) remained a legend for centuries after his death because he was not only witty but also an astute critic of the emperor Wu, castigating him for extravagance and for ignoring the interest of the poor, always surprising in his responses, capable of profound observation and of revealing that every question or event had more sides to it than anyone else realised. A fool, said a Jewish proverb, is half a prophet. And since truth cannot be easily swallowed whole or raw, jesters were usually also poets, magicians, musicians or singers, able to convey unpalatable insights in an epigram, a witty story or a song. To be amusing was not their deepest

The most famous Chinese jester

A fool is half a prophet

purpose, they were importantly artists in the search for truth. They point to one of the neglected sub-plots of history, which is the unmasking of sham.

It was not just kings who needed jesters; mediaeval noblemen who could afford it employed them too. Today, however, business tycoons expect something quite different from their 'coaches' and do not easily tolerate employees 'taking the piss'. The different arts which the jesters mastered have been divided among serious specialist professions. Musicians, magicians, poets have gone their separate ways and truth has become identified more with knowledge than with wisdom. The court jester's spirit, intent on speaking the truth, can be found still alive in the theatre, the mirror in which people can see themselves differently from what they imagine themselves to be, and the place where actors put themselves into the skin of another person and discover what it is to be someone else. Journalists are also unacknowledged heirs of the court jesters, when they denounce lies and obfuscation by public figures; but they do not enjoy the immunity of jesters. In some countries they are in danger of prosecution or even assassination, in others their voices are increasingly drowned by the rise of public relations experts, who are now four times more numerous than them.

Theatre and journalism versus public relations

Truth, which used to be imagined as an immovable rock that provided a firm footing for clear decisions, is today a diamond that radiates light in numerous directions and demands to be viewed from different angles. Just as diamond cutters could create only seventeen surfaces at the beginning of the seventeenth century and thirty-three at the end, while today

Truth is today a diamond

as many as 144 are possible, so truth is becoming increasingly dazzling, and indeed almost blinding, as hundreds of different disciplines each cast a different light upon it. Never has it been so difficult to understand the implications of even a small piece of knowledge, or to dissipate the clouds of misinformation in which it is enveloped. One jester cannot suffice. To be inspired by a single muse is no longer enough.

Sir Thomas More's playful joviality now appears too limited in its ambition. There is another role for humour beyond entertainment, self-defence or protest. Humour can also teach a new attitude to truth, as can be seen from the history of its development in England, where it seems to have consciously expanded to become an instrument for the appreci- *English humour expands* ation of strangers. Whereas traditionally comedy was supposed to 'correct the conduct of mankind' by ridiculing aberrations from the norm, the Irish dramatist George Farquhar (1677–1707), on migrating to London, observed that 'we have the most unaccountable medley of humans among us of any people on earth . . . as a consequence of the mixture of many nations.' Of course, other great cities were also mixed, but he confronted this as a dilemma, and asked 'How to please so many tastes?' In other words, how to respond to difference, instead of trying to stamp it out? 'A great diversity of character' was the inevitable result of a country becoming more commercial 'with a multiplicity of trades and professions', said Adam Smith's disciple John Millar (1735–1801), who influenced the drafters of the American constitution: 'Rapid improvements of arts and manufactures . . . produced a degree of wealth and affluence, which diffused a feeling of independence and a high spirit of liberty, through the

Triggers of
humour

great body of the people.' Another dramatist, Congreve (1670–1729), had been quick to notice that 'any man that has a humour is under no restraint or fear of giving it vent'. 'Every man follows his own [humour] and takes a pleasure, perhaps a pride, to show it,' wrote the diplomat Sir William Temple (1628–1699), who added: 'The first ingredient in conversation is truth, the next good sense, the third good humour, and the fourth wit.' A humorous person became not just someone amusing, but someone who is himself amused. Gradually, humour evolved to become more than a method for mitigating conflict and disagreement: it now stimulated interest in the peculiarities that made people different. The sympathetic perception of incongruity became a positive talent. A culture of sensibility encouraged a deeper interest in the unique nature of individuals. Instead of laughter being directed against people who were different, instead of it being antipathetic, it became sympathetic and an opportunity for good-natured play.

The phrase 'sense of humour' was first used in English in 1840. Having a sense of humour began to be seen as a desirable attribute around 1870. Increasingly valued ever since, not just socially but also as fulfilling an intellectual and moral need, it is now a force whose full potential has still to be realised. If Nobel had been more sensitive to the spirit of his time, he might have established a prize for humour, but the Swedish Bank that endowed a Nobel prize in the unfunny science of economics, and chose the year 1968 to do so – when youth was ridiculing authority of every kind – demonstrated that the rich and powerful, though they are often able to joke as well as anyone, persisted in seeing joking as no more than a piquant sauce to make a dull dish eatable.

The significance of humour has also been diminished by the myth that each nation has a distinct sense of humour, a myth invented to strengthen the exclusive loyalty that growing nations demanded. The humour of strangers has never been a secret language impossible for outsiders to appreciate. Humour all over the world makes fun of the same sort of targets. The oldest kind is the humour that comes naturally to ordinary people, disrespectful, scurrilous and earthy, preserved in folk stories that last for centuries, lose nothing of their savour from repetition, and require no book learning: they are despised but secretly enjoyed by those who aspire to refinement. Examples of universal humour abound. The jokes of Nasreddin, the fourteenth-century Turkish Sufi, have been endlessly reproduced across half the world from Budapest to Beijing, adopted by Afghans and Iranians and Uzbeks as their own, inspiring even the music of Shostakovich, and they are still laughed at. There is nothing arcane in the story of the emperor Tamerlane meeting Nasreddin in the bath-house and asking him, 'If I were a slave, how much would I be worth?' 'Fifty pence,' said Nasreddin. 'But,' retorted the emperor, 'this towel I am wearing is alone worth that.' 'Yes, of course, that is my offer for the lot.' Cervantes' Don Quixote likewise had an immediate universal appeal and has been appreciated in over seventy languages, including fifteen Indian ones. The same jokes reappear in the most unlikely places: those about the meanness of the people of Aberdeen are identical to those made by Bulgarians about the people of Gabrovo; they both say they stop their watches and clocks at night so as not to wear out the cogs. So how do they

Is humour a secret language?

Universal jokes

know the time in the dark? They blow a trumpet, and a neighbour shouts back: 'Who is the idiot making that racket at twenty past two in the morning?' Aernout van Overbeke (1632–1674), judge of the high court of the Dutch East Indies, included hundreds of English, French, German, Italian and Spanish jokes in his collection of 2,440 amusing *Anecdota*, which everyone could understand. Fakir Mohan Senapati (1843–1918) wrote his humorous novels in the Oriya language (spoken by forty-five million Indians) to assert the dignity of the people of Orissa, but he drew inspiration from the eleven languages he learnt, and from praying daily 'surrounded on all sides by befitting quotations from the scriptures of all the world's religions inscribed on the walls'.

Though many English people nowadays regard their sense of humour as an essential ingredient of their national character, and trace it back to Chaucer, a whole century elapsed after the poet's death before his readers decided that Chaucer was funny. As late as the early eighteenth century,

'The supreme humorists'

the third Earl of Shaftesbury, in his *Essay on the Freedom of Wit* (1709), said the Italians were the supreme humorists: 'It is the only manner in which the poor cramped wretches can discharge a free thought. We must yield to them the superiority in this sort of wit. The persecuting spirit hath raised the bantering one.' Before the age of nationalist conflicts, it was easier to recognise the universality of humour. Sterne's *Tristram Shandy*, much influenced by Rabelais and Cervantes, was initially more admired

Other people's jokes

in France than in England.

Though laughing at foreigners is a universal amusement, a closer look at humour in fact dissolves national stereotypes. The Chinese have not only been devoted to Confucius, but have made fun of him too, and even whimsically claimed that he might have been a woman; they have also worshipped a God of Joy, Hsi-shen, and participated in the Taoist fight against dogmatism, using the 'funny story' (*hsiao-hua*) and the 'side-swipe' (*ku-chi*) to protect their individual aspirations for freedom. The publisher of the German translation of my book on *The French* cut out the chapter on humour (though he did relent after many protests), and an international poll in 2011 did indeed rank Germany as the country with the least sense of humour. But the Germans invented the irreverent Till Eulenspiegel (the arse-wiper), internationally famous for his jokes in the Middle Ages, and in the nineteenth century Berlin was called the 'mother city of wit'. The comic magazine *Eckensteher* once rivalled *Punch*. The Berliners who laughed co-existed with straight-laced bureaucrats who tolerated hilarity in the hope that it would distract from political agitation. Jewish humour is universal too because it is an answer to universal problems, triumphing over vulnerability through self-mockery, revelling in reconciling irreconcilables so that disagreement becomes a spur to ingenuity, delighting in debate that takes logic to absurdity, and making seventy different ways of interpreting the Torah a source of pride. So a rabbi could settle an argument between two colleagues in the following way: when one gave his opinion, the rabbi agreed with him, then the other offered a diametrically opposed opinion, and the rabbi agreed with him too; when the rabbi's wife protested, 'They cannot both be right', the rabbi, after long reflection, answered, 'You are also right.'

A time for laughter and a time for boasting

There have, however, been differences in where laughter has been judged to be appropriate. Those Japanese who were worried about exposing their teeth to public view set aside their theatres as places where one could go to laugh and keep one's mouth perpetually open in hilarity. In China some demanded that full attention should be given to the serious business of eating at banquets and that laughter-making conversation would be a distraction, while the ancient Greeks brought entertainers to amuse them only when they had finished their dinner. What was peculiar about the English was that, once their little island was in command of a huge empire, they had the confidence to allow humour to invade almost every sphere of life; it became a proof that they had no fears. But the idea that their humour was radically different from that of their neighbours was mere bravado. Across the Channel, the French defined themselves as the most jovial country on earth when they were at the height of their power. It is a major defect of the tourist industry that it does not make the appreciation of the use of humour in every nation as important as the appreciation of its food.

Exchanging anxiety for serenity

Humour and anxiety are not opposites, but closely related; the two words once meant almost the same thing. None of the impressive discoveries about the genetic and neurological influences on mental well-being have yet found a reliable method of exchanging anxiety for serenity, and all that is known is that whatever theories or healing techniques are used, it is the quality of the relationship between the patient and the therapist that is 'the single most important ingredient of effective psychiatric care'. Humour does not automatically create deep bonds between people, because it is so often played at a shallow level; and it is still in an adolescent phase when, as with Thomas More, it has no influence on the harshness of official business. It may start as a private conspiracy between two people combining to narrow the gap between them and to sound out delicately each other's fears and defences, but it can progress so that they give each other the courage to question normally unassailable assumptions. It can lead to a superficial scepticism, but also to an almost scientific approach, mistrust for the apparently obvious. The compassionate element in it teaches how to see the world from another's viewpoint; the fantasy element to construct alternatives; while sarcasm reveals the limits of one's sympathies; but only when these are joined together, and create awareness of one's own absurdities, does it allow us to believe that we belong to the same species. This gives humour a central role in human relationships. If the cinema is the eighth muse, humour is the ninth.

The scowl of officialdom

But, of course, it is complicated by infinite gradations of sensitivity. I must confess that I laugh childishly at the most puerile jokes, just as tears pour out of my eyes at scenes of banal sentimentality, so I am not the person to censor or prescribe anything related to humour.

What stops people feeling completely at home in their own country?

> I was young once
> I wandered alone
> And I lost my way.
> I only felt rich
> When I met another.
> A human's joy is another human.

How much progress has been made in the art of meeting another human being since the thousand-year-old *Sayings of the High One*, the Nordic god Odin? They are full of fearful warnings about the difficulty of dealing with other people, and of distinguishing between friends and enemies. Has finding joy in other people been made easier or harder by the complexities of civilisation? The *Sayings* give this advice:

> If you find a friend you fully trust
> And wish for his good will
> Exchange thoughts
> Exchange gifts
> Go often to his house.

Since those words were uttered, the division of the earth's inhabitants into nation-states has made a big difference to whom one talks with and whom one trusts. Nations are often deaf to what their rivals say, but they have also brought apparently incompatible people together and have a magic power to make even those who have persistently been losers feel that they are winners. Most of their members have never met and are often left guessing about one another's opinions, so that many of the messages they exchange are platitudes which may give either true or false clues about the real extent of the familiarity, affection or resentment between them. Nations invent myths to suggest that, ever since a distant past, their members have been destined for each other and made to live in harmony, even when their unification has been relatively recent and their frontiers uncertain, and so they come to resemble immovable parts of the landscape like mountains or rivers. But with whom do they really like to talk?

Making losers feel like winners

I have decided to visit the descendants of the Vikings who worshipped Odin, because they are esteemed as having formed nations that make them among the most egalitarian, democratic, prosperous and happy people in the world. They have reached a pinnacle and so presumably may point to what nations might become in the future. I have chosen a half dozen of the heroes and heroines of Denmark – now ranked number one in the United Nations Happiness Report – not because they can speak for millions of Scandinavians, but to discover with whom they talked, who inspired them and why they felt the need to breathe foreign air.

The happiest people

Hans Christian Andersen (1805–1875) is one of the most famous of all Danes, having been translated into 152 languages. He is also the author of the most popular of all Danish songs, 'In Denmark I was born', which explains why he loved his native land: it is his home, its language is his mother's voice, and above all there is the song's emotional refrain: 'You love me, Denmark, You love me.' Andersen's stories, however, are also about his suffering. Denmark, he said, was 'where I have felt more unhappy than happy'. He complained that he was 'different from everyone' and that he 'must escape his roots'.

Underdogs and foreigners

In his early years, struggling to win recognition as an actor, playwright and poet, he thought Denmark was too poor and too small for him, unlike Italy, for example, 'filled with food and flowers'; and he escaped, becoming perhaps the most widely travelled Dane of his generation. When a woman once asked him, 'Tell me Mr Andersen, have you ever on any of your many and long journeys abroad ever seen anything as beautiful as our little Denmark?', 'I certainly have,' he replied. 'I have seen many things more beautiful'. 'Shame on you,' she retorted. 'You are not a patriot.' But European culture was a food Andersen could not live without, and the welcome and admiration he received from the great artists and writers of many countries were indispensable to him. He had to struggle hard and endure serious poverty before he won approval from his compatriots. The literary elite did not like his rejection of conventional literary prose and preference for colloquial language that everyone could enjoy. Others criticised him for being too conventional, or for being too keen to win the approval of the upper classes, and for his 'fawning servility' towards the aristocracy. He never quite overcame the handicap of being the son of a shoemaker, though he was lionised in the salons of the rich and powerful. He recorded with pleasure how 'the Grand Duke of Weimar pressed me to his bosom, we kissed one another. "We are friends for life," said the Duke. We both wept.'

Andersen was not a revolutionary, for all his sympathy with the underdog. His philosophy was that the Ugly Duckling could become a beautiful swan, but when that did not happen, he would say, 'God directs all things for the best.' He achieved his own transformation by escaping from adulthood into the fantasy universe of childhood. In his eyes, children were as excluded from the adult world as he always, to some extent, felt himself to be. Writing about childhood without moralising about it, but delighting in playfulness and humour, allowed him to use fairy tales to express thoughts he otherwise had to hide. Rebelling against the idea that literature's purpose was to create harmony, he wrote, 'I seek all the discords of the world . . . I believe I am myself the discord in this world.' He was indeed always tormented by anxiety: he imagined that his fellow travellers in stage-coaches were about to murder him; he remained so afraid of death that he carried a rope with him everywhere, in case he had to jump out of a house on fire, and he was so afraid of being buried alive that he always kept a note by his bedside which read, 'I only appear to be dead.'

Escape from the adult world

Denmark's national solutions to Andersen's perplexities have almost unanimously been judged to be impressive. The country has erected formidable barriers against anxiety, creating the most all-embracing and effective insurance institution in the world, guaranteeing freedom from the worries of unemployment, ill-health, ignorance and poverty. But

Guaranteed freedom from worry

Anxieties that nations cannot cure

there are fears that national institutions cannot touch, and there are new fears and new desires that rise up as soon as others are forgotten. Despite Denmark's top ranking in wealth and happiness, its children (according to UNICEF's comparisons with other countries) rank nineteenth in tests of reading, maths and science. Only 22 per cent of its children 'like school a lot' (but no country has more than 40 per cent). Only 70 per cent of Danish fifteen-year-olds spend time 'just talking with parents several times a week', less than Hungarians (90) and Italians (87), but more than Swedes and Australians (50), or Germans (42) and Israelis (who come bottom at 37). Denmark is ranked eighteenth in 'family conversation and interaction' and nineteenth in the proportion of those who live with step-families (though there is no information about what difference that makes). It comes three from the bottom, with only Finland and the United Kingdom below it, in the proportion of children under fifteen who have never been drunk. Still, it does much better than the U.K. and the U.S.A., which come near the bottom in many of the tables. If Andersen were to come back today, would his nation's acclaimed social institutions be able to cure him of his anxieties?

Escape from security

Karen Blixen (1885–1962) was also a Dane who found it difficult to be Danish and nothing else. She reacted against Andersen's philosophy and against the national search for security. She wanted more from life than what Denmark offered her. Escaping to Africa, she wrote: 'Here at long last one was in a position not to give a damn for all conventions, here was a new kind of freedom which until then one had only found in dreams.' Her father had gone off to serve in the French Army, identified himself with the revolutionary French Communards, then lived with the Chippewa Native Americans of Wisconsin, and finally committed suicide when he learnt that he had syphilis. She admired people like him who defied authority and enjoyed danger and struggled against fate, which she saw as a chance to attain heroism and immortality. Only people who had nothing to lose could have that courage, which for her meant aristocrats like herself and the proletariat. The middle classes, fearful of risk, craving for security, were, for her, 'the devil'. 'I cannot live with the middle class.' She despised the sacrifices they were willing to make to pay for the welfare state, which she found 'suffocating'. Never having recovered from having been 'watched over too much' by her mother, who was constantly trying to protect her from innumerable dangers, she believed that the only person who had 'loved me for myself' was her rebellious father, and so she had no sympathy for the pampering of children being turned into a national policy for pampering adults too. By contrast 'my black brothers here in Africa' loved adventure. 'My Somalis are happy whatever happens, as long as something is happening': they become 'quite desperate in an uneventful life'. Even the English wild-game hunter with whom she had a great love affair, 'who makes me tremendously happy, carries no weight in comparison'. Africa 'released' her so that she could 'discover herself'.

The courage of those who have nothing to lose

Discovering oneself in Africa

What she wanted above all was to achieve something 'as myself' and to discover ever more 'possibilities for beauty'. 'All sorrows can be borne if you can put them into stories'; that was 'the one perfect happiness that a human will find in life', and she turned the events of her own life into stories. But the need to do so was also 'a curse', for in real life she did not escape sorrow: divorced by her husband, who was also syphilitic, having her own health ruined by a false diagnosis of syphilis, she concluded: 'You know you are truly alive when you are living among lions.'

However, though her sensitive portrayal of Africa proved deeply moving outside the continent, it was a romantic vision. When her Kikuyu servant who worked for her for many years was suddenly arrested for being a member of the Mau Mau freedom fighters, she was very surprised. She thought she knew him well; but there was a lot he did not tell her. For all her kindnesses to them, Africans could not forget that when they worked on her 6,000-acre farm, it was African land of which they had been dispossessed. What a nation can expect from its relations with foreigners is still a question that has had no perfect answer.

What women can expect from men

Nor what women can expect from men. When still only twenty years old, Mathilde Fibiger (1830–1872), the first Danish advocate of women's emancipation, published a semi-autobiographical novel, *Clara Raphael*, protesting that women were 'excluded from all intellectual enterprise'. While emphasising the differences between the sexes, she demanded not that women should be like men, nor that they should have 'rights', but

Freedom of the imagination

that they should have spiritual and intellectual freedom, freedom of the imagination. Her book aroused an enormous amount of discussion and a torrent of reviews, but after two more novels, she accepted that she could not achieve financial independence as a writer and became a telegraph operator instead, the first woman in her country to obtain a civil service job. That was only a partial victory, for she hoped work would be a more effective weapon than argument, but though she succeeded in getting promoted to be a manager, the resistance of the men who worked with her was a constant irritation. When John Stuart Mill's book *The Subjection of Women* came out twenty years after hers, she welcomed it, but disagreed with it. Her mother had disagreed with her father and left him. It is impossible to count how many other women disagreed but either said nothing or did nothing. History does not record the silences behind which disagreement shelters.

Now that the women of Denmark and the other Scandinavian countries have won almost all the forms of equality that laws can guarantee, what is missing? They have freedom from their husbands, freedom from the constraints imposed by child-rearing and domestic chores, freedom from discrimination in the pursuit of every form of work. However, what no-one predicted was that public institutions that took over a large part of the education of children might create a void, a sense of not having lived fully, not having participated enough in the shaping of one's own offspring, a realisation that to 'be oneself' also means creating a unique relationship between parent and child, which is as profoundly a part of life and as elusive as creating a relationship between a woman and a man. A poll of young Scandinavian women suggested that after their efforts to improve the relations between the sexes, the next goal may be to try harder with the relations between generations. Laws cannot programme that very personal adventure, which is private to each duo.

What is left after freedoms are won

Denmark's most influential philosopher, Søren Kierkegaard (1813–1855), wrote a scathing and sarcastic review of Fibiger's first novel, suggesting it should not be taken any more seriously than a new sartorial

Sarcasm against feminism

fashion. 'If girls were brought up the same way as boys, then goodnight to the whole human race.' The emancipation of women 'is the invention of the devil'. 'Woman is personified egotism.' And he rejected the woman he was in love with because 'it is a superstition that something that lies outside a person is what can make him happy.' Kierkegaard was an escapist, though physically he hardly ever travelled outside Copenhagen. He built a whole philosophy around the idea of individuals being 'singular', with a mission to free themselves from the crowds and the stereotypes that menaced their individuality; they needed less knowledge, not more knowledge, to be truly themselves; they should reject the common opinions of the public and make their own minds up, relying on faith, not reason, to find God, a severe and dour God who speaks of sin and guilt. Unlike Andersen trying to escape anxiety, Kierkegaard insisted that 'fear and trembling' were necessary to attain faith, which was the main goal of life: 'Whoever has learned to be anxious in the right way has learned the ultimate . . . Anxiety is the possibility of freedom.'

How to be 'singular'

Making fun of his compatriots through irony and parody was one of Kierkegaard's ways of asserting his singularity. He has been called the most amusing of all philosophers anywhere, though it is not clear how much competition he encountered for that title. He is 'droll and rollicking . . . revelling in the comedy of the contradictions in human existence'. But he found humour even in suffering, even in religion, even claiming that 'all humour developed from Christianity itself'. Jest, for him, always springs from pain. His compatriots have developed a reputation for using sarcasm and irony as their weapons to prevent their ordered society

'The most amusing of all philosophers'

from being oppressive. When Victor Borge (1909–2000), the comedian nicknamed the 'unmelancholy Dane', said 'Laughter is the closest distance between two people', did he imply that the distance between them was normally huge?

All over the world, there have always been practical business and professional people who, while being pillars of conformity, could not help occasionally producing children who rebelled against their placidity. Peter Bang (1900–1957), founder of Bang and Olufsen, which became Europe's largest manufacturer of high-fidelity equipment, was the son of the manager of Copenhagen's biggest department store. He escaped to America as soon as he reached adulthood. He became passionate about radio, which for him symbolised the prospect of technology changing the world. He got a job in General Electric, and after some years wrote, 'I have worked for so many different people, I'm tired of working for others; now I want to work for myself.' He went back home having decided that independence, not money, was his goal. Olufsen was an aristocrat with a manor house, but with an unaristocratic passion for business. The two joined forces and started a factory in the rural wilds of Jutland, 350 kilometres away from Copenhagen. Bang always felt uncomfortable in the society of the capital city, which he avoided, preferring London, Berlin and the United States. The whole idea of his firm was to escape from banality, to combine technological research with beautiful products, to use avant-garde design as a language to communicate new ideas, and never to make a product until there was a new idea to express.

Bang and Olufsen's escape

The originality of Denmark's welfare state was that its inventors saw it as part of a movement for 'popular enlightenment', offering 'culture for the people', with an essential aesthetic ingredient, involving the creation of beautiful objects, furniture and buildings that taught people to distinguish between good and evil, and between the useful and the useless. Bang and Olufsen defined themselves in cultural terms, as rebels against the superficiality of mere consumption and entertainment. They insisted on discussing taste and quality before price. They employed Jacob Jensen as their designer who had originally been trained as an upholsterer, and situated themselves as an extension of the artistic movement that made Danish furniture and ceramics distinctive, 'democratising beauty', rejecting both 'bourgeois pomp' and mass production, and resonating with Japan's aesthetics of simplicity.

Rebels against mere entertainment

'Democratising beauty'

After the founders' deaths, however, new managers demanded that the products should be made more cheaply, since much of what was inside them was no different from what was inside products sold at half the price. Jensen was able to resist them for a while, protesting so forcefully that he was never interfered with again. But professional managers and American business ideas did increasingly infiltrate, and eventually designers and engineers lost their power to marketers. The advertising guru Jesper Kunde argued that what mattered was the 'brand', not the product, so that the firm should expand and make money in other domains: his book *Corporate Religion* was inspired by the success stories of Microsoft, Coca-Cola and Disney. Instead of the founders' single-minded idealism, some of the new managers now likened themselves to 'gentle priests guiding their sheep', while the consultants they brought in talked in highfalutin imagery

Corporate religion

about how they would re-educate the firm to become 'change agents' or 'wild flowers' or 'Masai who could look a lion in the eye'. At first, the engineers laughed at this mish-mash of ideologies, but soon they found that they could not escape the consequences of 'rationalisation'. More and more activities were outsourced, so that they ceased to make objects with their own hands, and spent most of their time writing specifications for external manufacturers. The company was now 'flexible' but also in thrall to the servitudes and jealousies of bureaucracy. Not everyone benefits when a firm becomes one of the most successful in the world.

The mish-mash of ideologies

To the novelist Aksel Sandemose (1899–1965), who spent his youth as a lumberjack, teacher and journalist in Newfoundland, Denmark was a 'living hell'. The furore aroused by his bestseller, *A Fugitive Crosses his Tracks* (1933), revealed how profound the divisions were about his famous denunciation of 'the Ten Commandments of the Jante Law', the codes of behaviour that prevailed in his native village, whose first commandment was 'Don't think you are anything special' and the last was 'Don't think you can teach us anything'. He protested against the widespread view that all achievements must be seen as collective, and that those who dared to stand out should be punished. In such an atmosphere, he wrote, 'knowledge was something despicable. Art was judged with a sneer. Science was something that occupied the lazy. Never hurry: that's the refrain all day long.' He ignored the fact that three out of four Danes said and continue to say they are not troubled by this and like their cosy life; for them *hygge*, cosiness, is what one should aim for. Sandemose could only dream vaguely of 'strong, erotic, intelligent women' solving his problem and he could

Against the 'cosy life'

propose no practical action beyond leaving the country. He was just one of about a million Danes who have emigrated in the last two centuries, from a country which had less than a million inhabitants in 1800, and has only five and half million today

National heroes nourished on foreign inspiration

Why should each of these six heroes and heroines of Denmark have been so uncomfortable in their own country? They were all international figures, they could not have been what they were had they not nourished themselves on foreign inspiration. Denmark itself lives only because it is international, depending for its prosperity on selling its talents and products all over the globe. Karen Blixen even wrote her books in English, before translating them into Danish. Nations in the past were established among people who spoke the same language, or who were forced to learn the language of the dominant partner, but sharing a language does not mean sharing the same thoughts or tastes. Today, nations survive only if they can talk to those who do not speak their language.

However, Andersen's statement that 'children speak the truth' re-awakens awareness that the adult world has always been afraid of saying openly what it thinks. Blixen's conclusion that the truth can only be told through stories, as though it is too dangerous to confront it face-to-face, Bang's desire to let objects speak for themselves, Fibiger's inability to get herself understood, Kierkegaard's obsession with contradictions, and Sandemose's protests at the obstacles that prevent the truth being spoken, are all indications that the conversations within nations and between nations have barely begun. The fear of foreigners has been one of the principal reasons why people with disparate provincial loyalties have united into nations. Nevertheless, foreigners have also had the opposite effect, injecting new ambitions and opening new vistas, and they are not condemned to being seen forever as mere aliens or tourists. The foreigner and the native are a couple, capable of interacting in ways as surprising as a pair of lovers: they are a muse to each other. Nations, like individuals, easily get absorbed in introspection, but that is only a first stage. These six national heroes, who were shaped as much by what they saw outside the place of their birth as by their origins, emphasise that the urge to explore competes with the need for a safe haven. To love one's country in an informed way requires one to know what others are like. As more and more people begin to do that, the sense of belonging comes to mean something else.

Strangers as couples

The Viking maxim that 'a human's joy is another human being' has for long been interpreted to mean meeting someone like yourself, and nations with the ambition to get bigger and more powerful have wanted their citizens to have a lot in common. Nations were created supposedly to bring together people who shared the same values, memories and hopes. In reality they paper over divergencies. Without relations with the rest of the world most of them would collapse.

The Scandinavians, despite all that they have in common, divided themselves into several nations, none having a population larger than that of mid-sized modern cities like London or Paris. They have decentralised most of their public activities into much smaller local entities (which the big nations borrowing ideas about unemployment and social welfare from them overlook): is that the way for humans to find joy in the humans they

The distance between neighbours

meet every day? Alas, village squabbles have been as annoying and have ruined lives as much as the internal and external hostilities of huge empires.

Where do you come from?

I do not ask you the question most people ask of one another: Where do you come from? I prefer to ask: Where are you going? I am interested in how one can build one's own collection of humans, independently of the nation one belongs to, as a supplement to one's own inheritance. 'Where are you going?' is a question about what outside influences and inspirations one can seek or choose or stumble upon. That is not different from falling in love. I shall try to discover more about the romance of such encounters in the next chapter.

How many nations can one love at the same time?

WHY IS NO-ONE ALLOWED to be a citizen of more than one or two countries, out of over two hundred? How can one feel a kinship with large complicated nations, or very small ones, which are also complicated? When people think of Denmark, for example, they rarely say that they must visit it at all costs and even learn its language. But every nation, or province or city opens one's eyes in a different way.

The 'father' of modern Denmark, the 'titanic figure' Frederik Grundt-vig (1783–1872), may superficially appear to be of little interest to those outside his country's frontiers. He was a pastor, descended from a long line of Lutheran pastors, who proclaimed that God had chosen the Danes to bring Christianity to fulfilment, at the same time as Herman Melville (1819–1891) was saying that 'Americans are the peculiar chosen people – the Israel of our time'. Grundtvig was a charismatic preacher, a popular poet of the 'simple, cheerful, active life', gushing with hope and pride, and above all a prolific writer of hymns – about joy rather than sin – which soon dominated the national hymn book, so that deeply emotional music and song carried his influence far beyond the limits that argument could reach. He idealised the common people, dignifying them with romantic

Danes and Amerians as chosen people

Nordic myths about their heroic mediaeval origins and their Viking

How to graft the new onto the old

heritage. Grundtvig's popularity came from his giving the Danes self-confidence. He saw that to embark on new adventures it always helps to feel that one is continuing an old one, so he grafted a new nationalism onto an old religion. His *History of the World* announced that it was God's plan that the Danish people should no longer rely on priests but should inaugurate an authentic Christianity in the language ordinary people spoke, so that even the most humble had a part to play in that grand endeavour.

However, to regard him as just another leader of a local patriotism is to miss out on what he had to say about people everywhere. His first message

The differ-ence between an individ-ual and a person

was that the world contains no individuals, only persons. Persons are crea-tures in relationships. No human being can develop without being united with the personal in others. A person is free if that relationship is one of reciprocity, enriched by a sense of community with contemporaries and predecessors. Despite being a priest, he insisted that his first concern was not to convert the masses to his faith. His slogan was 'First a Man, then a Christian', meaning that an individual needs to start by becoming a person, capable of having fruitful relationships, which could not be found simply by joining a church. For him, Christianity did not originate from the Bible 'translated from a foreign language', nor from the commentaries of theologians, but from the behaviour of its adherents. What made a church was neither preaching nor ceremonies but the interaction between its members. A community is born wherever people meet and utter the greeting, 'Peace Be With You'. Building a nation, for him, did not mean simply uniting people who spoke the same language: they had to learn how to behave. He proposed 'Schools of Life', the opposite of what he called the 'Schools of Death' in which everyone was still being educated. He called them 'Folk Schools' because people taught one another. They were part-time boarding establishments for adults, independent of the state, with no examinations or syllabus, designed to help working people become enlightened, self-sufficient and free. They did not inculcate dogma, but relied on conversation to encourage participants to initiate projects on the basis of their own experience, with a special kind of politeness that forbids individual arrogance and allows pride only in shared achievements. These schools reinforced the cooperative movement in Denmark, which enabled poor and isolated farmers to create in a remarkably short period a highly profitable exporting agricultural industry. All this may seem peculiarly Danish, but it is more than that. There are ideas in Grundtvig that make everyone, to a small extent, also a Dane.

Schools of Life and Schools of Death

Something of the Viking temperament that Grundtvig spoke of is to be found all over the world. The Vikings were rebels against boredom, which has been the well-spring of innovation since the beginning of time. Impatience with routine has repeatedly transformed apparently placid souls into restless adventurers, explorers of the unknown, importers and exporters of ideas and people. When the Vikings went marauding as far as Constantinople, Russia, Portugal and America for what they could not find at home, they pillaged, raped and killed, and would doubtless be called terrorists today, but they were also skilled traders and navigators.

Vikings as rebels against boredom

Priding themselves above all on being 'good companions' (*drengr*), valuing individual independence and (to a certain extent) women's autonomy, adopting foster-fathers and foster-brothers to cement their relationships, they intermarried with women whose language they did not speak, and left descendants far beyond Scandinavia. They were thus not simply ancestors of the Danes, but reminders that humans have spent longer *Humans as* being nomads, moving and migrating all over the world, than being seden- *nomads* tary tillers of their native soil. The recent great migration from fields to cities, and from poor to rich countries, is the latest episode in what has been a permanent feature of humanity's response to nature's diversity. Nations struggle in vain to raise barriers against these wanderings, but technology and communication and education all combine to encourage the new generations to become nomads again.

What the Grundtvig makes me think that being Danish and being Chinese may *Danes and* not be wholly different. Asia had its own version of the Vikings in the *the Chinese* Mongols, who, like the Vikings, rampaged over large areas in bands held *have in* together by loyalties created on a personal basis, between people who *common* knew each other as individuals. They had no trouble getting support from neighbours in what is today northern China, who had only distant relations with the rulers in the south. Alliances for war or booty between people of disparate origin and culture were easily made and easily broken, and there was no shame in changing partners, just as there is none in changing employers today. What Grundtvig was trying to encourage was an additional loyalty to one's nation, an impersonal loyalty, to people one did not personally know. In the eleventh century Chinese historians had the same ambition. They created a new interpretation of the past to convince Chinese people that they were a distinct species culturally incompatible with 'barbarians', that 'Chinese clothes and food and drink are not the same' as those of the Mongols, and rather than share such strange customs, 'it would be better to die than to live'. Biographies appeared idolising a new kind of hero, who rejected personal alliances with foreign warlords and was steadfastly loyal to the Chinese empire. The over-riding loyalty had to be not to an individual but to the state. Betrayal became treason. Even the emperor had to be loyal to the impersonal interests of the state, embodied in the *tao* or *dao*, the principles of the good life.

Historians create nations

Ever since, nations have been bringing together huge numbers of people with a wide variety of tastes and opinions and without any personal attachment to regions of their country that they may never even have visited; they have fostered a sense of belonging that made individuals who had never met feel passionately that they all shared the same values and interests, energised by a thrilling desire to unite to protect their beloved homes from foreigners, even though, when the foreign threat disappears, they are torn apart by innumerable and often insoluble disagreements. The difference between Grundtvig's nationalist creed and the Chinese one was that he aimed to make the people – the will of the masses – the arbiters of what was good, in contrast to the Chinese, who gave precedence to the teachings of their philosophers.

Population explosions dissolve nations

But in both cases rising populations encouraged this impersonal national loyalty. China's population almost quadrupled between A.D. 1000 and A.D. 1200, while these writers were inventing this new loyalty.

Nationalism grew into a universal phenomenon when the world's population exploded even more dramatically in the eighteenth and nineteenth centuries. Huge populations, however, have also made many feel lost in the crowd. Then the need for intimate and intense relationships reasserted itself, and that led to the construction of new kinds of friendships. The world is not what it was when nations were first conceived, and they now harbour affinities whichare not necessarily with immediate neighbours.

The Academy for nourishing intimate affection

Grundtvig insisted that affinities could not be left to grow naturally, but needed to be nourished throughout life. His Schools of Life or Folk Schools were remarkably successful, though his ambition to make his country the pioneer of a new popular Christianity was foiled, and Denmark is now one of the least religious places on earth. He might have adopted other tactics if he had remembered how the Chinese, many centuries before him, also tried to improve the world with 'schools of life', not unlike his. Mencius (372–289 B.C.) was the first to advocate them, and the White Deer Grove Academy established by Zhu Xi (Chu Hsi, 1130–1200) made them a much-copied model through succeeding centuries. These Chinese schools offered part-time seasonal education for ordinary farmers who had no ambition to climb into the elite and no interest in preparing for government service entrance examinations; for them, the true elite was not that which flaunted wealth or power but practitioners of morals and culture. They were not concerned with business success, nor with profit from buying and selling, but with the encouragement of mutual respect, 'worthy deeds' and the fusion of public and private interests.

Communal granaries, self-defence clubs, wine-drinking ceremonies and 'country compacts' developed similar goals. Disappointed by the bureau-cratic and authoritarian official system, some Confucians moved the emphasis from obeying the law to developing relationships based on moral behaviour and, as Zhu Xi insisted, 'intimate affection'. But these village schools gradually lost their original purpose and decayed into insti-tutions cramming for official employment. China's first famous woman scholar, Ban Zhao (A.D. 45–116), who argued in her *Admonitions for Women* that 'husbands and wives must be worthy of each other' and that girls should therefore get the same education as boys, discovered even more rapidly that what moralists have said and what people do has always been very different. But the yearning for bonds not based on pure self-interest remains inextinguishable.

Grundtvig's statement that the sign of a community is that its members say to one another 'Peace Be With You' spills over every kind of wall and frontier. The Muslim greeting, *Salaam Aleikum*, is identical, as is the Hebrew *Shalom*. The Chinese character for Peace, written in three parts, begins with *ping*, which means equality: there is peace only when there is equality and no-one is trying to dominate or attack another. The second part is *pa*, represented by a woman under a roof, which means that peace involves a peaceful home and that a mother's affection is at its heart. The third is *ho*, picturing a mouth and grain, meaning there is peace only when everyone has enough to eat. To which the Hindu greeting *namasté* adds: 'I bow to you', which means I am no better than you, we are all human with the spirit of life or a spark of divinity in us. All this challenges the idea that

Peace between persons

humanity's ultimate destination is to be separated into nations proud of

Civilisations and empires can vanish

their uniqueness. Civilisations have vanished leaving only dust behind them; and most of the mighty empires ruling over multitudes of different tribes and languages no longer exist. Nations may not be immortal either.

The world looked different, with different constraints and freedoms, before nation-states appeared, only a few centuries ago, and it was not because people in certain regions suddenly discovered that they were all alike that they decided to unite. Far from being representative of any supposedly common Danish characteristics, Grundtvig was a rebel against almost every aspect of the established order, despising the ruling class, criticising church leaders so violently that he was for a number of years forbidden to preach, condemning the educational system as 'dull, empty and boring', whose graduates were 'cold, self-opinionated and earth-bound', a polemicist pouring out innumerable books and articles on a vast array of subjects, and relentlessly attacking those who disagreed with him. As a scholar he quoted from German philosophers, and from Shakespeare, *Beowulf* and Anglo-Saxon literature. He cherished memories of summers spent in Oxford and Cambridge, but also of visits to Robert Owen and the pioneers of the English cooperative movement. His enthusiasms were a smorgasbord of lucidity and wishful thinking: for all his admiration for

'Inordinate English busy-ness'

England, he wrote 'I have a strong suspicion that a great deal of desperation lies at the bottom of this inordinate English busy-ness. Everybody is so inordinately busy . . . just as busy gadding about the world as others are working, just as busy squandering money as others are earning it', unlike the Germans who 'pursue industriousness as a virtue for its own sake'.

By contrast, the Danes 'allow themselves good time'. But then Prussia's annexation of a sizable part of Denmark in 1864 drove him into a nervous breakdown. His passion for a stronger resistance to foreign threats was ignited. Different kinds of patriotism have always battled against each other within Denmark.

So what is the relationship between patriotism and cosmopolitanism? At present, most people see themselves as exclusively citizens of their own country. But 51 per cent of French people include citizenship of the world as part of their allegiance, as do 50 per cent of Chinese, and significant numbers of Italians (48), Indians (46), Mexicans (44), Britons (38), Thais (38), Germans (37), Argentinians (34), Indonesians (29), Americans (27), Palestinians (27), Egyptians (26), Turks (19) and Russians (17). The more education people receive, the younger they are, and the more they travel, the more likely they are to be citizens of the world, with 47 per cent of those who know people from five other regions of the world seeing themselves in this way.

Part-time citizens of the world

These multiple loyalties emphasise that a government is not always the core of a nation, and that ordinary people are busy creating their own affinities, infinitely extendable and retractable. The Islamic Umma, with its vision of a world-wide community, neither tribal nor national, regarded governments as too ephemeral and superficial to generate permanent loyalties: *Allahu Akbar* meant that no human owed total obedience to any other human and an imam was not a chief, only a 'guide of a caravan', though, of course, struggles for power have replaced unity by bitter divisions. The celebrated physician Abu Bakr al-Razi (841–926) even argued

Infinitely extendable affinities

that there was no need for organised religion, because all humans had the ability to distinguish between good and bad; they could all use their reason and inspiration (*ilhan*), the word *ilhan* being not very far in meaning from what the Greeks called their Muse. The Danes by contrast claim to have contributed to the art of keeping the peace in disagreement by redu-

*The tempera-
ture of
disputes*

cing the temperature in the outward expression of dispute and difference.

Nothing, so far, not even technology, has been able to engineer the seismic shift that would make the 'fellowship of humanity' a reality. The difficulties were already apparent in ancient Greece, when Diogenes (412– 323 B.C.), the wayward son of a Black Sea banker, possibly the first man to call himself a citizen of the world, mocked the pursuit of security and prosperity by posing as a street beggar and sleeping in a tub, to show he could live well without luxuries; he went around carrying a lantern in daylight, explaining that he was searching for an honest man; he mastur- bated in public, saying he wished he could get rid of hunger by rubbing his stomach; he named his philosophy Cynicism (literally, dog-ism), asserting that dogs were the true philosophers because they lived without anxiety, able to distinguish easily between friends and enemies, and without

*A place to be
proud of and
a place to
hate*

shame, unbothered about making love in public. But his audience felt insulted rather than amused; horrified by the thought that foreigners and barbarians and even animals might be as worthy of respect as the cultured citizens of Athens. People have persistently wanted both a place they can be proud of, and places to hate.

Cosmopolitanism could not be imposed by force. Ever since the Sumer- ian king Sargan destroyed the city states around him in the twenty-second century B.C. and conquered what he imagined to be the whole known world, proclaiming himself 'master of the four regions of the earth' with the 'obedience of all men', an endless succession of military rulers have tried to unite humanity using military might, but in vain. Alexander the Great, aspiring to winning more than obedience, made his 'cosmopolis' a union not just of the Hellenic and Persian civilisations but of individuals who, he declared, should consider themselves as all part of one family, intermarrying and accepting one another's gods, with himself setting the example by wedding a Persian princess and wearing Persian clothes. But one man could not change ancestral traditions.

Empires of the mind

The philosophers of the Enlightenment believed they had the answer to that difficulty. They appealed to the masses to share in a dream of a world in which freedom would have no boundaries, redefining patriotism as a sense of community with everyone who believed in freedom, wherever they lived. In place of the ancient model of the citizen of the world as a serene sage who finds harmony within the diversity of languages and tribes, they substituted the activist fighter for liberation from tyranny, in which even the most humble could join. However, in the last two hundred years, national self-interest has won far more adherents. Even Soviet Communism, while inviting all workers of the world to unite, used national feeling to extend its empire. Though the United Nations Organisation supports supranational welfare agencies concerned with universal problems, it is also a guardian of jealous national sovereignties.

A sage or a fighter

It is no longer possible to behave like the libertine wanderer Fougeret de Montbron, author of *Le Cosmopolite* (1750), who poured scorn both on those who had never been out of their own country and on those who gave all their admiration to just one foreign country, like the French 'anglo-maniacs'. When he asked for a passport to visit England, and was told 'Have you forgotten that France is at war with England?' he replied 'No, but I am an inhabitant of the world, and I maintain a perfect neutrality between the belligerent powers.' It is no longer possible to do what Humphry Davy (1778–1829) did in 1813, and travel to France while the Napoleonic War was raging, to receive a medal from the emperor for his scientific discoveries, insisting that though the two governments might

Choosing between loyalties

be at war, scientists were not. Cosmopolitanism remains a mirage partly because it is not believed when it insists that it is no threat to national or any other local loyalties, and partly because less than 5 per cent of the world's population is fluent in a language other than their own. A world government, assuming that one will ever come into existence, would not necessarily be more benign that the ones about which citizens presently complain. Even in the twenty-first century, a majority of voters in the United States have shown that they are not worried about electing as their president a person with only the haziest notions about countries outside his own. The exchange of insults or worse between nations remains a favourite safety valve for many frustrations. Rousseau's scepticism is still widely shared: 'Beware of these cosmopolitans who search in books for duties to fulfil in distant parts, which they disdain to carry out at home . . . They love everyone so as to have the right to love no-one.'

An alternative to cosmopolitanism

The answer to this is that there is an alternative to the cosmopolitan ideal. I cannot love a person I have never met, or at least heard or read. It is the same with nations: I need to be moved not only by its appearance but even more by its dreams and its memories, and by its ancient and present struggles, and to become strongly aware that the individuals in it are not identical pebbles on a beach. When chance led me to write my doctoral thesis on France, and when I then spent many years trying to understand French people of every sort, both alive and dead, I discovered three Frances: one was an imaginary one, made up of the myths that French people like to believe about themselves; a second one consisted of sixty-five million individuals, each with their own unique peculiarities and different opinions, revealing that there were as many minorities in France as there were inhabitants; while a third France was made up of people of every nationality all over the world who have imbibed something from French culture, and who are many times more numerous than the citizens of France. Anybody whose tastes have been influenced by French ideas, or food, or literature, or art, or any other experience of the country, has an ingredient of France inside them, side by side with ingredients derived from other countries too. *I discover three different Frances*

Beyond the cosmopolitanism caricatured by Rousseau, loving everybody whoever they are, another chemistry of ideas can be envisaged, which each individual concocts with elements from different parts of the world, combining appreciation of particular people and places to produce affections of a unique composition. Unlike the cosmopolitanism that is immediately at home anywhere, this more personal approach is nourished by knowledge that is only gradually acquired, and is sustained by a reciprocal feeling on the part of both the stranger and the native that they have each had their minds opened to new ways of looking and think-ing. Like artists who paint a picture of a landscape in which they see

Catalysts of the imagination

features that the natives may notnotice or value, they become catalysts to each other's imaginations.

The *exception française* – the insistence on doing things their own way – though irritating to many – is as significant as the protest against the earth being re-afforested with identical fir trees or its architecture being homogenised with identical glass skyscrapers or its inhabitants all wearing the same style of clothing. It is balanced by the tradition France has inherited from its eighteenth-century thinkers of extracting universal

The capacity to extract universal implications

implications from particular or local facts, the most powerful antidote to narrow perspectives. The France that has been a muse to me has therefore not been a jealous muse, but one that has urged me, and made it easier for me, to seek inspiration from other countries. And each one suggests new thoughts, like a dictionary that reveals a multiplicity of nuances to the meaning of each word. Just as a person's age is not measured simply by the number of years since birth, but by the intensity with which those years were lived, and the variety of the experiences absorbed, from which is deducted all the time spent in vacuous semi-existence, so each human being's homeland can be made of many fragments and gradations of gratitude, loyalty and inspiration.

Why do so many people feel unappreciated, unloved and only half alive?

WHY HAVE THE IDEALS OF Liberty, Equality and Fraternity been so difficult to turn into reality? Why have they failed to deliver all that they promised? If ideals inevitably lose their delicate and intoxicating flavour when frozen into laws, what future is there for them?

There have so far been two ways of keeping ideals alive after repeated disappointment. The first is to insist that it is good to have noble ideals, even if one cannot put them into practice. In Japan, in particular, many have come to this conclusion, that since failure is so much more common than success, the way you fail matters more than failure itself. Though Japan has as strong a tradition as the U.S.A. of seeking success in the conventional sense, it has a parallel tradition that exalts noble failures and admires those who bravely defy established authority in the name of a worthy moral cause, ignoring the possibility or likelihood of failure. There was a time when the Japanese had riots or 'smashings' almost every ten years, which were often futile, but were repeated nonetheless. Some of the country's most popular heroes are not the rich and powerful but these noble failures. Oshio Heihachiro (1793–1837) is one of them, a humble police inspector in Osaka who made it his mission to fight against

The way you fail

corruption. When the chief magistrate of the city turned out to be corrupt too, Oshio resigned and devoted himself to teaching the public better morals, with the message that it was wrong and cowardly to resign oneself to injustice. Even if the power of authority seemed invincible, one should 'do right for the sake of doing right'; one should not just know what is right, but act to assert what is right. He gave revolutionary meaning to *Living a lie* the Chinese philosopher Wang Yang-Ming's dictum, 'To know and not to act is the same as not knowing at all.' It did not matter if action was ineffective; a sage should not be afraid to act 'like a madman', foreshadowing what Mishima wrote a century later, 'The journey not the arrival matters.' So when in the 1830s a famine lasting four years had devastating effects and over 100,000 died of starvation, Oshio Heihachiro protested that the bureaucrats were in league with the rich merchants in keeping the price of food beyond the means of the poor. He sold his most precious possession, his library, and gave all the money away to the poor; then he started a rebellion, not to win political power, but to give expression to what most people 'sincerely' believed, that the wicked should be punished and that justice should reign on earth. What mattered above all was to act with 'sincerity', rather than to live a lie. He set his own house alight, so as to burn down the houses of the merchants around him, and ultimately 3,300 houses were destroyed and many shops looted. But his rebellion was hopelessly disorganised and easily and brutally quashed. Oshio committed suicide, but he lives on as a hero of all those who believe that life should not, and need not, be 'hell', the word he used to describe the lot of the many. Reverence for failure, both heroic failure and that of 'the little man', reappeared as a frequent theme in American literature centuries later: *The Death of a Salesman* echoes the Japanese lament that though the body may live longer, the spirit too often dies an early death.

The second, more common, response to the demise of ideals is to keep on repeating that ideals rule one's life, even though one constantly betrays them and even though one is less attached to them than one claims. Ideals salve the conscience. Humans have in practice not been as devoted to Liberty, Equality and Fraternity as the slogan suggests. They have repeatedly abandoned these ideals, often without a struggle. Even the English, justly proud pioneers of free speech and freedom from arbitrary arrest, have demonstrated how readily people will give up their liberties when they get frightened. It does not require a brutal tyrant to destroy liberty. All that is needed is panic. At the turn of the twentieth and twenty-first centuries, in the space of a single decade, a huge number of new criminal offences were created, supposedly to protect liberty, but sometimes having the opposite effect. The people of England are now watched daily by about five million cameras, under closer surveillance than any other country, to the extent that an average person is apparently observed 300 times a day and the movement of every car is recorded. Freedom of speech and the right of public protest have been curtailed. Individuals have been held in jail without charge, or placed under house arrest without ever being convicted, on the basis of evidence inadmissible in a court of law. Governments have given themselves legal authority to conceal actions which might lose them votes. The media have far fewer resources to reveal the truth than in the past. Trial by jury is under threat, and freedom from

The betrayal of ideals

libel is available only to the very rich. According to a poll, the majority of British people no longer believe that Human Rights laws increase justice. In the U.S.A., Human Rights have been called 'the last Utopia', briefly popular when other ideologies lost their appeal, but already going out of fashion. Amnesty International has only three million members, compared to ninety-seven million Red Cross volunteers. Survival is more highly valued than freedom.

What Americans did not choose freely

The message from the U.S.A., despite its dedication to freedom, is that its citizens did not freely choose to be what they have become. They did not voluntarily abandon Benjamin Franklin's injunctions in *The Way to Wealth* (1756): 'Buy only what you need. He that goes a borrowing goes a sorrowing.' They were carried away by their brilliance in technology, which enabled them to produce far more than they could consume, so they had to seek new markets and entice everyone to buy as much as possible relentlessly, cajoling them into betraying the simplicity and thrift they once cherished. They did not intend to become the world's most publicly and privately indebted nation. They did not freely choose to be dominated by huge corporations; on the contrary, as a nation of independent pioneers and family businesses, they battled hard to avoid them with anti-trust laws, and failed. They did not decide after careful deliberation to give so much importance to material possessions, and over three-quarters of them still complain that their country is too materialistic, selfish, ungenerous, uncaring; but they have difficulty in following the morality they believe in: when asked what their main ambitions are, the same proportion replies that they want a beautiful home, a new car, nice clothes, and a highly paid job. Desire, possession and distraction govern them willy-nilly as much as liberty, equality and fraternity. John Adams, the second president of the United States (1735–1826), told his wife that he busied himself with politics and war only so that their sons could 'have the liberty to study mathematics and philosophy, geography, natural history, naval architecture, navigation, commerce and agriculture, in order to give their children a right to study painting, poetry, music, architecture, statuary, tapestry and porcelain.' The vision for the grandchildren has still not been reached. Many insist that America's essential business is business, which was not the original intention.

These disappointments have not stopped Americans from continuing to pray for success from the graveyard of their moral defeats. What they have done has influenced almost everyone on earth, but what else could they have done? They give expression to their idea of liberty and equality by having as their prime hero the self-made man who delights to sing 'I did it my way'. America's gospel is that anyone who works hard can succeed, simply by their own efforts, with the comforting conclusion that all the privileges of the successful are deserved, and there can therefore be no quarrel about inequality of wealth. But the American dream is of course only a dream. In reality, large numbers do not succeed, and those who get to the top do not necessarily work much harder than those who stay at the bottom, certainly not five hundred times harder, as their salaries suggest.

The American Dream

Bob Dylan said 'If you try to be anyone but yourself you will fail', and 'A man is a success if he gets up in the morning and goes to bed at night and in between does what he wants to do.' However, it is not that easy to be oneself, and to know what one wants, and what caricature of oneself one is becoming as the years go by. One needs others to speak honestly about how one appears to them, or at least one needs the encouragement that comes from two people finding each other beautiful, despite what the whole world might think. Whatever is believed about relying on oneself, few succeed without the right friends. Most people have only their small families and a few friends to help them, often failures like themselves. So where can they find more friends? 'I don't mind failing in this world,' sang Malvina Reynolds (1900–1978), 'because those who succeed are the sons of bitches.' But what is the alternative to devoting one's energies to joining the ranks of the sons of bitches?

The 'sons of bitches'

When ideals become too obviously a sham, a third attitude to them might be to question whether there is something vital missing from them. This became clear when the acquisition of the vote and the control of political power were adopted as the world's primary goal and as the essential precondition for happiness, directing attention to public debate away from private understanding, and to legal rights away from personal relationships. Liberty, Equality and Fraternity are unable by themselves to provide sufficient emotional sustenance, because they leave too many people feeling unappreciated, unloved and only half alive. Though it is wonderful if the law gives us the freedom to say and do what we please, without hurting others, what if no-one listens to what we say and no-one values what we do? Then increasingly the desire to be appreciated and understood becomes more important than the theoretical possession of

Legal rights versus personal relationships

constitutional privileges. For everyone to have an equal vote and for all discrimination to be abolished is hugely satisfying, but what if greed, malice, envy and pride take the joy out of equality? Then, increasingly, equality looks like a mirage and instead it is affection that is seen as making the differences between individuals bearable. To know that fraternity will come to one's aid in moments of difficulty or in old age is a great relief, but what if that help is given impersonally, meanly, grudgingly, with no gratitude for what one has given to others in better times? Then, increasingly, mere survival no longer seems enough, and there is a yearning for a greater sense of being properly alive, to be a source of energy with something valuable to give others, able to animate others and be animated by them.

Greed versus equality

Liberty, Equality and Fraternity is a recipe from which an important ingredient has been omitted. The lawyers who draft constitutions do not like to mention facts of life that are too personal or intimate. Though an enormous amount of heroism and sacrifice has been devoted to making each of these three values the real foundations of society, none are anywhere near being so. The French took a century of hesitation before they finally decided on their famous slogan, having previously toyed with Friendship, Charity and Sincerity. The three magic words that decorate the walls of almost every official building in France, accompanying warnings that it is forbidden for anyone else to put up notices on walls, have survived only because they are protected by numerous myths and wildly different interpretations. This may suggest that without myths nothing can endure. But it is precisely because the magic words have been cocooned

Ingredients missing from Liberty, Equality and Fraternity

in myths that they have not changed lives as much as they could have.

Appreciation, Affection and Animation

Today people need Appreciation, Affection and Animation as a supplement to the political, economic and social preoccupations of the past.

But what about that large part of humanity that is not bothered with ideals and lives passively under dictators, apparently even admiring them? Forgetting that power is a bitter-sweet poison that causes bizarre forms of blindness and deafness, normally sensible people can still be stirred up into handing it to every charismatic would-be messiah promising to solve all problems, even though infatuation with persuasive heroes has repeatedly been followed by disappointment and panic, almost as inevitably as storms and hurricanes bring sunshine to an end.

> 'When the land is kingless, the rich are unprotected,
>   and shepherds and peasants sleep with bolted doors
> When the land is kingless, the son does not honour his father,
>   nor the wife her husband'

Faith in power

wrote Kamban in the ninth century, in his *Ramayanam*, the national epic of the Tamil people about the god Rama, who came down to earth to 'chasten, uplift and guide men'. This faith in all-powerful rulers has survived even though kings – and those who imitate them, whether petty domestic tyrants or masters of vast conglomerates – have, as often as not, brought less security and order than they promised. War, for long the sport of kings, has also become the sport of politicians desperate for popularity, while competition, purged of physical violence, is the sport that animates innumerable aspects of life, work and play. 'As soon as a king has established himself on the throne, he should, as a matter of course, attack his neighbours,' said an Indian treatise on the 'science of politics' (the *Arthasastra*), probably written in the second century A.D. Every civilisation has had otherwise intelligent men urging kings to place aggrandisement above morality; even the brilliant first master of Arabic prose, Ibn al-Muqaffa (720–756) did that, despite his father's having been tortured and crippled by royal command. 'The king who is weaker than the other should keep the peace, he who is stronger should make war': Machiavellianism came to be accepted all over the world as the un-avoidable method for maintaining oneself in power, however devoted to virtue one might be. It was not that Machiavelli wanted princes to be ruth-less, he simply observed that they had to be ruthless to remain princes. *How princes remain princes*

Though governments have thwarted Liberty, Equality and Fraternity by usurping the tradition of absolute obedience to the divine, in practice they have often not had as much control of their subjects as they pretend: they are sabotaged by bureaucratic resistance, and those expected to obey laws have through long practice become expert in evading them. More important has been the encouragement given to the ambitious to seek prosperity as a compensation for being excluded from government, because eventually the prosperous conclude that winning small personal favours from those who monopolise political power is more advantageous than entering the struggle for power, for that struggle has time and again had more losers than winners. *More losers than winners*

Liberty as a unique goal has suffered many defeats because it exhorts individuals to go their own way, with the unintended side effect that the differences between them increase. Disagreements and rivalries multiply. Minorities are side-lined and cry out for appreciation, which liberty by itself does not give. Few humans feel sufficiently appreciated and fully understood, and many meekly agree to wear the labels given to them by others. There are so many obstacles in the way of knowing the truth about anyone, so many disguises worn to create an illusion of respectability, so much increase in the lies and half-truths told by governments and businesses, so much imaginative fiction masquerading as publicity, that the isolated and ignored individual suffers more poignantly from being misunderstood than from being powerless. Only intimate private relationships can provide the reassurance that one is not the caricature one is taken for, but private life has been denigrated as a distraction from civic engagement, so little thought has been given to how private and public life could collaborate rather than compete.

Caricatures of oneself

One alternative to expecting politics to supply all the kinds of dignity that humans desire is to investigate what can be achieved outside the election voting booth, in the places where colleagues, customers, strangers, rich and poor meet, namely at work. So far most people have not invented their own way of earning their living. They have not freely decided that working for an employer is the best of all possible methods of avoiding starvation. They do not often remember that commercial companies were once regarded with such suspicion that, following one of the financial crashes into which they periodically fall, for a whole century (between 1720 and 1825) it was a criminal offence to start a company in England,

Rethinking the idea of 'earning a living'

which was a period of great prosperity nonetheless. Humans are mistaken if they imagine that agriculture and industry and the service society are part of the natural order, rather than inventions for purposes they may no longer share. They are not taught at school that the reigning corporations of today owe their existence to an accident of history, that there were once two kinds of corporations in the land of liberty that America aimed to create, those that were established to carry out specific tasks democratically deemed to be of public interest, like building canals (Ohio was the state that was most noted for ensuring that corporations did not abuse their privileges for private gain), and those that obtained charters that allowed them to do whatever they liked (charters which were granted most easily in New Jersey). Gradually the New Jersey system prevailed and the public lost control over what corporations did. But corporations are a system that is only a century old, not necessarily the only one that can nurture prosperity or pleasure. Likewise, agriculture was not invented to please everybody equally; and the peasants who have laboured at it have consistently failed to get as much benefit as the townspeople they fed. It was not from free choice that the unemployed flocked into the grim factories of industrial civilisation. There was no free vote to approve that speculators should be the minority that derived most profit from humanity's toil.

Outdated working habits

Surprisingly few people now have a completely free choice in how they earn their living, but even for them, liberty is being undermined by the kind of work they do. It is not only governments who panic and invite their citizens to panic. Employers panic that their profits might be reduced if their workers allow their minds to stray from their allotted tasks. Their panacea has been to use technology to oversee every movement their employees make, exercising far greater control than has ever been possible in the whole of history. There is no reason to believe that liberty will gradually spread throughout the world, in imitation of the few countries which became famous for valuing it in the past. The idea that free markets encourage appreciation of the value of liberty has been disproved by many countries which combine economic competition with authoritarian rule. Investors panic when they are not manic, destroying savings and jobs. Pericles said that happiness depends on being free, and freedom depends on being courageous. But society has not been constructed to make people courageous.

Too many forms of work seem to have been invented to grind the mind into pulp and drain the body of energy; too few have the goal of making people more lively, interesting and fully awake. One of the most important ways of feeling more alive is by winning appreciation for what one contributes to society through one's work, exercising a valued skill with talent and artistry, and doing something more than simply being obedient to the whims of the more fortunate. But awareness of this need has penetrated into organisations only as a tranquilliser to minimise the stress they generate. In ancient Athens employment was for slaves; it was dishonourable for a free person to kow-tow to another by working for wages; but today it is shameful to be unemployed and regarded as an achievement to sell oneself into part-time slavery, meekly accepting as natural that one is not free for half one's waking hours; and this despite the fact that the more

Society not constructed to make people courageous

In ancient Athens, employment was for slaves

prosperous a country becomes, the more its inhabitants dream of being free humans in their work, choosing how they use their talents and their time without having to grovel and flatter. A huge terrain for exploration has opened up in which to search for ways of being in control of one's own work, to be inventive, to be indispensable, to be appreciated. Many forms of work do not allow that. Quite a lot of people do not even demand it, because they assume that work has to be the way it is and they have acclimatised to the limited rewards it offers, or because they have learnt to find their satisfactions outside it. Very few realise that they are being forced to fit into patterns created centuries ago, sacrificing themselves on the altar of efficiency.

However, work can be reconceived instead as an entrance ticket into a fuller life. In the Revolution of 1848 the Right to Work was proclaimed, but it is possible to go beyond the idea that any kind of employment is better than none. There will soon be another billion young people demanding not just the right to work, but the right to work at jobs that will neither stupefy nor bore them. Who is going to invent a billion new kinds of fascinating, mind-enhancing, purposeful jobs? Every occupation and every profession is waiting to be re-thought to discover how such expectations can be met. Without a Reformation of Work the wonderful aspirations of Liberty, Equality and Fraternity cannot grow to be more than an incomplete slogan. Work is just one activity which can generate Appreciation, and also some Animation. Affection is more difficult. I shall now look at how women and men have grappled with its mysteries, before going on to explore what new ways of working can contribute.

Inventing new ways of working

*What ideas
are worth
dying for?*

The Japanese police inspector may not have found the final answer to the problem of how to achieve worthy aims, but he raised the most important question: What ideals are worth dying for, or working for, or living for? Politics is the art of putting ideals into practice. Unfortunately, once turned into realities, ideals cease to be beautiful butterflies with multi-coloured wings fluttering among the flowers, and become mere worms that eat the corpses of hope. It is time to rescue ideals from the grave where they do not rest in peace.

How else might women and men treat one another?

WHICH IS THE CRUELLEST and most long-lasting of all wars, which has made the most victims? The war of the sexes has, in varying degrees, disabled half the world's population, and impoverished the other half's sensitivities and imagination. It is the war that has mattered most to me because friendship with women has been so decisive in my own life. Changing the law, winning the vote, obtaining an education, organising a mass movement, challenging male monopolies in the professions, breaking the glass ceiling, should by now have changed men's attitudes towards women. But the weapons women have used in their struggle have been largely those that men have used before them, forgetting that men have never won anything like the amount of liberty, equality and fraternity they expected. In Islamic countries women have likewise used traditional methods such as reinterpreting holy books, but still with very limited results. When the Soviets decreed the abolition of gender inequalities, they discovered that legislation was not enough to dislodge ancestral habits. In the U.S.A., ever since the pioneering Margaret Fuller (1810–1850) proclaimed that 'there is no wholly masculine man, no purely feminine woman', there have seldom been advances without subsequent

Mistakes in the war of the sexes

retreats and backlashes, and withdrawals from reality, like Fuller's saying, 'I now know all the people worth knowing in America and I find no intellect comparable to my own.' The status of women has gone down as well as up over the centuries, and there is no certainty that it will always improve in the future. The suggestion that if only women ruled the world, gentleness and kindness would prevail forgets how inexorably power corrupts. After so much discouragement, should I conclude that it is futile to imagine that the war of the sexes can ever be ended, any more than the war of predators in the natural world?

The struggle for privilege and power has so far distracted attention from something much more elusive. The war of the sexes has been like a battle on land, with bitter hand-to-hand fighting for territory, gaining or losing a few yards, while the command of the air remained unchallenged. By the air I mean the atmosphere surrounding the relations of men and women, the dream-clouds they live in, the mentalities that refuse to change. So what other kinds of battles still need to be fought? This is not a war that can be won by battles. I am more interested in three pollutants that are very difficult to avoid breathing, and which have had a profound effect on humanity's energies.

Mentalities that refuse to change

The first is the idea that 'the human condition' is unalterable. Writing my *Intimate History of Humanity* liberated me from that illusion. But mind-sets that have existed since the beginning of time never vanish completely and it is dangerous to forget about what keeps them alive.

You, whether male or female, and I have the same name, *Homo sapiens*, given to us by Carl Linnaeus (1707–1778). Despite the apparent compliment suggesting that we were wiser than other creatures, his esteem for men was low, and for women lower still. After a long career devoted to careful study of thousands of plants and animals, this is how he defined the human race: 'Our daily task is to prepare from our food disgusting shit and stinking piss. In the end we must become the most foul-smelling corpses. Why did God create us more miserable than any other animal? . . . For his own enjoyment, not for man's.'

Is Homo sapiens the best name for humans?

Linnaeus is famous for inventing the system by which each plant and animal is classified as belonging to a genus and a species. He found a way of satisfying the need most people feel to be identified as belonging to a group of one kind or another, and to be able to place everything around them in clearly labelled categories – on the assumption, still widely held, that this makes life simpler. The criterion Linnaeus chose to separate plants was their sexual characteristics. At first, prudes condemned him as a 'botanical pornographer' advocating 'loathsome harlotry', but his classification became universally accepted, because he brought an easily understood order into nature's confusing diversity. When every plant had a name which everyone used and agreed on, ordinary people could feel they could make sense of nature. Linnaeus was hailed as a liberator: just as the metric system freed people from the chaos of innumerable local weights and measures, his system created a consensus about the relations between different forms of life. However, his passion for simplification was not a liberation designed to encourage independent thought. He felt comfortable only when he could label each creature on the basis of one easily established characteristic. This is the attitude of mind that has

Why simplify?

continued to have a profound effect on how men and women treat one another. It limits their expectation of what each can do for the other.

A universal hobby

Linnaeus came from a family that had been Lutheran pastors for five generations, and he regarded the study of botany as performing the same task – teaching that there was a divine order, and that everything had to be the way it was, as God had made it. His mission was to reveal the law of nature, fixed for all time; his scientific books were written like sermons, and indeed he described himself as a new Luther. Having obtained a medical degree after eight days' stay at an obscure Dutch university, by writing a dissertation thirteen pages long, he become a doctor, specialising in syphilis. He believed that epilepsy was caused by washing one's hair, and was unable to prevent his own health being ruined by gout, migraine, rotting teeth and numerous small strokes. However, he was a brilliant exponent of taxonomy, the science of classification, as well as an impressive preacher, who won popularity also for the enjoyable plant-gathering outings he organised. Collecting and naming plants became a universal hobby. He democratised science, as Luther had democratised theology.

But when science popularises a particular approach to the world, it also directs attention away from other approaches. Linnaeus illustrates how people value limits on curiosity. Mostly, they do not welcome new ideas. New ideas are disturbances. When they seem to accept them, it is usually by modifying them so that they appear to be old ideas. The brain is constructed to fit unfamiliar ideas into familiar categories. Changing

How new ideas are accepted

mind-sets, and particularly about something so ingrained as the relations between men and women, cannot be done by law or by mere persuasion;

it is a slow process that grows from example, experiment and experience.

Far from wishing to change mind-sets, Linnaeus's ambition was to reinforce his own basic assumptions. He wanted to use his knowledge of plants for practical ends, to bring stability to his life and to his country. He proposed that Sweden should become self-sufficient economically, that it should start growing rice, tea and spices, and that instead of venturing for exotic produce in the West Indies, it should be content with what it could find in Lapland. He urged his compatriots to adopt the simple diet of the Lapps, promising that it would make them live twice as long. Determined to make everything less complicated, he held up the 'noble savage' as a model and the courtly sophistication of the European elite as a plague, and he stopped travelling abroad. To speak only his native Swedish and academic Latin was enough for him. Life he saw as a long tragedy of sin. He was an avid collector not only of plants, but also of horror stories, of villainies and tribulations of all sorts, and of 'whores' who were punished by fire or boiling water. In his world, men and women would always be worlds apart, in the same way as good and evil, and that opinion was locked in by all his other convictions. His outlook and temperament survive. Having security, certainty and a clearly defined order is still a top priority for a large part of humanity, even though, and doubtless because, security remains as elusive as ever. A different kind of relationship between the sexes is impossible without a very different vision of the world as a whole.

The resistance of habit

Could a dose of urbanity and enlightenment bring that about? This is the second assumption most people have made about what is needed to

Beyond being civilised and polite

make a society truly civilised. Linnaeus' arch-critic, the French scientist Buffon (1707–1788), whose imagination was less dark, had broad interests and artistic tastes. He ridiculed Linnaeus for using only one characteristic to place animals and plants into fixed categories. Superficial resemblances, he insisted, were less significant than the 'profound reality' that lay behind them, which comprised all that enabled each creature to live and reproduce and degenerate, and to form relationships of many kinds. 'We cannot know any object in isolation; it must always be seen in relationship to others.' So he described in minute detail not just the physical structure, but all the peculiarities and habits of each species, and also how humans could use and connect with them. He expanded the study of the world so that it stimulated thoughts about how to view nature and to meditate on the suffering that each creature has experienced, from the 'ass's misfortunes' and the 'horse's servitude' to the 'black slave's misery'. He accepted the contradictions of existence: 'Everything works because with time everything collides with everything.' His thirty-six volumes of *Natural History, General and Particular* were bestsellers throughout Europe, outstripping Voltaire and Rousseau, though his success annoyed the experts who despised him for being popular with 'women and children'. He was a master of literary style, a painter in words, delighted by the nuances and infinite variety of nature, which was, above all else, charming. Nature was there to inspire wonder.

'A man of the world'

Buffon opened the doors of curiosity and imagination wider than Linnaeus, but only to a limited degree. He was 'a man of the world', and for him women's role was still off-stage. Though absorbed by the search for happiness, he lamented that 'we are unhappy as soon as we desire to be happier', and at the age of forty-five he married a girl of twenty, saying that love was an animal passion that gave pleasure to the body but not happiness to the soul. His biographer summed him up thus: 'He loved money and became rich. He loved power and frequented those in power . . . He loved women, and not just for their beautiful souls.' He deserves an inextinguishable place in history for having made the Paris Jardin des Plantes into a great centre of research, but though he observed animals in his zoo with great attention, he did not listen much to women, and learnt nothing from them. His central preoccupation was not human relationships. He did not apply his vast knowledge to the way he conducted his private life. It is this inability to link up the public and the private that has been one of the greatest obstacles in the way of mutual understanding. So for all the culture and learning and charm of this great Enlightenment figure, the barren conclusion of his studies was that the earth would eventually, one day, freeze up and die. The war of the sexes could only be concealed, and no more than interrupted, by a smokescreen of politeness.

Learning nothing from women

The third kind of fog that has made it difficult for humans to recognise one another is the belief that private life is something quite separate from public life and cannot make much difference to it. Narcyza Zmichowska (1819–1876) deserves to be remembered for beginning the shattering of this illusion. She was the daughter of a clerk in a Polish salt mine, and briefly governess to a Polish prince in Paris, until she was sacked for showing too much independence by going to the National Library to read Kant, Leibnitz, Schlegel and Fichte. Her first novel, *Paganka* (meaning

Narcyza Zmichowska the outsider

the pagan or heathen, the outsider, the rebel, which is what she felt herself to be) is a series of barely fictionalised portraits of each of her friends, who called themselves 'The Enthusiasts'. She dissected the predicaments and emotions of men as well as women with extraordinary acuteness, while insisting that 'there was no way we could understand one another. Each has a different experience of love.' And of almost everything else too. Determined to liberate women, and men also, from all stereotypes, she took care not to replace old clichés with new male or female 'identities', which she believed would isolate them each in a 'ghetto'. Men did not benefit from being idealised, she believed, though she found infinite reassurance from their friendship. Men's dedication to political solutions had ended in failure too often; too many had been locked up in prison or exiled. So women needed to find another way, in alliance with men, but aware that there would be no consensus among them or among women either. Women could now ask 'more audacious questions' and 'risk impossible experiments', rejecting the abstractions of masculine philosophies. Her group was 'free of all dogmatic thinking . . . it never occurred to any of them to tie themselves to the shared dogma of some creed. They were united by sincere friendship . . . and by quite contradictory understandings, by opposite principles.' Friendship was what she valued most; friendship was her solution. As an orphan, she understood loneliness, and prized the creation of hybrid links to replace or supplement what families did not provide.

Daring to ask more audacious questions

Friendship, she argued, needed to be sought beyond its normal confines, beyond the safety of the literary clique in which writers lived, and to reach out to artisans and people of every kind, but without preaching. 'Have I really got to tell them what they lack? No, don't tell them – the fruits of someone else's morals quickly go rotten; only truth found through one's own searching cures and gives succour, enriches and enlightens.' In her eyes, each individual was a potential artist. One became an artist if one used one's anxiety and curiosity to search for opportunities to serve others. Was not her friend Jadwige 'a real poet?', she asked. 'Oh! I tell you she was, though not everyone guessed it because she spoke little . . . and has never written a single couplet of verse. She had a strong exterior and only sometimes, sometimes did her soul flicker sincerely in her eyes, through her fiery glance . . . She finds my opinion of her very offensive, but, believe me, she has within her so many of the elements needed to make a real poet that she should share them out among the whole bunch of Warsaw literati.' Zmichowska's passion for finding the artist in others involved getting away from the normal boring conversation topics with which families anaesthetised themselves, 'about crops, vodka, poultry and waxing floors'.

Each individual is a potential artist

Finding the artist in others

Her novels have no climax, no resolution, and each one is a completely different kind of novel, their aim being to discover different angles from which to penetrate into the minds of others. Of course, she never reached her ideal. 'In the hierarchy of human achievements, the book occupies the lowest place; whole volumes of burning utterances are not worth a single spark that warms a living heart; the wisest systems are not worth one noble deed'. She never escaped from her own frustration and sense of failure. That is the challenge she bequeathed. Zmichowska was jailed for a time on suspicion of fomenting a conspiracy, even though she was opposed to political activism, and imprisonment permanently damaged her health. She has been called Poland's 'most accomplished female author', but one 'whose potential was never fulfilled'. She illustrates *The big* another big obstacle in the way of men and women getting on better, *obstacle* which is that, despite the marvels of education and technology, they have had enormous trouble communicating.

Today, it may seem that science is redirecting attention back to what traditionally was more important than anything else: who one's parents and ancestors were, and the names in one's genealogical tree. The discoveries of genetics have encouraged the conviction that the most useful way to think about the diversity of animals and plants is to understand their descent and common origins. But science is also doing something much more original: focusing attention on minute details whose very existence no-one suspected. Both Linnaeus and Buffon confined themselves to species, and ignored individuals. Now it is not only individuals, but the smallest detectable ingredients inside them, that are being given names, and producing ideas and puzzles hitherto unforeseen. Humanity's thinking about what is most significant in the relation between the sexes has yet to catch up with this. The quality of relationships, though influenced by outside forces, is felt by each person with individual nuances, *A micro-* vulnerable to the most microscopic variations. It is at this nano level that it *scopic* is possible to imagine a different approach. The war of the sexes cannot be *approach* ended by a universal cease-fire, because it is a war with no high command. The example of the heroines of the women's movements is most inspiring when to it is added the intimate history of the endless trials and errors that each person pursues in private life. Every record of such endeavours is like another candle lit to illuminate the truth as it is actually lived.

Oscar Wilde wrote, claiming to sum up the wisdom of the ages: 'Between men and women, there is no friendship possible. There is passion, enmity, worship, love, but no friendship.' That is historically false. There have been times and places when such inhibitions were overcome, though not very often. Friendship is an art that people are supposed to discover for them- *Friendship* selves, and it is no wonder chaos rules about how to set about it. So long *as an* *untaught art* as women were regarded as property, friendship with men was out of the question; and it was one of humanity's most radical innovations for husband and wife to see each other as their best friend. Though some theologians interpreted religion to mean that men and women must not look each other in the eye because that creates 'temptation', the Prophet Muhammad said of his wife Zainab, 'She who makes the heart flutter strengthens mine.' The intoxication of romantic love has never guaranteed that friendship *The intoxica-* will grow out of it, any more than out of sexual intercourse. Many ancient *tion of* *romantic* interpretations of friendship still survive, involving superficial alliances *love* built on expediency, opportunism or even fear, while modern networking is more often about competitive advantage rather than moral renewal.

When I attended the inaugural meeting of the British Women's Liber-ation Movement, held in Ruskin College Oxford in 1970, inspired by the friendships and conversations with women that had shaped much of my life, friendship was not on the agenda because other goals seemed to be more practical and urgent. The feminist movement focused on the power of men rather than on their vulnerabilities, so what men and women can achieve together, in mutually sustaining friendship, has yet to be explored. When I was asked to contribute a volume on France to the Oxford History of Modern Europe, and to the consternation of its editors produced *A*

What universities do not teach

History of French Passions, with long chapters on friendship and love and women, no-one had ever thought of including such supposedly private topics in a university syllabus. Since then, however, public opinion polls have repeatedly shown friendship to be a top priority, very close to love. The internet is a parade of friends one has never met and it is now even possible to hire 'friends' for the day, but these imitation friendships have not reduced the demand for real ones. Many women complain that many men do not listen. Friendship is built on listening. I translate the war of

A world kept rigid by its silences

the sexes as a war of silences. The world is kept rigid by its silences.

In friendship, disagreement does not imply hostility and it can be avowed without losing face or losing interest. The historical importance of friendship between men and women is that it offers an alternative to the age-old idea that war and other forms of competition provide the most

Consensus is not the only glue

convincing proofs of manliness. Consensus is revealed as not being the only glue that can hold civilisation together, and the most inspiring exchanges as those where there are no victories.

Liberation for one sex only is futile. The war between men and women cannot be ended by little concessions, nor by a truce, nor by piecemeal negotiations for minor modifications to professional and social customs that no longer please either men or women. Men are waiting for many forms of liberation too.

What can replace the shortage of soul-mates?

I S IT BECOMING MORE DIFFICULT for people to like one another? Are there too many who pride themselves on having an independent mind, or who see themselves as very complicated, or unconventional, or jokers, or mavericks? Has finding a soul-mate who is a perfect partner, and will remain so, become too laborious?

An independent mind

Being different once meant being in a minority, but the story of Samuel Augustus Maverick (1803–1870) leads to other conclusions. His ancestors had landed in New England in 1624, and prospered, but he was determined to become richer still, and moved to Texas, taking with him forty-five slaves and twenty horses. There he became a legend because he refused to brand his cattle, when everyone else did. Why did he not conform? Some said it was because he thought branding was cruel, others that he was craftily intending to claim that all unbranded cattle belonged to him. Or perhaps being mayor of San Antonio and a state senator, widely rumoured to be the largest landowner in the world after the Tsar of Russia, gave him the confidence to ignore custom. His celebrity resulted in the word 'maverick' entering the American language, meaning an unbranded yearling. Then the word was applied to politicians who were unbranded by any party label. In 1886 a San Francisco newspaper, the *California*

Maverick, defined 'a person who holds maverick views as one untainted by partisanship'. In 1905 a politician stood for office in Massachusetts as a 'maverick', saying, 'I have no man's brand upon me.' Recently, an American writer concluded: 'The maverick is now being hailed as representing the American ideal, a person who goes his or her own way. A loner [the word first appeared in the language in 1907] may be loony, but a maverick is an independent thinker.'

In real life, Sam Maverick was a reserved and prudent lawyer, simple in his dress and manner, and it might seem strange that he should become the symbol of waywardness. He excelled in the business of buying and selling land, eventually accumulating an estate of over 300,000 acres. His wife, fifteen years his junior, was no revolutionary either; she wrote, 'I do not understand why knowledge and science is forbidden to women – but I am glad to live in the time-honoured custom, to love, honour and obey.' However, they both talked of themselves as 'adventurers'. He saw himself

as a man of the frontier, who delighted in his 'rambling adventurous life', his 'land-loving fury', his bargaining with immigrants and the challenge of the unknown. She also was proud that 'we find ourselves a family of adventurers . . . going to the extreme limits where it is possible for Americans to go', though for her adventure meant turning to religion as a first step out of her domestic role, and regarding the world as 'a large home' in need of women's moral and spiritual involvement. In their intimate letters, there is a sense of collaboration between them 'in the direction in which we both wish to go', though they never made that precise. 'I fear nothing,' he said. Contempt for fear, or at least for certain kinds of fear, allowed him to be partly nonconformist. The staid and the adventurous co-existed in him. Maverick showed how just a small mutation, or a spark of courage in a single branch of life, could make someone apparently 'normal' in most respects appear to be a model of independence. And conversely, people who have regarded themselves as nonconformists have conformed in many aspects of their lives.

Since Maverick's time, the whole notion of being different has been jeopardised by scientists realising that what distinguishes living organisms from lifeless objects is that each one is different. 'Every grain of salt is identical with every other, but every organism is a novelty.' You and I are 99.9 per cent identical, 'we differ by only one letter in a thousand in our genomes . . . but out of a genome of three billion letters, that one in a thousand difference means there are three million differences between us.' Even individuals with identical endowments differ from each other because they combine these endowments in unique ways. Each immune system rejects intrusions, however similar, as foreign bodies (with a very few exceptions). Humans diverge so much that some require twice as much energy as others, just to keep alive. Every human brain is slightly different, with every experience making it more different still. There is no normal genome sequence: 'We are all mutants.' The mutations associated with cancer do not appear identically in different cancer patients. Medicine, which traditionally placed individuals in categories as fellow-sufferers from ailments shared with others, now regards individual variability as the great mystery. No remedy is expected to suit everyone. The individuality of fingerprints has been known since Babylonian times, and

The million differences between each individual

Personalised medicine

now computers have established that a hundred different portions of the human face can each vary in a hundred identifiable ways. Even identical twins have been found to develop epigenetic changes so that they cease to be perfectly identical physically. Normality is taking on a new meaning: each individual is different, and it is abnormal to resemble anyone else too closely.

Everyone a nonconform- ist of sorts

Everyone today is forced to be a nonconformist of sorts, at least in some part of their life, because it is more difficult to know to what exactly one should conform. Social classes and categories of many kinds are no longer so clearly defined. Even the institutions originally established to develop consensus are encouraging independence of mind, and under- mining the respectability of conformity. Families, which used to regard the accumulation of property and prestige as a priority, are giving more importance to the nourishment of autonomy and sensibility. Teachers are attempting to stimulate a critical spirit as an expression of individual talent and self-reliance, and they no longer preach the sanctity of disci- pline. At work, individual initiative is demanded as much as obedience. The majority of wage-earners in prosperous countries dream of being self-employed and not having to lick their master's boots, even if in real life they succumb to the attraction of regular pay cheques. Individual spirituality is increasingly valued above the mere performance of ritual. Independent thinkers are no longer burned at the stake, and powerful business people now pay large sums to be trained to 'think out of the box'.

This may seem to be a conclusion applicable only to the West, contrast- ing with the subordination of individuality to family and community which is regarded as characterising the East. But the ancient Chinese were just as interested by individuality as the ancient Greeks. The appreciation of individual character is supposed to have begun with the book on the subject by Theophrastus (371–287 B.C.), Aristotle's successor as head of Plato's Academy, who asked 'Why is it that, while all Greece lies under the same sky and all the Greeks are educated alike, it has befallen us to have characters so variously constituted?'; but the answer he gave was superficial, little more than a series of amusing sketches of bores, flatterers, gossips and idiots. The Athenians produced some wonderfully independent minds, but they also wanted citizens to be virtuous and rational, and they devoted much energy to defining what that meant, condemning Socrates for being too individualistic in his ideas, and denying citizenship to most of the inhabitants of the city, who they thought did not have the necessary qualities. *Individuality in ancient Greece*

In China, already in the sixth century B.C., a royal text stated that 'men's hearts are no more alike than their faces'; and in the fourth century a protest declared that 'we should follow our inclinations' or it would be 'like being in a prison, shackled by irons'. Between the first and fourth centuries A.D., after a long period of compliance with Confucian orthodoxy, a movement of rebellion by the young, supported by the frustrated of all ages, denounced the collective social norms as 'unnatural', and resulted in some people actually trying to live with greater individuality and saying of themselves that they 'competed to be strange and excellent, each wanted to surpass others with his unique behaviour'. The *New Account of the Tales of the World* (A.D. 430) described over 600 historical figures in terms of *Individuality in ancient China* their peculiarities and their 'petty talk'. Petty talk was what Confucius had condemned as frivolous chatter, but now it was seen as the key to understanding what made each person special: how people actually spoke, and how they showed rudeness, extravagance, anger, infatuation, meanness and a multitude of other qualities, each of which was worthy of being carefully observed. Whereas previous generations had reserved their admiration for moral behaviour, or, in times of crisis, for practical organisational skill and courage, now aesthetic and psychological traits were found more interesting. What made this change even more original was that the decisive criterion became the ability to express one's attitudes and feelings in a forthright way, to genuinely reveal oneself to others, to be open with strangers, treating them as though they were old friends, to be spontaneous, 'as spontaneous as nature itself'. Instead of treating personalities as static, and focusing on abstract virtues or faults, this book, which

Looking at the whole person from many angles

has remained endlessly popular throughout the centuries and been frequently imitated, described individuals in relentless conversation and confrontation with others, showing interest not only in 'inner qualities' but also in responses to the outside world, and in looking at the whole person from many angles. Previously, individual character was considered mainly from the point of view of suitability for recruitment into positions of power, but now the gentry class became interested in its complexities and regarded understanding these as central to the art of living.

Political disenchant- ment

Young people, and others who were disenchanted with the futility of political engagement and resentful of the repression of dissent, and who wanted more freedom for their imaginations and their wit, began organising what they called 'Pure Conversations'. These were early precursors of Europe's eighteenth-century salons (they did not exclude women) and in some ways of the twentieth-century counter-culture. Participants were consciously aiming to upset the established order, and sometimes deliberately engaged in outlandish behaviour, assisted by much wine drinking. Their goal was to search for the truth rather than self-interest, to encourage openness and independence, the discussion of poetry and sex, and to reach what they called the Profound, the possibility of more meaningful change. This movement died in due course and the grey clouds of obedience returned to shield society from the dangerous light of independent thought. But sparks of independence have continued to reappear sporadically ever since.

'Pure Conversations' in China

The belief that only the West has been interested in the individual is also belied by the history of many religions, which beyond collective allegiance have also encouraged the cultivation of personal spirituality, each individual engaging in a unique search for an understanding of the truth, with each having to give an account of their choices and behaviour. The early Muslim Sufis often liked 'to shock their contemporaries by outrageous behaviour and paradoxical statements calculated to bring out the moral irrelevance of conventional institutions', sometimes deliberately neglecting their appearance and inviting the contempt of others, ignoring gender and social distinctions, saying that 'freedom is freedom of the heart, nothing else'. A Sufi followed his own 'path', which historically has varied from near-atheism to solipsism, from asceticism to political ambition, participation in government, and military and worldly pursuits, from

Sufis challenging convention

self-denial to using music, dance, drugs and drink as aids to becoming a 'friend of God', a 'mirror in which others see their own faults reflected'. And Sufis were divided into a multiplicity of fraternities which appealed to numerous opposing temperaments. The Egyptian Sufi saint Dhu'l Nun al-Misri (*c.* 796–859) mocked the establishment and its claim to having a monopoly of learning, saying, 'I have learned true Islam from an old woman and true chivalry from a water carrier.' The 60,000 lines of poetry and song that Rumi (1207–1273) wrote rejected imitation and conformity: 'If you want certainty, jump into the fire,' he sang, and concluded: 'To open windows, that's religion's role.' Sufism is the hidden side of Islam that is the counterpart to outward conformity. The more minutely a civilisation is examined, the more deviations are revealed. In *The Argumentative Indian* Amartya Sen has shown how disputation has been refined so that it becomes one of the pleasures of sociability, and there are many other countries where having your own opinion is celebrated.

'To open windows, that's religion's role'

By the sixteenth century European painters and sculptors were increasingly making portraits of individuals designed to show them as unique, as opposed to mere representatives of a type. Now photography is officially used to prove that no-one looks exactly like anyone else. Literature has delighted in the description of distinctive characters as opposed to types. Nobody would dare repeat what the poet Pope once wrote, that 'most women have no characters at all', or what Karl Marx said about French peasants, that they were like 'potatoes in a sack', with 'no diversity of development, no variety of talent, no wealth of social relationships'. It

Art and literature in search of individual character

is no longer taken for granted that people are forever stuck with the aptitudes and peculiarities with which they were born, or that they cannot throw off the pretences they put on for the world.

It is true that the world has always been organised, and, despite all the talk about the triumph of liberty, is increasingly organised to prevent too much independence or at least its open public expression. When the Chief of Staff of the British army questioned the wisdom of his government's persistence in keeping troops in Iraq, he hastened to add that he was 'not a maverick', and that his very conservative aim was to save the army. At the same time, when one of the world's most successful investment bankers was called a maverick, his public relations team sprang to his defence, terrified that it would damage his reputation. Only in private will he reveal that he is bored by office routine and management meetings. Only on holiday or in free moments can he indulge his interest in art, philosophy or theology, and reconnect with his youthful passion for choreography; but all that is private, it is dangerous to be a maverick in public. When a boss lectures his employees on the need for creativity, but says in private that there must be limits to that creativity because he does not want them to challenge his own position, why do they not call his bluff? Why is a tycoon compassionate only in private but unforgiving at work?

The dangers of being a maverick

The reason is that institutions were invented to inject predictability into human waywardness, and most are still based on the assumption that people are neither unique nor unfathomable, but categorisable and needing to be categorised, if no longer by the old measures of class, gender or race, then by psychological tests and other 'behavioural markers'. So job

Injecting predictability into human waywardness

descriptions are now written to suit a professional ideal, to which people have to approximate as best they can, forgetting their individual tastes or temperaments, and accepting that their independence might be squeezed out of them. Classifying humans (at school, at work, and in every social encounter), rewarding them according to the category to which they are assigned, and then consoling them for being wrongly classified, still consumes a large part of every national budget. Admiration for originality may be growing, but it has been counterbalanced by new inducements to pretend to be like everyone else, or at least like people who are admired, and a whole industry is devoted to urging people to believe and buy as others do. Climbing the social ladder has been raised into the ultimate ambition, which means adopting the obsessions of those higher up.

However, while the desire to 'belong' to a group of some sort remains as profound as ever, traditional loyalties are fragmenting or dissolving. In *Britishness* Britain, while governments insist that 'Britishness' needs to be inculcated and celebrated by every child learning the names and dates of every English king that ever reigned, only 13 per cent of Britons say they feel they belong to the community in which they were born. Less than half (44 per cent) consider that they are best described as British. One-third say that their sense of belonging has changed significantly in the course of their lives. Only 22 per cent believe that it would be relevant for them to mention their occupation when introducing themselves. Commitment to voluntary activities is often short-lived and changeable. Only 15 per cent of men and only 5 per cent of women regard the political party they support as an important element of their lives. Only 15 per cent are proud to belong to a trade union. To be a fan of a football team is often a more significant affirmation of allegiance than religious belief. But the real cement of society for 65 per cent is friendship, finding and keeping friends being a permanent preoccupation; 88 per cent say that the family is their most important attachment, but the family is increasingly taking on the characteristics of friendship, needing constant maintenance and repair and reinvention as affections grow cool or warm.

The war between conformists and nonconformists, which has dominated all history and caused so much havoc, is running out of ammunition. There are no longer two opposing armies, but seven billion guerrilla fighters, or guerrilla victims, with shifting grievances, uncertain aims, never wholly predictable. Being an ordinary person, just like everyone else, now has a new meaning – being different from everyone else. The whole of history has been a huge effort to deny or postpone or avert the implications of this fragmentation, but it is now possible to imagine how something more interesting might be constructed from the pieces.

Being 'an ordinary person' has a new meaning

The first implication is that the most fundamental, enchanting and puzzling of human needs, the desire to find a permanent partner, has not become any easier to satisfy. Though 55 per cent of marriages in the world today are, according to UNICEF, still arranged by parents, with a divorce rate of only 6 per cent, this majority is dwindling, as ever more people in different countries search for partners independently of parental guidance. It is as momentous a change as 50 per cent of humans moving into cities. It means that humanity is parachuting itself into an open sky and over unknown territory without any clue as to where it will land, for never

New difficulties in finding a life partner

has there been so much disagreement about what a perfect partner is, or what a soul-mate is. A soul-mate used to be the person chosen in heaven or by destiny who was one's other half and who made one complete. But losing oneself in another being is no longer a universal ambition; the safe retreat into a cocoon of mutual admiration, despite all its pleasures, can end in claustrophobia, when couples find they have nothing new to say to each other and routine replaces excitement. Excitement is not what everyone wants, far from it, but the more education stimulates criticism and curiosity and the more culture becomes exploration of the unfamiliar and not just reassurance from habitual rituals, the more individuals seek to discover others, to acquire from them capacities and sensitivities they never had, and to be recognised as being interesting persons in themselves, rather than half of someone else.

Soul-mates in crisis

Sociologists say that those who believe they have found their soul-mate are breaking up more often than anyone else, because as soon as they clash with some fault in the chosen one, they decide they must have made a mistake, and try again and again, endlessly repeating the discovery that they cannot find their elusive ideal. Psychologists add that women are attracted by the odour of men different from themselves, but when they are on oral contraceptives they prefer men similar to themselves, as though they need a different partner to conceive a child from the one with whom they can cohabit harmoniously. All these uncertainties have only reinforced the popular wisdom that to fall madly in love and to be idolised as the most wonderful and beautiful person in the world by at least one person is the foundation of the good life.

Concentrating attention on how to find love, how not to lose it, how to cope with desire, possession and compromise, has resulted in much less being known about how the experience of love can deepen understanding of the vast numbers whom one does not love but whom one wants to know nonetheless. Love can be an introduction into seeing the world through another's eyes and also a foretaste of what experiencing other people's feelings does to one. There is room for more experiments in human relationships, rather than just repairing those that break down. Love between two people is the first step in the expansion of compassion beyond concern for oneself, and then beyond the selflessness that children provoke, until it becomes the source of the courage that no individual ever has enough of, to confront alone the fears that are the bane of life, the fear of rejection, of loss, of inadequacy, and all the fears concealed behind happy façades.

All those whom one does not love

The Renaissance ideal of proud individual originality no longer suffices because it is often too fragile, tortured by an insatiable desire for approval and applause. The Romantic ideal, a thrilling liberation from the constraints of calculating or rigid reason, can often end up as slavery to figments of the imagination. The twentieth century's antidote for its debilitating uncertainties – self-absorption in self-definition – is the Identity ideal that leaves introspection pacing unceasingly round its animal cage unable to free itself from its doubts. So not finding a soul-mate of the traditional kind need not be a cause for lament. Safeguarding one's peculiarities by surrounding oneself with those who agree with one and resemble one leads only to this question: What prevents people from being interested by every form of life, since life is what is most precious to them?

Dangers of the romantic ideal

The answer is that humans are so often inscrutable that the instinctive, elementary response is to treat them as buzzing, biting insects best swatted away indiscriminately. The search for consensus and harmony has resulted in far less attention being devoted to appreciating difference than to instilling obedience and encouraging imitation.

Gastronomy and affection

    The domain in which difference and inscrutability has won the right to be celebrated is gastronomy, though habit still rules within it. Yet only the brave follow the example of the Boston lawyer Jeffrey Steingarten (born 1942), who, on abandoning his profession to become a food critic, immediately recognised that he could not succeed until he got rid of his 'intense food preferences, whether phobias or cravings'; and he then systematically and perseveringly ate a lot of what he hated and learned, if not to love it, at least to appreciate it. Most people are still avoiding what they do not like, as the ancient Greeks did when they used perfume on a lavish scale to conceal their faults and enhance their attractiveness. Men as well as women anointed each part of the body with a different scent: each 'steeps his feet in rich Egyptian unguents; his jaws and breasts he rubs with thick palm oil; and both his arms with extract of sweet mint; his eyebrows and his hair with marjoram; his knees and neck with essence of ground thyme'. Guests at dinner were not only fed but sprayed with many perfumes, as were spectators at theatres, and dogs and horses too. It was the aroma of a kiss that was held to be most memorable, while the Greek gods fed on scent. King Darius III of Persia (380–330 B.C.) kept fourteen perfumers in his retinue. It was only when equality became the supreme virtue that deodorants triumphed to prevent discrimination on the grounds of smelling foul or different. Only when masculinity felt threatened did it proclaim that perfume should be reserved for women.

The hope of finding a soul-mate is the hope that there must be somebody, even if it is only one person, who understands one. There are all sorts of obstacles, and not the least is that people are encouraged or intimidated into pretending to be what they are not. Private life should be the one refuge from that pressure, but no statistic reveals how often it is or is not.

Where there is no need to pretend

Is another kind of sexual revolution achievable?

IN 1763, IN SUCHOW, NOT FAR from Shanghai, Shen Fu married Chin Yun. They were both seventeen years old. 'We lived together', he wrote, 'with the greatest mutual respect for three and twenty years and as the years passed we grew ever closer . . . We were inseparable.' She said, 'I wonder whether there is another couple in the world as much in love as we are.' On her death-bed she told him, 'I have been happy as your wife . . . You have loved me and sympathised with me in everything, and never rejected me despite my faults. Having had for my husband an intimate friend like you, I have no regrets.'

A marriage based on the love of her poetry

He had resolved to marry her the moment he saw her, when they were only thirteen, not because he was overwhelmed by her looks – all he ever said about them was that she had beautiful eyes, which compensated for her protruding teeth – but because he admired her poetry. She had taught herself to read and to love poetry using her brother's books, but she could not step out of the limitations imposed on her by her sex, and had to spend most of her time using her skill in embroidery to help her family survive; the word 'woman' in Chinese is written as a picture of a person with a broom, as though women are eternally condemned to domestic tasks. Only later did Fu discover her generosity, her gentleness, and also how emotional she could be, 'too sensitive to be completely happy'.

Fu failed his examinations, never completed his studies, was unemployed for long periods, and gave up what jobs he had because he
disliked his employers or colleagues. The little shop he opened was unsuccessful, as was his attempt to earn a living as a painter. He quarrelled
with his parents and was ashamed that he 'seldom gave his father any
happiness'. Poverty haunted him to the extent that he once had nothing
left to pawn but his underclothes. However, 'the sorrows of misfortune'
did not weigh heavily on him. 'I like to have my own opinion and not
pay attention to other people's approval or disapproval. In talking about
poetry or painting, I am always ready to ignore what others value and to
take some interest in what others ignore. And so it is with the beauty of
famous scenery . . . There are famous scenic spots which I do not feel are
anything extraordinary, and there are unknown places that I think are
quite wonderful. A man's honour lies in being able to stand on his own two
feet . . . All my life I have been honest.' He remembered best not his many
woes but whole days discussing the great works of literature with Yun,
roaming through the countryside with her, admiring the flowers 'compet-
ing amongst themselves over which was the most beautiful', holding hands
with her in the moonlight, drinking wine and laughing loudly. 'She understood what my eyes said and the language of my brows. She did everything
according to my expression, and everything she did was as I wished it.' So
he too, by assuming his wife was there to do his bidding, was unable to
escape from the traditional masculine role, but at the same time he failed
to do what a man was supposed to do: be the financial provider for his

*Not quite the
ideal man*

family. Nevertheless, in the end, he did do something extraordinary, turning failure into inspiration by writing down his 'true feelings' about their life together, the 'joys of the wedding chamber' and 'the delights of roaming afar'. When his manuscript was published sixty years after his death

*China's
favourite
love story*

it became and has remained one of China's favourite love stories, because it suggests that the love of two people is enough to blot out adversity.

But it has a deeper significance. It was by their relations with other people that the couple judged themselves. Yun believed her life was a failure because it was all her fault her husband had lost the affection of his parents. 'While I have tried to do my best to be a good daughter-in-law [which for Chinese wives was as important as satisfying a husband], I have failed.' Fu's father adopted twenty-six sons, and his mother nine daughters: that is how parents could get nearest to immortality, proliferating descendants who would remember them. Yun herself, while looking after their two children and doing everything to please her husband including making his clothes and developing frugality in housekeeping into a fine art, wanted something more, to be able to do what men were allowed to do, to accompany him on his journeys and see more of the world. Above all she wished to expand the range of their affections, and that extended to people as well as places. Yun as a woman did not have the freedom that men enjoyed, but would winning it have satisfied her? She

*The next
sexual
revolution*

did not see that men were not free either. Fu revealed the limits of what men could do when he said, 'I have never been able to search out and explore secluded places on my own.' This is a clue to where sexual revolutions could go next. Too much is left out when sex is thought of only as a force of nature, or an expression of love, or a criterion of morality, or a struggle for power, or a theatre in which genes and hormones are the main characters. It is also about what one person cannot do satisfactorily on their own.

One day, Yun announced to Fu that she would find him a concubine who would come to live with them. How, he asked, could they possibly afford such a luxury? The practice of taking a concubine, not out of desire but to produce descendants, ideally with the approval of a loyal wife free of jealousy, had become a tradition that had spread particularly among the wealthier classes, supported by the emperor, who even provided concubines for his senior officials. 'We are so happily married,' Fu said. 'Why should we look for someone else?' Yun refused to be deterred and found a young woman who was 'both beautiful and charming . . . her eyes were as lovely as the surface of an autumn pond' and 'her literary knowledge was extensive.' 'I love her too,' Yun explained, and she took an oath with the concubine to become sisters. Fu asked: was Yun trying to imitate the heroine of the famous play by Li Yu (1610–1680), in which a wife falls in love with a woman and brings her into her home as a concubine for her husband? 'Yes,' replied Yun. The novelist and actor-manager Li Yu was another examination failure who became a bold analyst of eroticism (and gastronomy too), and an advocate of originality and invention. His message was, 'Even if your tastes are mistaken, if you cultivate your own mistakes, they are not mistakes anymore.' In the end, nothing came of the concubine idea, and Yun died aged forty, too poor to afford a doctor.

The wife loves the concubine

She was unintentionally a pioneer by living with Fu as a couple, separated from his parents, who practised what was then and has in many places remained normal, to have a large family of many generations all in one house, sometimes with employees or servants too. However, innumerable modern couples who have replaced this with the ideal of independence and privacy have been struck down by an unforeseen epidemic: boredom, having nothing more to say to each other. The entertainment industry has struggled to offer short-term relief for this recurrent affliction, but it is not a cure, for entertainment can also become boring. Yun's attempt to bring a third person into her home so as to extend the range of her experience of life has been widely rejected as a solution and couples have defined themselves by their exclusion of third parties. According to surveys, the majority of American women believe it wise to give up their close male friends when they get married because their jealous husbands feel threatened. From the beginning of human history, how to be a couple without jealousy has been a problem: the very first recorded conversation between two lovers, in Mesopotamia about 1750 B.C., centres around a woman suspecting that her lover was too interested in another, and her determination to win him back: 'No, she does not love you,' says the woman. 'I shall win over my rival . . . I shall win back my beloved . . . It is for your love that I thirst.' But jealousy is only one of the obstacles in theway of making the relations of couples more beautiful.

Jealousy

Sexual revolutions are not a modern invention. In the third century A.D., Chinese moralists complained that the Celestial Empire was entering an age of debauchery, that people were interested only in gratifying

An age of debauchery – 3rd century A.D.

their senses and were giving way to 'lustful impulses', that even well-bred women 'jest lewdly, drink and sing as they go along'. Well-to-do provincials, excluded from power and disgusted by the incompetence and corruption of the emperor and his courtiers, made sexual conquest an alternative form of politics. For these men, it was another way of asserting their independence of state-supported morality and their ability to do what they pleased, at least with women, another way of building their own little domain of authority and of finding an inspiring purpose. But the result was nothing more dramatic than the growth of an industry of ever more sophisticated courtesans to entertain frustrated gentry and newly rich merchants. Even when the Taoists turned sex into a cosmological experience, promising longevity with elaborate sexual ceremonies, liturgies, massages and varieties of copulation, though they sometimes gave women an active role, they often degraded them too.

Sexual conquest – an alternative form of politics

'Debauchery' stimulated a lot of questioning about what men and women wanted from each other, but offered few practical answers. Juan Chi (A.D. 210–263) questioned whether traditional sexual morality was out of date: 'Were the rituals established for people of our time?' The wife of Hsieh An (A.D. 320–385) said, 'If the rules on sexual conduct had been written by a woman instead of by a man, they would be different.' Liu Ling (A.D. 221–300), notorious for wearing no clothes when at home, issued one of the first declarations of the right to privacy: 'The rooms of my house are my trousers. Gentlemen, what are you doing by entering my trousers?' A wife, reproached for not addressing her husband with the habitual ceremonial circumlocutions of respect, dared to reply, 'I am intimate with you

What men and women wanted – 3rd century A.D.

and therefore I call you *you*.' Through the centuries that followed, every time people lost their respect for government, or their fear of it, and felt they could ignore imperial controls on their behaviour, they attempted a sexual revolution. Every time emperors reinstated their authority, they brought intermittent periods of sexual freedom to a close. This see-saw between sexual freedom and sexual repression was repeated time and again. In the twentieth century, under Mao all talk of sex was silenced and energies diverted to economic progress, but immediately after his fall it reappeared, with a vast range of publications on the 'bedchamber arts' and social surveys describing the precise sexual techniques people could use.

From sexual freedom to sexual repression

The goal of these sexual revolutions was to keep private life separate from public life and free from public censure. But freedom has proved to be too limited an aim. 'Sexual liberation' has repeatedly aroused puritan reactions, and it has not necessarily enabled men and women to understand each other better, nor increased the amount of affection exchanged between them, nor expanded their idea of what life has to offer.

Freedom too limited an aim

In the lifetime of Fu and Yun, parts of Europe also experienced a similar flux and reflux. In 1763, the year they were born, John Wilkes, sometime member of parliament and Lord Mayor of London, the popular campaigner for liberty in England and the American colonies, wrote:

> Life can little more supply,
> Than just a few good fucks,
> And then we die.

This was an extreme application of the doctrine that the pursuit of happiness was the most important aim of life. Lust, hitherto condemned as dangerous, was now celebrated by some as 'the most exquisite and most ecstatic pleasure in life'. Male appetites were freed from restraint: 'A woman being enjoyed by a dozen . . . can never render her less agreeable to a thirteenth.' England's Hellfire Club crowned itself with the motto: 'Do what you want', and brought together respectable clergy, leading politicians, army officers, noblemen, merchants and academics to ogle naked women, read pornography, compare their penises and masturbate in 'elaborate rites of phallic celebration'. However, as in China, that phase passed and by 1800 piety and modesty were back in fashion. Though the 1920s and the 1960s revived the celebration of sexual freedom, they also produced a backlash. In 2012 Alain de Botton concluded that there was 'no solution to the majority of the dilemmas that sex creates for us' and that humans have to learn to live with their disappointments. Today indeed individuals are more rigorously categorised by their sexual orientation than they were in the past. And no public figure would dare openly conduct a relationship as King James I and the Duke of Buckingham did in the early seventeenth century, communicating in unsealed letters, with the king addressing the young duke as 'my sweet child and wife' and signing as 'your dear dad and husband', with the duke writing back, 'My only thoughts are bent on having my dear dad and master's legs soon in my arms', and ending, 'your majesty's most humble slave and dog.'

India, in contrast to China, had clearly expressed divine support for the pursuit of sexual pleasure as one of the goals of life. There was therefore no need to fight for freedom, but obeying the rules of religion implied

Lust as 'the most ecstatic pleasure in life'

The aftermath of freedom

respecting social structures too. The *Kama Sutra,* (written possibly as many as eighteen centuries ago) gave the sub-continent the reputation of being nearer than any other place to reconciling conscience and carnal knowledge, by showing how its sixty-four ways of love-making could be raised to the level of art and religion. Each gesture, each embrace, each position was given a meaning, orgasm was turned into a mystical union of male and female, elaborate play-acting during intercourse transformed quarrel into theatre, and the exchange of bodily fluids was made into a ritual for the expiation of sins. Temples, moreover, were filled with erotic works of art that assimilated sex into a search for the divine. European visitors were astonished by the sophistication and variety of sexual teaching and believed they had struck on a golden remedy for adultery, because in their own sexual practices 'monotony begets satiety'; but in this civilisation it seemed possible to 'live with a wife as with thirty-two different women, ever varying the enjoyment of her and rendering satiety impossible'. They were amazed that Indian women 'cannot be satisfied with less than twenty minutes'. But outside the bedroom, social hierarchies remained untouched. Ancient constraints on individual behaviour, often ambiguous, were sometimes even reinforced. The great Sanskrit epic, the *Mahabharata*, which dates back as far as the ninth century B.C., suggests it could have been otherwise:

Love-making as art and religion

> 'The wife is half the man, the best of friends . . .
> With a wife a man finds courage . . .
> On her depend the joys of love, happiness and virtue.

But ten centuries later the *Arthasastra* insisted that all that was expected of a wife was obedience: 'She should do nothing independently, even in her own house. In childhood subject to her father, in youth to her husband, and when her husband is dead to her sons, she should never enjoy independence . . . The virtuous wife should ever worship her lord as a god.'

Sexual intimacy did not dismantle the barriers between men and women. 'Love Poem for a Wife' by A. K. Ramanujan (1929–1993) ends by saying 'what keeps us apart is an unshared childhood': they are brought up too differently. According to the *Hindustan Times* surveys, three-quarters of people aged under twenty-five in today's India are in favour of arranged marriages. In Bollywood films, love is not generally expected to triumph over family. The harassment of women remains a major complaint. Sexual freedom is not enough to change the relations between men and women.

Sex and intimacy

Nor are prosperity and luxury, nor the rise or decline of civilisations. The problem with the cultivation of sensuality has been that it then raises the question of what comes next, beyond more sensuality. Just when the Roman empire, in the first two centuries A.D., was at the height of its power, people who seemingly had everything rebelled against the ideal of sensual pleasure, and Christianity joined the rebellion, adding its religious authority to Stoic philosophy. The flesh dies, the spirit lives, said the preachers; spiritual pleasures were more important. The worldwide monastic movement exalting celibacy was not just about sex but an expression of a different idea of what humans should be. Monks, nuns and hermits attempted a heroic experiment: to have such complete faith in the

Rebellions against sensual pleasures

divine that they did not need children to care for them in their old age. For many, in any case, the end of the world was imminent. They wanted to distinguish themselves from mere animals by their will power in resisting all natural temptations, and to be able to love everybody, not just one partner. Their ambition to free themselves from the domination of sex was as bold as that of communists who later tried to free themselves from the domination of money, but it proved just as difficult. Pachomius (292–346), the Egyptian saint who was the founding father of Western monasticism, said that between the ages of fifty and seventy he had not spent a single night or day without desiring a woman, even when he tried to concentrate on prayer. St John Cassian (360–435), who introduced monasticism to Europe from Egypt, claimed that he could guarantee perfect chastity in six months: all that was needed to purge oneself of lust, desire and gluttony was to live on nothing but two loaves of bread a day, changing the meaning of what it meant to be alive. The idea of accepting suffering so as to test one's ability to triumph over it, and of overcoming sexual desire in favour of spiritual rewards, was for many centuries admired, as was rejecting contact with another human body because flesh was a reminder of mortality and sexual desire a sign of human weakness in the service of God. Women embraced asceticism by becoming the brides of Christ. But when Catholic priests tried to interfere in the sexual lives of lay people, allowing copulation for only 184 or 185 days a year, and used the confession to punish them for unorthodox sexual variations, they found the limits of their power. Instead today's economic system was built, in part, on the rejection of self-control.

Loving not just one partner

The discrediting of sexual desire

To change one's understanding of what life is about is one way of having a sexual revolution. But another is to change what is understood by sex. In 1905 'sexy' meant to be engrossed in sex; in 1923 it meant, for the first time, to be attractive. Could a 'sexy' person today be one who appreciates the complexities that the existence of two sexes involves? The Chinese encourage such a view because their word for sex, *xing*, had a broader meaning before the twentieth century, describing an individual's whole personality rather than referring specifically to the genitals. But the whole personality is still far from being what initially attracts humans to one another. According to researchers who like to put numbers even on such matters, people are attracted first of all by appearance (55 per cent) and then by the style of speaking (38 per cent), and much less by what is actually said (7 per cent). Is that an additional clue to what another sexual revolution might concern itself with? In 1511, the word 'conversation' was used to describe sexual intercourse. In the eighteenth century, 'criminal conversation' meant adultery. In the twenty-first century an 'intimate conversation' is a reminder that the magnetism that draws people to one another is not always the product of a desire to penetrate bodily orifices, and that they also enjoy exploring each other's minds, tastes and experience. The sex manuals which give precise instructions about how to produce arousal and orgasm may eventually become a quaint relic of faith in mechanical efficiency, with the realisation that if you repeat what someone has told you to do and to say, you become a mere shadow of a person.

In China, Yun could not know that almost at the same time as she was talking to Fu, a member of the Constituent Assembly of the French

Changing what is meant by sex

Revolution was demanding that after the Declaration of the Rights of Man, which 'made man free and happy in public life, it remains for us to assure him liberty and happiness in private life'; but the only result was a law to allow divorce and another to abolish the power of fathers over their adult offspring. The politicians failed to notice that though French novels had hitherto been about rebellious children quarrelling with authoritarian fathers, they were increasingly portraying fathers seeking the affection of their children. Providing affection has never figured in any election manifesto, and the slogan 'Make Love not War' did not follow from any careful research to discover whether making love does generate affection. The word 'love' does not occur in the Universal Declaration of Human Rights, nor do Liberty, Equality and Fraternity concern themselves with it. It is as though public authorities still agree with Confucius who said 'I have never met anyone who loves virtue as much as he loves sex', and recognise that they are powerless when it comes to promoting love, the most deeply desired of all blessings, even though they wish to be loved themselves. Those who have power or money have their own idea about how to make everyone happy, which is by giving everyone more power and money. But it is possible for those who have neither power nor money to attempt something different, to make more inventive use of that mysterious magnetism, the attraction and repulsion that humans have for one another.

Politicians' views on love

The obstacles are formidable. Each sex clings to its ancient prerogatives even when it protests against them. Sex is still associated with conquest and domination, and there is little sign of its demilitarisation.

Three-quarters of the men in the world, according to a 'survey of thirty-five cultures', are hungry for one-night stands. Marriages based on love *One-night* rather than on duty still leave women as caretakers of men, with love *stands* providing an alibi for continuing their traditional domestic chores – 'I wouldn't wash his socks if I didn't love him.' A century ago, having a husband who brought a wage home was considered more important than his insults, violence and infidelity, and there was nothing shameful about Saturday night fights between spouses; but today women who have won financial independence are still not always immune from more subtle forms of contempt. Is there really no remedy for these stubborn grievances?

The efforts of public authorities are very far from having succeeded. Could ordinary couples do better in private and personal experiments? Only they can clarify what they want from sex and love; only they can develop more satisfying forms of communication. It is true that Yun failed in her attempt to open up her hermetically sealed couple and that Fu *The hermeti-* failed to act as heroically and independently as he believed males were *cally sealed* supposed to. Two centuries later, however, they might possibly have seen a *couple* way out of their dilemma. In the U.S., at any rate, a recent survey has found that what men and women disapprove of above all else is being lied to, almost twice as much as they did forty years ago, when the conceal-ment of sexual infidelity was widely accepted: now, however, 91 per cent regard cheating on one's partner as much more heinous than all the *Cheating on* taboos of the past, like divorce, pre-marital sex and babies out of wedlock, *one's partner* which used to be punished with private humiliation and public censure.

Openness between lovers was one of the first remedies that intelligent women imagined for dealing with boring marriages back in the early nineteenth century, but men were not ready. Attention was therefore switched to winning the same rights for women as men enjoyed. But for women to become more like men is not an improvement. There are still innumerable men unwilling or unable to reveal their emotions or to understand the complexities of intimacy. Couples who hardly ever talk abound. One of the rare investigations of what couples say to each other found that half remain silent while making love, and the other half 'say loving words'. Experts advise lovers to say 'romantic things' and some give a list of suitable sentences, of remarkable banality, as though a sexual performance is comparable to a religious liturgy, at which everyone should be repeating the equivalent of the same favourite prayer. The experts remain baffled by the bizarre thoughts and seemingly uncharacteristic sexual fantasies that often emerge during intercourse, and the rare serious scientific studies of them limit themselves to connecting these with pathological categories like anxiety, rather than investigating them as interesting openings of the imagination and invitations to conversation about ideas that each partner is often incapable of understanding or is even unaware of harbouring. There has been so much concentration on the physical and emotional delights of intercourse, and the drug-like high it produces, that there is still much more to be discovered about what it can do to stimulate mutual appreciation, affection and animation.

Openness between lovers

Couples who hardly ever talk

Bizarre fantasies

*

There is no longer any need to regard sexual desire as comparable to hunger for food. One reason why there has been more progress in cooking than in sex is that cooking does not simply aim to feed individual appetites but also fosters conviviality, making eating into a feast dedicated to entertaining, charming and surprising guests of many kinds, and expanding knowledge about the variety of foods and tastes the world over. By contrast, sex has become private and secret. Once upon a time it was at the heart of a universal conviviality, with whole communities publicly and festively worshipping the fertility of everything that lived, celebrating copulation in public in the same way that they honoured sowing seeds in the fields; the growth of the crops and the birth of children were all one. But now that having as many children as possible has ceased to be the main purpose of sex, and that the ambition to be 'fruitful and multiply' has been replaced by the search for pleasure and love, and for equal opportunities for that half of humanity whose role was for long limited to procreation, it is clear that old myths about masculinity and femininity need to be sent to the cleaners. This is no simple matter, because stereotypes about sex are so deeply entrenched and seduction is such an absorbing game that relationships may long continue to be theatrical performances, relentlessly repeated. The fourth-century Chinese woman who hoped that the rules of sex would be quite different if they were drawn up by women rather than men would find today that not only has that not happened, but it is not obvious what the result would be.

More progress in cooking than in sex

Seduction as theatrical performance

The new factor is that private life need no longer be perceived as somehow inferior to public life, as more trivial and selfish; it need not be a mere refuge from public life, the secretive custodian of truths hidden by worldly hypocrisies. It is on the contrary where the relationships on which public life depends are forged, and where an infinity of gradations of attachments are nourished, a busy workshop brewing sympathy and curiosity, knitting emotional and intellectual bonds, and sometimes also breaking them. So it has a crucial part to play in furthering equality, which remains a mirage despite all the efforts of politics and economics. Ineradicable disparities in appearance, character or talent between individuals can only be metamorphosed into valued advantages through private affection. No law, no treasure, no pill can equalise the fears that torment each person and that ultimately determine how much of a life a person has; equality of opportunity is an empty promise if achievement depends on victory over so many fears, and the haunting presence of one's own inadequacies. The unequal distribution of anxiety is intensified by the unequal distribution of affection, which is what private life creates. People are so starved of affection, not only of receiving affection but also of opportunities to give it, that they offer it to celebrities they have never met, and do not complain that they get none back in return. Private life, when it is a nursery of affection, is an indispensable catalyst for equality.

The haunting presence of one's own inadequacies

In private also it becomes possible to deepen the meaning of fraternity beyond what governments and philanthropists do, who are concerned with reducing the distress of disadvantaged minorities. But everyone is in need of fraternity, to give and receive it, to convey what one possesses across the barriers that self-regard imposes, to acquire qualities one does not possess, to incorporate sensations one has not experienced, to enter into the thoughts of others, to be more aware of possibilities one has not dared envisage. It is above all through private conversations that people obtain the reassurance and courage to attempt what they may have never thought possible before, find partners enabling them to do something they could not have done alone, and become animated with the feeling that by discovering others and being discovered by others, and by assimilating what each gives the other, they have become more fully alive. Appreciation, affection and animation are what private life can add to public life. Political revolutions have neglected them. It remains for sexual revolutions to expand the idea of the couple, to see the problems that lovers encounter as part of the more universal issue of one-to-one relationships that affects every branch of existence.

Becoming more fully alive

The story of Fu and Yun is an unfinished one. The fruits of being a couple are still being discovered.

[20]

What can artists aim for beyond self-expression?

IN MEDIAEVAL JAPAN, in one of the most rigid of hierarchical societies, a hereditary ruling class of tough Samurai warriors discovered that when they wrote poetry they could become unrecognisably gentle, and their attitude to strangers was transformed. 'Even when we are meeting for the first time . . . we feel an intimacy with one another . . . and are just as close as cousins.' This quotation is from the poet Sogi (1421–1502), the master of 'linked-verse', poetry written by two or more people, composing alternate verses. He has a place in humanity's common memory because he was unrivalled in creating sensitive links between different collaborators: his charm united the most unlikely strangers in a common search for beauty. Poetry conceived of as intimate conversation goes back even to before the ninth century, when the *Dialogue between a Poor Man and a Destitute Man* was composed, but Sogi went further. Travelling around the country, carrying only his writing kit, lodging in a grass-thatched hut, he held poetry parties that revealed how, in a country plagued by violent *Art creates* political conflict, art could create bonds between strangers. His amateur *bonds* fellow poets felt such pleasure in their collaboration that, he said, 'We *between* have also thought that we might perhaps be together in the next world.' *strangers*

They 'do not feel uncomfortable socialising with their juniors, and those of noble birth do not shun their social inferiors'. Anybody could attend these meetings with complete anonymity, guaranteeing equality: they concealed their identity under loose-fitting clothes and wide-brimmed rice-straw hats that obscured their faces. Often sitting in the shade of a cherry tree, 'under the flowers', empathy for the natural world added another dimension to their feeling of community: Sogi's favourite flower, the pale yellow wild rose, inspired the belief that 'the essence of linked verse [*renga*] is to give a mind to that which lacks a mind and to give speech to that which cannot speak'.

His poetry was in some ways the predecessor of sport in that it encouraged social classes to mix, temporarily equal in their club shirts, but it did so at a deeper level, because it involved the careful expression of aesthetic emotions, and the ability to respond elegantly to those of one's partners. The Japanese 'philosophy of the artistic way', *gei-do-ron*, was the art of socialising with strangers. However, this kind of poetry had to be composed according to fixed rules, so it initially remained impersonal, the emphasis being on creating a coherent whole out of disparate elements, rather than recognising or encouraging originality in each individual. It was only a first step in the search for inspiration from strangers, by getting them to participate in an activity that blurred their singularities.

The Japanese philosophy of the artistic way

The second step was to make being a stranger a virtue that anyone could practise and refine. Again, art was used as a catalyst, inciting different professions and classes temporarily to set aside the barriers that separated them, ignoring status. In the practice of art, people could learn to live two separate lives, one official, determined by their birth, occupa-

Having two separate lives

tion and wealth, and the other personal, shaped by artistic activity. Officially everybody had fixed and lifelong obligations, with good manners meaning respect for superiors, but privately, by joining artistic circles, they could find freedom in their social exchanges. Artists invented the 'floating world' as an alternative reality, where moral rules could be broken, where sensual pleasures could be cultivated both light-heartedly and with sophistication, and where the joys of sharing could be intense.

An alternative to political protest

Art also became an alternative to political protest. In seventeenth-century Japan, young men from the fringes of the aristocracy – masterless or low-ranking Samurai with no hope of battle honours in peacetime – became 'skinheads'. With their foreheads and temples shaved, their hair hanging long at the back, rather than tied in a topknot, they smoked tobacco while they loitered in public places, dancing and singing in the streets, proud of their trendy clothes, with velvet collars, short kimonos and wide belts. Some flaunted their homosexuality, discarding traditional loyalties. They came to be known as *kabuki*, 'crooked' or eccentric people.

The first female entertainment star

Then independent women made the protest even more radical. They were led by Izomo no Okuni, whose importance as the country's first female entertainment star was finally acknowledged in 2003 when a statue of her was erected in Kyoto. A froth of legend surrounds her biography, as it does that of her contemporary Shakespeare, but ancient sources speak of her as though she was almost divine. She 'had a face which was unique in the world, clever hands, a heart that allowed her feelings to express themselves in song, and her gentleness had profound colours. Holding a flower, she could suggest the whisper of a lover in the moonlight . . . She was a true poetess.' Another wrote: 'She deserves to be called The First Woman of the Universe. But I cannot become the first man of the universe: not to be the equal of this woman mortifies me and I feel destroyed.' Originally, she worked as an attendant at a Buddhist shrine, but travelled widely as a performer to raise money for its repair, inspired by priests who believed that the doctrines of Buddha could be more easily appreciated 'not by boring and difficult sermons but by plunging into ecstasy through song and dance'. Okuni won instant success and national fame, and invented *kabuki* theatre.

This was originally a ribald, satirical, sexually suggestive song-and-dance show, interspersed with comic sketches. The all-female cast, wearing elegant male clothes, mimicked and mocked the 'crooked' men. The government closed their theatre down as immoral, but beautiful boys replaced them. So actors became the trend-setters of fashion, with clothes and hairstyles that fascinated men and women alike. A huge fashion industry blossomed. Personal appearance became an obsession, and those who could not afford silk could pride themselves on the latest trends in striped cotton. Stylishness became the escape route from vulgarity. Art expanded sensibilities and refined eroticism. Ordinary people were able to accept their inferior place in the 'real' world, the hard-headed world, by diverting their protest into the floating world and aesthetic rebellion. They expressed their private emotions in 'women's hand' (Japanese script) to distinguish themselves from the official class which used Chinese in public documents, as Europeans used Latin. This was an

Aesthetic rebellion

early challenge to the idea that men and women are irrevocably strangers.

Artists as intermediaries

However, though artists have been important intermediaries not only between individuals, but also between civilisations that see themselves as strangers, exercising an influence more subtle and more long-lasting than diplomats, there have so far been limits to what they could achieve. Being sensuous and generous in the floating world, in the evening or when not at work, did not necessarily make patrons of the arts any less ruthless in the daily struggle for power and profit. On the contrary, it had disas-

The divorce of art and work

trous consequences for work, by giving plausibility to the belief that the most delightful pleasures should be sought after hours, and that work was for more serious and practical purposes. In the past, when left to themselves, humans thought otherwise. Early visitors to America were astonished to find the indigenous population apparently spending most of their time doing nothing from morning to night, and a few said they could 'live with less labour and more pleasure and plenty as Indians' than they could in their home country. Even in England before the Industrial Revolution, despite the poverty and seasonal unemployment and the absence of all those comforts now judged to be essential, work was more casual and sociable than it later became, with frequent pauses for rest, talking and drinking, more free days balancing the longer hours; work was integrated into the rest of life rather than segregated from it. The Japanese may have been made more skilful at switching between a plurality of identities by their art, accepting ambiguity and fragility in their aesthetic mode, while insisting on hierarchy and obedience in their business mode, and that may have helped them to accept some strange Western innovations while simultaneously retaining their traditions. However, art has not sufficed.

Today, though Japan's achievements in many fields have been brilliant, 80 per cent of its present inhabitants say that they expect to die of over-work – suggesting that they are becoming estranged from their jobs, just as they are becoming estranged from the idea of being happy to die for their country. When cartoons show the lavatory as the only place once-revered fathers can find to read their newspaper in peace, when women's magazines declare that women no longer envy men, when two-thirds of women want a daughter rather than a son, when, despite the vast increase in every kind of entertainment to make the floating world exciting, more and more say in opinion polls that their life is meaningless and that 'they are becoming stupider than their computers', in other words they are strangers in their own country, strangers to one another. Art has not protected them, any more than their faith in their social cohesion and ineradicable traditions, their world leadership in technologies or their businesses that became almost surrogate families.

The mean-ingless life

The rich all over the world display revolutionary paintings on the walls of their mansions, in the same way that sinners built churches or temples to purge their crimes, but as patrons of the arts and religion they have not necessarily altered the methods that enabled them to acquire their power. This has meant that 'culture' could flourish in one small corner, some-times brilliantly, while brutal force and boring work could continue to dominate the rest of existence. The separation of art from work is one of the tragedies of history.

The tragedy of art

The place where one meets most strangers is at work. What makes seemingly prosaic jobs appealing is that they bring one into contact with people who open windows into worlds one does not know. Work has been completely redesigned twice in the past, by the agricultural and industrial revolutions. To redesign it once again to suit contemporary aspirations would involve transcending the separation between commerce and spirituality, between power and friendship, between the floating world and the hard-headed world. The hard-headed world is no more the real world than the floating world of the imagination. Both exist, though they are strangers. Do supermarkets, offices and factories, where art is no more than decoration liable to be eliminated when costs are cut, have to be the way they are forever? Can the different occupations and professions which absorb so much of human energy, and which require constant negotiation with strangers, evolve more relationships that are not just mercenary, but widen understanding? Is it possible to be more ambitious than just seeking 'work–life balance', which holds out the hope of a better life by exalting activities outside work, and in doing so distracts attention from the mind-numbing effects that many jobs still impose on all but the very privileged? In later chapters, I shall describe my own efforts to discover, through practical trials, how else work can be organised to suit people who want to be more curious, adventurous, intelligent, sensitive or artistic, without relying on leisure pursuits to compensate for its frequent futility and boredom.

The floating world and the hard-headed world

Mind-numbing jobs

Those who make the big decisions in the world may have been short-sighted when they decided to marry management science and treat art as a mistress for the entertainment of their spare moments. Their marriage may not be – to use their now favourite word – 'sustainable'. Management science is all about constant change, but the more innovation there is, the more uncertainty there is about the future, the more the young avoid placing faith in skills that may become obsolete, the more frequently they fall out of love with increasingly hectic, relentless and unforgiving work. Not that work was universally loved in the past; but people resigned themselves more frequently to the work to which they were limited by the accidents of birth. The more the specialisation of tasks and firms increases, the more do those who work together become strangers incomprehensible to one another. The more technology makes it possible to have longer hours of leisure, the more time becomes available for worry, not just about 'What kind of work do I want?' but 'What kind of world do I want?'

Art as a mistress

Whether people say they are happy or dissatisfied with their work depends on how many minutes they are given to answer the question, and how deeply they dig into regrets they normally dismiss as pointless and unrealisable. A manager at Marks & Spencer could tell me how proud he was to work for such an excellent firm, and how honoured he felt when the big boss once asked him for his opinion, but after singing its praises for about two hours he suddenly blurted out, 'I hate my boss', and revealed how he was planning to turn his theatrical hobby, which was what he really cared about, into a full-time occupation. It is the doubts of the privileged in 'advanced' countries that are the most significant warning signs.

'I hate my boss'

The hesitations of the French are particularly revealing, they being the people who in 1789 started a revolution when they were the most powerful and prosperous nation in Europe, but they still wanted something more than prosperity and power. It is not just destitution and oppression that produce revolution, but, quite as often, disappointment among those who succeed, and then have doubts, and ask what else there is to aim for. Today the French are still among the richest people on earth, and they work fewer hours than most others, but once again, they want something more. Of course, many love their job and are proud of their skills and there are many kinds of work that are exhilarating and a privilege to be involved in. However, to the question 'What is the priority in your life?' they have replied that family is by far their highest priority (63 per cent), with leisure (18 per cent), and work (12 per cent) trailing well behind. There is still work that is soul-destroying, and innumerable people are still forced by their work to sacrifice deep ambitions, or regret having spent too large a part of life working too hard and missing out on activities they discovered too late to pursue. Is it enough that work should provide status and a sense of purpose and social pleasures and mastery of a skill? Why does it so often degenerate into no more than a way of keeping body and soul together and earning enough money to pay taxes, or reimburse money-lenders, or shop for goods one may or may not need, or impress one's neighbours so that they do not treat one as a stranger?

Could art play a different role, and not just be a distraction? Could it expand beyond its ancient focus on worship and its modern preoccupation with self-expression? Could it become a seedbed that grows another kind of courage, able to rescue ordinary working life from the torments that too often afflict it? Could it prevent professional rivalries and jeal-

Successful people also start revolutions

ousies from turning colleagues into strangers? Do the pleasures of work have to be spoilt by having one's inadequacies pointed out, making one a stranger to oneself? These questions may seem to ask too much of art. However, art has contributed much more to humanity's achievements than is usually acknowledged; it has not been merely marginal decoration or distraction. Probably no religion and no ideology would have spread without the aid of art. Art has been enormously influential in destroying prejudice, in championing independent creativity, and in giving respectability to 'whatever the human mind, fancy or whim may invent'. Its prestige has survived even when self-expression deteriorates into self-worship or is bruised by the frustration of discovering that others do not share one's opinion of one's own 'genius'. But artists have not exhausted all the roles they could still play.

The contribution of art to civilisation

New roles for artists

The biographies of artists are, in many cases, a litany of struggle and suffering, of drama and disappointment, because they have increasingly been engaged in a search for a form of existence different from that of the vast majority. That search is now of greater relevance than ever before. The more people are educated, the more they become interested in the artistic life, which is often explored, too late, in retirement. But there is more to aim for now than trying to revive the idealised world of the artisans who created objects with their own hands. How to make one's life into a work of art is the new challenge.

Making one's life a work of art

The clue that art provides is that it seeks more than a predictable purpose, and more than competent craftsmanship. It expresses an individual vision that is discovered in the process of being constructed, so that the direction of the search, the perspective and the goal may change as new

An adven-
ture into the
unknown

discoveries are made; it is an adventure into the unknown. No recipes or instruction manuals can do more than teach very preliminary skills. Each work of art is individual, but it is also an adventure in communication, stimulating ideas and emotions in others which it cannot control. It is

The taming
of fear

therefore a training in courage and a small step towards the taming of fear.

Teaching children to be 'creative' by drawing and painting has had only limited results. It may give them self-confidence, but when they come out of school, they have no choice but to work for organisations which demand that they perform specific tasks, rather than freely exercise their imagination. Creativity is in any case not an adequate goal; it is possible for it to produce useless and harmful results. Procreation is more interesting, coupling two imaginations to generate something that is a surprise to both, and then continuing to experiment until a desirable result emerges.

The divorce of work and art was consecrated by Frederick Winslow Taylor (1856–1915), whose ideas on 'scientific management' captured the whole world's imagination in the first half of the twentieth century, even more influentially than Henry Ford's assembly line. What Taylor proposed

F.W. Taylor's
'mental
revolution'

was a 'Mental Revolution' which applied to all forms of work, even to education, even to gardening, and not just to manufacture as Ford's did. Taylor believed that science could solve the problem of how humans should work. He started by analysing in minute detail how machines could be made more efficient, and often succeeded in trebling their productivity. He then studied every movement humans made in different kinds of work and showed that they too could vastly increase their productivity if they followed his instructions precisely, doing only what his stop-watch and slide rule calculated to be the optimum use of their energy, what a day's labour could ideally achieve if pursued with total dedication. As a reward, he doubled or trebled wages, and the results were impressive: at one paper mill he increased output from twenty to thirty-six tons a day, reduced costs per ton from seventy-five to thirty-five dollars, and labour costs from thirty to eight dollars per ton. Everyone should have been made happier and richer, and Taylor claimed that the conflict of employers and employees would be ended because the surplus of wealth would become so enormous that there would be no need to quarrel about its distribution.

But his system involved all initiative being transferred from workers to expert managers. The workers protested that they were being humiliated, *The cost of scientific management* enslaved, turned into mere automata; more goods might be manufactured, but 'as far as man is concerned it means destruction,' said a union leader; what Taylor considered to be a wasted movement or gesture or an unnecessary pause 'is frequently that moment when the divine spark of a new thought' comes to the worker. But the worker was not supposed to think. That, said the union leader, was to ignore the precedent of James Watt, who used precisely such a momentary pause to watch a kettle boil, which inspired his revolutionary ideas about steam engines. Taylor persisted in pushing workers to extreme effort by offering ever-higher rewards and bonuses, but they responded by saying it left them so exhausted that their lives were ruined and their wives threatened to leave them. Those who were willing to do anything for money also worried Taylor because they became 'extravagant and dissipated . . . Our experiment', he wrote, 'showed that for their own best interests it does not do for most to get rich too fast.' At the same time he reminded all employees that the purpose of their work was to pay dividends to the owners; 'They should never lose sight of this fact.' Skilled mechanics were replaced by 'drones' who just minded machines; many were made redundant and told to become teachers or carers; a new class of white collar managers was created, quite separate from workers; foremen lost their traditional wide-ranging role and had their duties divided between several specialists to ensure that each gesture exactly obeyed the rules.

Efficiency as America's new ideal　　In 1910 efficiency became America's new ideal, when a national dispute about railway companies demanding an increase in fares was opposed by a sensational demonstration of how, using Taylor's scientific methods, they could easily make a hundred million dollars of efficiency savings so that no increase would be needed. Cutting the cost of living became a popular slogan, despite the price that had to be paid in harder work and redundancies. Europe and Japan quickly followed the American example. The leisurely pace of traditional work and individual pride in personal craftsmanship became inefficient and impossible to sustain.

Scientific management has learned many lessons since Taylor's day and what is understood by it is now hugely different; his reminder that the purpose of work is to pay dividends to the owners is not spelled out in the same way; workers are no longer dismissed so arbitrarily for refusing to work harder, and when a few commit suicide because they find the strain of work unbearable, they attract international headlines. But it is worth thinking about how scientific management could change still further and how it could be inspired by art. A poet after all, in the original meaning of the word, was a maker and a builder.

21

What is more interesting than becoming a leader?

T HERE IS ALMOST UNIVERSAL agreement that leadership is needed to solve the challenges of life. Leaders are our heroes, until they fail. So I propose to look at the side-effects of their achievements.

Sir Francis Bacon (1561–1626) was one of the first to excavate below the surface of leadership. Thomas Jefferson called him one of 'the three greatest men who ever lived', and he was considered so exceptionally talented that it was claimed he was the real author of Shakespeare's plays. Bacon reinvented scientific enquiry, transforming it from a contemplative pursuit to one of experimental research directed at practical inventions to 'alleviate mankind's misery'; he was a pioneer in the colonisation of America, and he had visions of religious freedom and legal reform. He was a leader in everything he touched, and eventually became Lord Chancellor of England, the equivalent of prime minister. But his life was also a disaster. He was dismissed for corruption, pleading guilty to the charge, begging for mercy and confessing that he was 'a broken reed'. His wife, thirty-one years younger than himself, turning out to be a spendthrift who complained he did not give her enough money to satisfy her extravagant tastes, was unfaithful to him and eventually left him. He was in debt for most of

A disastrous life

his life and died owing huge sums, at least three million pounds in today's money. He was admired but also disliked and mistrusted, because he used hypocrisy and betrayal to achieve his eminence. After his downfall, he was lampooned as the 'wisest, brightest, meanest of mankind'.

Bacon's importance today is that he was able to distance himself from his misfortunes, and analyse the problems of ambition with a lucidity that has a universal relevance. He was not ashamed to admit that he had not been able to follow the principles of virtue and honesty that he preached. He had lived two separate lives, he said, and his ideals had been defeated by unforeseen temptations: 'My soul hath been a stranger in the course of my pilgrimage.' The rewards of ambition had not been what he had expected. Only too late did he realise that he had unthinkingly been trapped by 'the strange desire to seek power and to lose liberty, or to seek power over others and to lose power over . . . [one]self'. He could not *The strange desire to seek power and lose liberty* explain it, nor why so many others suffered from that strange desire. High office, to his surprise, had reduced him to the status of a 'servant' of the routines of administration. The process of achieving power was 'sometimes base'; retaining it was 'slippery', and losing it 'is a melancholy thing [because] when a man feels that he is no longer what he was, he loses all his interest in life'. Success comes at too high a price: 'By indignities men rise to dignities.' His hunger for power had indeed made him master of the art of licking the boots of the influential, of making promises and betraying those who were once friends but were no longer useful. He concluded that power had isolated him from other humans; he was the first to find fault with others but the last to recognise his own faults. Worst of all, 'in the puzzle of business [the powerful] have no time to tend their health either of body or mind.'

Two and a half centuries later, Sir Robert Barlow (1891–1976), starting from a poor illiterate home in East London, became the founder and head of a multinational, the Metal Box Company, employing over 50,000 workers, a giant of the packaging industry, surpassed only by the titan American Can Company, but never surrendering in the battle against it. He used a mixture of cunning, courage, ferocity, ruthlessness, generosity and kindness 'with such charm that even those he injured would speak of him with affection', while others called him 'an evil man'. He was hailed as one of the most brilliant businessmen of his generation, but he said, 'I get no happiness from it.' He was constantly fighting rivals and colleagues challenging his power. 'I don't know why I go on with it . . . I'm sick of this life. They are all plotting against me . . . Never be ambitious. Only misery can come of it. Never hold a job like I hold. You'd better be dead.' But he continued to resist all the efforts to oust him, fighting back with outbursts of rage against the 'personal conflicts which loom so large in the minds of [his] executives', 'the exceedingly bad atmosphere' in the company and 'the clash of personalities'. Though he was a great success in his lifetime, no sooner was he dead than the worst blow came: his achievement was condemned (in 1976) as being an 'undesirable manifestation of the consumer society, adding unnecessary frills and expense to the process of distribution, using scarce materials extravagantly, disfiguring the landscape with litter and contributing, especially in the food industry, to the debasement of taste with products cultivated and processed by unnatural

'They are all plotting against me'

means'. He could not have foreseen this change in society's expectations.

Heroes and saints have a necessary place in the history of ambition, but so too do the far more numerous people who throughout the ages have regarded ambition as dangerous, because it contradicted the ethos of acceptance of one's lot that most religions recommended. 'An ambitious man is a sick man,' wrote a doctor in 1841, when there were still very limited opportunities for ambition, with only 1 per cent of the jobs in industry being managerial, and only about 7 per cent in commerce. It is only recently that the ambition to be promoted to a higher rank has become an almost universal passion, and that 'incentives' have become the aphrodisiac of the workplace. In the twentieth century, Britain increased the number of managers sevenfold; and many of the world's armies trebled or quadrupled the proportion of officers: one third of the Chinese Army are officers and one third NCOs. But now ambition is in crisis: there cannot be more supervisors than subordinates who have no-one to whom they can give orders. Rising expectations make the fulfilment of ambition ever more elusive, even if aristocracy is endlessly expanded into merit-ocracy. Thomas Hobbes' brutal claim remains unanswered, that all distinctions imply superiority and inferiority and that there was no way for everyone to enjoy equal respect, for 'if all men have it, no man hath it'. More importantly, never has there been such pitiless scrutiny of the weaknesses of the successful, the powerful and the rich. Never has there been so much questioning of whether they do more harm than good. Only in countries emerging from poverty do they inspire awe; once their numbers multiply, their spell is shattered.

Ambition in crisis

In 2000 an MIT professor of economics simplified the criterion of success: 'Wealth has increasingly become the only dimension by which personal worth is measured . . . It is the only game to play if you want to prove your mettle. It is the big leagues. If you do not play there, by definition you are second rate . . . Wealth gives one the power to do what one wants. The greater one's wealth, the happier one becomes.' But this may not be the last word. It has become evident that the big players cannot do everything they want. If they run big corporations or organisations, they find that power is often elusive. Their orders are constantly reformulated, reinterpreted and resisted. Their problems are frequently too difficult to solve. They are spending ever more time worrying about the risks that threaten them. They call themselves 'leaders' but they are now not even 'servants' in the way Bacon described: they are prisoners of the shareholders and analysts and pension-fund managers who are constantly pressing them to make bigger profits. Political leaders disappoint because they do not work miracles and seldom even carry out the programmes on which they won their election. All leaders now devote enormous amounts of time to nurturing their 'image', as though they dare not show their face

Triumphs of self-delusion

without make-up. Some become characters of pure invention, triumphs of hypocrisy or self-delusion. However brilliantly they can talk about any subject, however much affability or humility they display, and whether they write poetry or watch birds to keep sane and show that they remain ordinary humans, they have never been so vulnerable to being suddenly destroyed by mistakes that are hard to avoid. Though they may enjoy their privileges, the excitement of being at the helm and a sense of achievement, few can avoid constant stress and broken private lives. The price to be paid for the fulfilment of ambition is rarely fixed in advance. Voltaire complained that 'the only reward to be expected from the cultivation of literature is contempt if one fails and hatred if one succeeds'. Education, though conceived to help everyone succeed, can throttle imagination as well as make it sing.

Two thousand five hundred years ago, when Athens was establishing the first democracy, it hesitated between slow and fast ambition. The philosophers said that its citizens should simply strive to maintain moral standards, honouring truth and virtue for the common good and not expect instant rewards. Itinerant teachers called Sophists offered courses in the application of these ideals to practical life and were influential in developing Athenian democracy. But the more impatient among the Sophists, simplifying traditional wisdom, taught that since human beings were intent on pleasure and wealth, and were moved by passions and self-interest, the strong would inevitably dominate the weak; so all they needed to understand was how to get what they wanted, for which there was just one magic tool, the art of persuasion. They were the first professional teachers of success, who claimed that anyone could learn how to get others to follow their leadership. Instead of physics and mathematics, they focused just on the art of persuasion (which is not so far from management). Power, they said, came from control of the emotions (an idea revived many centuries later as 'emotional intelligence'). They attracted vast numbers of students because they promised rapid rise to influence and demonstrated how to get any argument accepted, if only one acquired

Slow and fast ambition

The first professional teachers of success

the skills of rhetoric. Foreshadowing the belief that people only value what they pay for, they charged fees for their lessons, unlike the philosophers. This caused a scandal, all the more so because the fees were enormously high. Whereas a judge got half a drachma for a day's work, the Sophists charged up to fifty drachmas. One of them was even said to have been paid as much as 10,000 drachmas, more than the ten most celebrated sculptors of the city put together. Only the rich could afford them, which made them unpopular, but that did not diminish their appeal.

These Sophists saw Athens not as a beacon of civilisation, but as essentially a centre of maritime commerce, accumulating wealth so as to enjoy luxury and feasting. Their writings have not survived, because they did not write for posterity, any more than the authors of business books today. A second wave of Sophists appeared among the Romans, and had even more success, touring the empire, attracting huge crowds by their skill at improvised persuasion, almost forerunners of modern motivational speakers. Sophists were practical, not idealists.

Since their day, business schools have been the most prominent institutions directing and encouraging ambition. Fifty years ago a graduate of the Harvard Business School said, 'We are not the intellectual elite, nor the hereditary elite, nor the artistic or creative elite. What we are being groomed as is the competent elite. We're being trained as the guys who stay sober at the party. We are being handed the tools to get out there and run things', and these were tools which 'like aspirin or like dynamite would work on just about anything'. This mixture of modesty and arrogance, however, ultimately proved inadequate. Business schools were originally

'We are not the intellectual elite'

established to transform managers and merchants into a more highly esteemed, cultured and respectable profession, but by concentrating too narrowly on finance and administration and forgetting about culture, they left the managers they trained one-legged, vulnerably dependent on always succeeding in making profits, unable to switch to any other basis of support. So business schools had to think again.

The person who in 1977 first publicised the notion that to be a manager was not the height of achievement, and that the real goal was to be a 'leader', was a Harvard Business professor who believed that psycho-analysis held the key to a better future, and who wrote a book on 'how Freudian theory can turn good executives into better leaders'. Abraham Zaleznik (1924–2011) attacked managers for being too rational, imper-sonal, interested only in efficiency and process rather than ideas, intuition and empathy. He offered them a chance to be 'born again' and to find self-esteem. The way to do this, he said, was by 'convincing others of the validity of one's own conclusions'. To be able to do that, one needed to 'empower oneself' by liberating oneself from the doubts in one's unconscious which prevented one's talents emerging. The problem with too many managers was that they lacked a father figure, physically or metaphorically, resulting in anxiety, a desire to control uncertainty and a longing 'to be born again'. Zaleznik married this idea with a second source of inspiration that became fashionable in the 1980s – Japan, which was threatening the industrial supremacy of the West. He idolised Konosuke Matsushita (1894–1989), the self-made electronics industrialist, whose company is now called Panasonic, whose philosophy of management was enshrined in

The height of achievement

an Institute of Peace and Happiness through Prosperity (founded in 1946), and whose biography was written by Zaleznik's successor in the chair that Harvard established with an endowment from Matsushita.

Leadership courses have ever since become barometers of the ruling class's changing moods and expectations. Every year thousands of books and articles appear incorporating some new preoccupation or ideology into leadership, and there are now 284 million references to it on Google. Since leadership does not eliminate the frustrations of those who do not become leaders, an egalitarian version has been added, proposing that almost everybody can be a leader (of sorts). 'Followers' have been held up as being as important as leaders, because no amount of teaching can prevent leaders making mistakes, and their success depends on having followers who will correct them. A leader has even been redefined simply as someone, however lowly, who 'makes things happen' and who 'creates change'.

What business schools borrow from the military

Leadership was of course originally a military idea, but what the business schools borrowed from the military was an outdated version that had already been abandoned by generals. The U.S. Army, preparing for the next war, began investigating the psychology of leadership in 1945, but revised its ideas completely following its demoralisation after defeat in Vietnam and the uncovering of a vast amount of cheating at West Point Military Academy. It invented a completely new idea of leadership. Henceforth, an officer was expected to expand his knowledge far beyond military matters; sixteen optional scientific and engineering subjects were brought into the syllabus and eight from the humanities. The new reading lists were a complete contrast with those proposed in 1910, which were dominated by forty-eight books about war, with only three books on general history, plus *Roget's Thesaurus* and a list of 'words frequently mispronounced'. The most recent discussion of leadership in the U.S. Army emphasises that officers increasingly have non-combatant roles, and need skills in technology, diplomacy and business, but that these needs are being inadequately met by specialist training, because only generalists could provide the coordination that was absent, and generalist education is still a distant ideal. The business schools have not got round to this. So soldiers are now more admired than business leaders, and are preferred to them as presidential candidates. 'Line management' remains as one of the ambiguous legacies that business has inherited from the army.

In 2008 yet another economic recession made it clear that leaders were responsible for a world catastrophe. Professors of leadership were forced to rethink everything they had taught, almost like professors of communism after the collapse of the Soviet Union. The dean of Harvard Business School confessed that leaders, having 'caused so much hardship for so many . . . have lost legitimacy'; their failure was manifested not only in the economic collapse of firms but also in their 'moral collapse', and 'the attendant confusion and loss of meaning they have engendered'. He castigated the teaching of leadership as being based on scholarly research that not only 'lacks intellectual rigour' but also fails to provide answers to the important questions. A professor of leadership at the Harvard School of Government announced 'the end of leadership', but without saying

Confessions of the Dean of Harvard Business School

what would replace it. The idea of leadership has nowhere been jettisoned, even though the experts in it reported that the leaders they had studied often suffered from 'the fear of seeming ignorant, stupid or at the edge of their competence when dealing with matters they must inevitably get involved in but don't feel deeply informed about'. 'They can easily get so consumed by the myriad demands (both from inside and outside the organisation) that they dissipate their attention and fail to accomplish anything substantial.' They find it 'surprisingly difficult' to obtain reliable information and 'get cut off from the informal channels' that could reveal reality to them, but they 'have to be careful about whom they ask for information' in case they undermine the authority of senior staff. 'Although ostensibly they are masters of their time, the reality is that the demands on their time are endless.' They 'often find themselves over-committed, or spending time on things they regret'. They blame their subordinates: 'Their greatest regret is not having acted sooner to replace underperforming members of their top management team.' But they are themselves constantly blamed and are mercilessly evicted from their jobs because expectations are so often followed by disappointment. The effect they have on the organisation they lead, whether for good or ill, is disputed, one calculation measuring it with a characteristic claim to exactitude as 14 per cent on average, varying from 2 per cent to 21 per cent in different branches of activity, whereas others have been more sceptical. One study concluded that it might be wiser to have mere figureheads at the top of organisations instead of powerful leaders. And 77 per cent of Americans, echoing these concerns, told pollsters that there was a 'crisis of leadership'.

It was as dramatic a collapse as the 'crisis of the aristocracy' that afflicted seventeenth-century Europe.

Leaders have been extraordinarily vague about their goals. Harvard's official mission was 'to educate leaders who make a difference to the world', Stanford's to 'change the world' and M.I.T.'s 'to improve the world'. But how? The uncertainty, and the self-questioning of Western leaders who are asking themselves whether the sacrifices needed to climb to the top were worth making, have not worried newly industrialising countries. According to *China Youth Daily*, two-thirds of its readers aim to become leaders and say that this is the ambition of 91 per cent of all young people. But though universities and corporations continue to sprout leadership institutes and programmes, there is increasing doubt as to whether leadership is a skill that can be taught, and whether it is so different from wisdom that it can be learned in a short course lasting a week or a year.

One of America's most admired and humane writers on leadership, Warren Gamaliel Bennis (born 1925), has been unusually frank and illuminating about his personal experience of leadership. He wanted to be a leader, he says, because 'I did not want to be like the people I already knew.' He grew up 'depressed' by his modest background and by having an unsuccessful immigrant father. As soon as he could afford it, he underwent six years of psychoanalysis, five days a week for three years, and four days a week for another three years. Later he took a course in the 'technology of transformation' developed by the New Age guru Werner Erhard. Bennis was convinced that he was looking for a parent who corresponded more closely to his ideals. His elder brother, ten years his senior, appeared

Self-analysis of a leader

to him to be a natural leader. Ever since his childhood, he said, he had thought about how he too could become a leader. During his military service, his captain became his model, and at Antioch College he switched his admiration to its president (the psychologist Douglas McGregor, who said that he valued his own four years in psychoanalysis more than his four years as an undergraduate). 'I tried to be like him in every conceivable way. I was shameless at sucking up to mentors. I was so drawn to genius perhaps because I felt so ordinary myself.' At the Massachusetts Institute of Technology, 'I imitated my professors and the brightest of my fellow graduate students . . . When I began teaching [psychology to] undergraduates. I didn't always know who I'd be that day. On some days, I thought of myself as a total fraud.' His 'fatal desire to please' tormented him. The refugees from Hitler's Germany who played a leading role in the growth of psychology in the U.S., having tasted the grim reality of charismatic leadership, were of course suspicious of all leaders, but Bennis felt he needed 'structure and support', the perfect father who would combine authority with love.

Dreaming of power

Being a powerless junior professor, he dreamed of power. Having a 'terrible sense of uncertainty, I need the illusion of understanding to feel safe'. He was attracted by people who seemed to have found certainty, who had a convincing vision, and who could satisfy 'my natural impulse to poetize . . . I am a sucker for vision'. So he moved out of teaching into administration, as provost of the University of Buffalo, which had a 'visionary' president who was trying to turn it into 'the Berkeley of the East'. This was in the 1970s, the epoch of student riots. The dream 'never got out of the administration buildings . . . We undermined the very thing we wanted most: our actions, even our style alienated the people who would be most affected by the changes we proposed.' Many years later he summed up his effort at leadership thus: 'I did not learn how to integrate intimacy with ambition. I still have not.'

But he had learned something. 'Without history, without continuity, there can be no change.' He decided that he had moved too fast, ignoring tradition. So he had another try, this time as president of the University of Cincinnati. But different problems once again smashed his enthusiasm. 'When I had most power, I felt the greatest sense of powerlessness . . . After a year I said: 'Either I can't manage this place, or it's unmanageable.' I have become the victim of an unwitting conspiracy to prevent one doing anything whatsoever to change the status quo. Unfortunately I was one of the chief conspirators.' The routines of the bureaucracy left him no time for deep rethinking or fundamental reforms. 'I believed in the false dream that people would love me if only they really got to know me . . . Leaders should not look to being loved.' He collapsed with a heart attack. Three months of convalescence writing poetry convinced him that he should abandon trying to be a leader, he would never be happy as the leader of an organisation. So instead he would write books to tell other people how to be a leader, which he did with enormous success and brilliance. Somebody ought to turn Bennis's autobiography into a requiem mass for the twentieth century, when the privileged publicly sang songs of self-congratulation and privately dreamt of being liberated from self-doubt.

Bureaucracy versus deep thinking

The conclusion Bennis reached after a lifetime of personal obsession with leadership and thoughtful observation of it was that ultimately being

Becoming a decent human being

a leader meant only being a decent human being. (But is business or politics organised to make behaving decently easy?) He discovered also that he had got his priorities wrong, deciding that 'My three children are more important than anything else'. (Why then is family life so often damaged by work?) Above all, he insisted, no leader is complete without a 'vision', but the only vision he proposed was 'to be yourself'. (Is that sufficient for the vast population that is profoundly and sadly conscious of its own inadequacies?)

I live in a country that leaves everyone free to choose how they earn their living, but in which 57 per cent of the workforce says that they have chosen the wrong job. It is no longer possible to believe that they would feel differently if they were all magically promoted to the top of the greasy pole and were hailed as charismatic leaders. There are alternatives to this kind of success. Bacon, Barlow and Bennis illustrate just a few of the

The personal lives of leaders

pitfalls that the idea of salvation through leadership entails for the personal lives of those who aspire to it. To judge leadership on the results it produces for organisations ignores what it does to the character of the leader.

In the late seventeenth century, in Hangzhou, which Marco Polo had called 'beyond dispute the finest and the noblest city in the world', educated women met at the Banana Garden Poetry Club wearing simple raw-silk outfits, with no jewellery and their hair in a bun, to reflect on what was important in life, or as they put it, to 'investigate things thoroughly', and their conclusion was that the men who competed for power while claim-

Moral fakes

ing to be moral were 'fakes'. But these women did not know how to win the support of 'women who care about cosmetics and dressing up', for whom they 'felt sorry', and so they concluded that their ideal of more honest ways of working was 'unattainable'. Ignoring the obsessions of men, they decided to pursue an 'aesthetic life' on their own, by cultivating the arts and creating beautiful gardens. Women have had only a limited influence on the organisation of paid work ever since. Many men have continued to believe that their hunger for power and its rewards is attractive to women, and some perpetuate the tradition of turning to women only for consolation for their failures and humiliations, like the noble mediaeval French warriors who having just lost a battle said, 'We'll talk about it in the ladies' chamber.' The desire to please women has sometimes encouraged the cultivation of gentler manners, but it has not led men to reassess the value of their competitive struggles in search of wealth and influence. The 'unattainable ideal' is being made more attainable every time women extirpate the old-style leadership from private life, but it has yet to be linked to the business of earning a living.

Ignoring the obsessions of men

The danger in the cult of leadership is that its devotees can end up as actors trying to play the role they believe is demanded of them. Calling almost everybody a leader is rather like raising everybody into the ranks of the nobility by giving them the title of Monsieur or Señora. After ten years as CEO of IKEA, Anders Dahlvig was unusually honest in saying that what he valued most of all was to receive recognition, and that this was 'the most important driver of mankind'. But very few people believe they are properly recognised and appreciated. Public recognition is too often a façade, idealised and then suddenly withdrawn after a mistake. Private

Recognition – 'the most important driver of mankind'

recognition goes much deeper and is worthless if it is fake.

Other kinds of leaders, the prophets, sages, saints, sufis, gurus and zaddiks who have pointed away from the vanity of worldly ambition, have still not found how to put the qualities they exalt – wisdom, spiritual emancipation, loyalty, moral refinement and dedication to the welfare of others – into a financial balance sheet. Confucius' injunction to the *The* 'profound person' (*j untzi*), as opposed to the petty person – 'Never impose *'profound'* upon others what you would not choose for yourself' – remains the very *and the* contrary of what the world of work practices. Most success still involves *'petty' person* big sacrifices, assuaged by therapy, and protected from criticism by the doctrine of being non-judgemental. Francis Bacon's question, why people continue to seek power over others only to lose their own liberty, remains unanswered.

An alterna- There are alternatives to the ambition to be a leader. One is to be an *tive ambition* intermediary, who neither receives nor gives orders and who helps those who have too little knowledge, or money or imagination or opportunity to acquire it from those who have some to spare. The service society might have been the paradise of intermediaries, but it too is often poisoned by greed or deceit. But the arrival of a billion young people for whom the world's economy has no room, plus the growing disappointment of women finding that the role it parsimoniously offers them is not all that attractive, mean that ambition is waiting to be rethought.

Agriculture, industry, service were all invented to respond to sudden huge increases in population. Today, many humans, aware that they may become centenarians, may find that climbing and falling off the career ladder is not the most amusing way of spending so many years, and that the idea of being a leader – for all the changes, profound and cosmetic, that it has recently undergone, without casting off entirely its heritage of the warrior chief who survives by defeating rivals and enemies – is less exciting than the more up-to-date one of being inspired by the example of the astronaut exploring the unknown. To give new meaning to work, so that it is more than the exercise of a valued skill, more than the enjoyment of collaboration with others, more than a price that has to be paid in the search for security or status, means using work to redefine freedom. This could be one of the great adventures of our time.

The heritage of the warrior chief

Using work to redefine freedom

    It is an adventure that implies a renewal of attitudes to competition. How these are already beginning to emerge can be glimpsed in the history of women's tennis. Chris Evert, world champion between 1974 and 1981, was obsessed by her determination to win at all costs, to 'destroy' her opponents. Her rival, the immigrant, nonconformist heroine of gay liberation, Martina Navratilova, wanted to become friends with her opponents, to win the affection of the spectators and to be accepted, despite her unconventional views, by her adopted country. Suzanne Lenglen (1899–1938) increased the appreciation of women's tennis and introduced elegance into the game with ballerina-like movements and astonishing chic in her clothing and shoes. But I shall leave consideration of the unused potential of sport (and of outdoor activities and relation-ships with nature) to another volume, and meanwhile pursue, in the next chapters, the challenges of competition and ambition.

Alternatives in women's tennis

22

What is the point of working so hard?

'I HAVE NEVER BEEN A VERY reflective person,' said Sam Walton (1918–1992) the founder of Walmart, whose family now owns the biggest business in the world, employing over two million people. But he was clear in his own mind about 'the one element in my life that has made a difference to me'. It was the 'passion to compete'. 'Any competition is great,' he said. He played tennis with a merciless determination to win; he boasted that no football team of which he was a member ever lost; and the contest of a man, a gun and a dog against a little bird – shooting quails – was for him the ultimate sport. He admired his father (a farmer and banker) for 'squeezing others to the last dollar', being willing to make a deal for just about anything – horses, cattle, houses, farms, cars – and readily trading his watch for a hog if that meant getting the better of a bargain. He summed up his father-in-law (a lawyer) as 'a great salesman, one of the most persuasive individuals I have ever met'. Walton's energy went into persuading people that he was giving them what they wanted. He 'loved merchandising' – 'an absolute passion of mine . . . I really love to price an item, maybe the most basic merchandise and then call attention to it. So we would buy huge quantities of something and then dramatise it . . . I love to get in front of a crowd and talk up something.' Successful business

The passion to compete

for him meant not merely reducing expenditure and increasing efficiency, but spotting how any object could 'explode into big value and big profits, if you are just smart enough to identify them and take the trouble to promote them'. Working all hours, proud of every advantage astutely gained, his mission was to buy and sell at a lower price than anyone else could offer, and still make a profit. Competition made him feel alive, just as battles did to soldiers.

But is competition an end in itself? In the past, shopkeepers and craftsmen used to be wary of it, and kept out of each other's territory. Sam Walton, however, was so successful so quickly that he became wealthy enough to buy up his competitors, and the thrill of capturing or destroying one, and then another, made him think 'we could conquer anything'. To talk of conquest is to borrow the ethics of the military, rather than to invent an ethic of one's own. Sam Walton's descendants now wage retail wars in fifteen countries; when their invasion is repulsed, as it was by Germany, they move on to another target, like India. Sam Walton never saw a reason to place a limit on his ambition. It was not money that he wanted, but excitement. A friend who knew him well summed him up as simply wanting 'to be on top of the pile'. But he wanted to be that discreetly and modestly: millionaires who showed off their wealth by displays of extravagance horrified him.

Not money, but conquest and excitement

Sam Walton was proud of doing things differently, breaking everybody else's rules, being more astute than others, even favouring mavericks who challenged his own rules. But it was not originality for its own sake that he valued; he was a mediaeval rather than a renaissance man; taking ideas from competitors delighted him; he watched them closely and visited them endlessly, so that his empire was an amalgam of other people's inventions. His was not the first company to adopt self-service, but quickly copied the one which did; he borrowed the idea of giving employees shares in the company from the John Lewis Partnership, his encouragement of team work followed a visit to Japan and his Supercentres were modelled on those of Carrefour. At the end of his life he concluded that there was 'a big contradiction in my make-up that I don't completely understand to this day. In many of my core values, I'm a pretty conservative guy. But for some reason in business I have always been driven to buck the system, to innovate, to take things beyond where they've been. In the community, I really am an establishment kind of guy; on the other hand in the market place I have always been a maverick who enjoys shaking things up and creating a little anarchy. And sometimes the establishment has made me mad.'

Both a conservative and a maverick

There was no contradiction. He was using the instruments of modernity to protect himself against it, and the awe-inspiring, up-to-the-minute technology he mastered behind his firm's logistics was directed at preserving tradition. Though he often persuaded his customers to buy what they may not have really needed, everything he sold them was a bargain, at an amazingly low price, so that he and they believed they were actually saving not spending money; they were enjoying the satisfaction of demonstrating their loyalty to the ancestral virtue of thrift. Moreover, he was not urging his customers to be greedy or selfish, because they were buying for their families, and the preservation of the family against the onslaughts of

Modern instruments to combat modernity

modern licentiousness was the mission he and they shared.

Small-town America was his religion, and also his wife's, who insisted that they should never live in a town with more than 10,000 inhabitants. The headquarters of this giant corporation is still in the middle of nowhere, in the very small town of Bentonville, Arkansas. Walmart was modelled on the old idea of the family as an economic unit, and it was for long largely staffed by local people – with as many as thirty relatives working in the same store – serving local people. Their mission was not to encourage cold or obsessive consumerism, but to give people what they needed to win the respect of others. 'I am a friendly fellow by nature, always speaking to folks in the street,' said Sam. When he got out of the helicopter that he was constantly piloting to keep an eye on every one of his stores all over the country, he would sit down at the counter and help a saleswoman with her work, or pack up purchases at the cash desk, chatting and listening to what his employees said to him; and they felt that he really listened to them. He often did his interviewing of candidates for jobs in his own home, inviting spouses and children to come too. He urged his employees to talk to customers about 'their chickens and pigs and cows and kids' and maintain extreme courtesy in all relations, though his own enormous charm was occasionally interrupted, like lightning, by a lashing tongue.

Sam Walton's attachment to the past was reflected also in the traditional amusements he encouraged to 'fight the monotony' of small towns where nothing ever happened. 'We have always tried to make life as interesting and as unpredictable as we can, doing crazy things to capture the attention of our folks and lead them to think up surprises of their own.'

The religion of small-town America

A 'friendly fellow' with a 'lashing tongue'

Playing practical jokes

Relying on local amateur talent, playing practical jokes, including cruel ones, dressing up in bizarre costumes, parading in the streets with cheerleaders, interrupting routine with carnivals, even the Saturday morning strategic meeting of managers was unpredictably relieved by singing or comedy acts. Ten thousand shareholders were invited annually to Bentonville for a weekend of wild and raucous entertainment, in the hope that the strangers in Wall Street could 'know us and understand us'.

Though Sam Walton would not have called himself pious, simply valuing church-going and Sunday school as pillars of stability, his employees and customers increasingly found in their involvement in Walmart a religious justification for their patience in accepting their humble role in society. The corporation's management adopted the gospel of Servant Leadership, propagated by the founder of one of the world's largest advertising agencies, BBDO, Bruce Barton (1887–1967), the son of a clergyman and a staunch conservative opponent of Roosevelt and the New Deal.

Jesus as a businessman

His bestseller portraying Jesus as a businessman popularised the idea that business was a spiritual calling, so shoppers and salespeople were encouraged to see themselves not as automatons, like factory workers obeying orders, but as helping their fellows in Christian service, serving their neighbours and enabling families to lead honourable lives. Walmart

Reconciling religion and business

reconciled religion and business, becoming the largest merchandiser of Christian goods, but nonetheless remaining business-like and open on Sundays. The religion many customers adopted, while maintaining the Biblical superiority of the male, consoled women by exalting motherhood, elevating domesticity into a Christian rite, persuading men to make the

family the centre of their interests and attacking abortion and homosexuality as the great threat to the family. The company teamed up with
other business giants to support small Christian colleges against what
they considered to be the subversive anti-authoritarian influence of the
major universities. Sam Walton was even suspicious of what he dismissed
as 'the charity business', and preferred to make donations directly to local
causes himself, maintaining that his corporation was a public benefactor
by saving customers' money through its low prices. He said he wanted
Walmart to be 'a force for change', but the most important change it has
made has been to grow. Despite Sam's delight in doing things differently,
Walmart's 8,500 stores around the world, trading under fifty-six different
names, are more or less clones of its original self. Trade unions are shunned
and complain in vain that most workers are kept on the very lowest wages
and that the share of profits they receive is minute; they deny that Walmart
is providing employment, claiming that it causes more job losses by
driving rival shops into bankruptcy. Walmart's American customers are
now predominantly the one-third of the country who have lost in the
struggle for prosperity, and who sustain their pride by adherence to the
age-old values of neighbourliness against the anonymity of the city. In the
twenty-first century, three-quarters of them voted for President George
W. Bush. The 'Walmart Mom' is a political force.

Mistrust of intellectuals

The 'Walmart Mom'

It may seem that there is no reason for Walmart to change. Financial
analysts are satisfied that it has a winning formula for making a steady
profit, and even more in times of recession; its expenditure on advertising
is one-quarter that of its nearest rival, and its sales are six times greater,

so it can get bigger discounts from its suppliers. Its ability to save on costs is so technically perfect that even the thermostats in every store are controlled from Bentonville. It has become the most successful business in the world, but also the one with the most enemies, repeatedly assailed by protests and lawsuits and accusations of hypocrisy, as, for example, that many of its staff never get a share of the profits, because they have to serve for two years before they qualify, by which time those on low wages may have moved elsewhere. Whereas in the 1950s the CEO of General Motors, which was then the model of a successful business, was paid 135 times more than assembly-line workers, fifty years later the CEO of Walmart earned 1,500 times as much as the ordinary employee; a factory supervisor at General Motors, in charge of two or three thousand workers, used to be paid five times as much as them; but a district store manager at Walmart earns ten times as much as his sales staff. Retail wages used to be half of manufacturing wages; today they are down to two-fifths.

Enemies of success

If the most successful company in the world has not said the final word about the best way of spending one's time on earth, and if most people still feel that they are not as well rewarded for their labours as they deserve, and that dedicating their lives to earning a living has not produced the result they wish for, then what is the alternative to earning a living? What is the alternative to sacrificing one's energy making money, obediently doing what everybody else seems to be doing, in the hope that whatever meagre wealth one can accumulate will make it possible, at last, often too late, to embrace all those parts of life that one has not touched or even seen?

Earning a living without living

How far can one get following the European answer to Walmart, which is IKEA? Ingvar Kamprad (born 1926), who founded it at the age of seventeen, came, like Walton, from a small town in the middle of nowhere (in southern Sweden), which remains the headquarters of his firm. He too sought to perpetuate the traditional rural values of hard work and thrift, but whereas Sam's Ten Rules for Building a Business were all about commitment ('I overcame every single one of my personal shortcomings by the sheer passion I brought to my work'), appreciating one's colleagues and celebrating success with them, giving customers what they want and a little more ('the two most important words I ever wrote were on the first Walmart sign: Satisfaction Guaranteed'), the Nine Principles in Ingvar's *Testament of a Furniture Dealer* added a vision of 'the joys of discovery', 'developing ourselves as human beings', 'becoming freer human beings . . . with a more natural and unconstrained way of life . . . creating a better everyday life for the many people' with limited financial resources, contributing to 'democratisation all over the world', and producing 'cheerful' and more beautiful goods that give long-term enjoyment. 'Why do poor people have to put up with such ugly things?' asked Kamprad: it was unfair that only the rich should be able to afford beautiful things. 'I have always disliked the harshness of American capitalism,' he said, 'and I do admit I do have some socialist principles . . . I can combine the good in a profit-making business with a lasting human social vision.'

His nostalgia for the simple life of rural Sweden did not divert him from being both fearful of the future and imagining how it could be made wonderful. After every task accomplished he would say 'most of the job

IKEA, the European answer to Walmart

The Testament of a Furniture Dealer

remains to be done'. There was always a 'glorious future' to look forward to. He refused to sell shares in his company because he was determined to remain free from the demands of greedy investors who might deflect him from his goal. Instead of paying dividends, he preferred to save money so that he would not be in danger of being bought up by rivals. 'Always think and prepare for bad times,' he repeated. Profits were hoarded in a non-profit foundation that would ensure perpetual independence with an impenetrably complex set of legal arrangements as protection from taxation by governments and from the apocalyptic collapse of nation-states that he feared. He wanted to preserve not the past but the achievement of his lifetime, to ensure immortality not for his soul but for his business, and 'eternal life' for his ideals, which he called the 'sacred concept'. 'We are a concept company. If we stick to the concept we will never die.' Wealth was 'too burdensome' for any individual to bear and while bequeathing an influential role to his children, ownership of IKEA was locked into the Foundation.

A substitute for religion

There was a substitute for religion in IKEA, secular and unmystical, with humility as its watchword and something of the Viking cult of soft-spoken egalitarianism as its ritual. Whereas Sam Walton called his employees 'associates', Kamprad saw himself as the father of his 'co-workers', defining leadership as 'love'. In the firm's early days, which he remembered as the happiest, 'we were working as a small family'. There was a subtle difference between his ideal of the family and Sam Walton's. 'We were as if in love. Nothing to do with eroticism. We just liked each other so damned much.' He chose his co-workers because he liked them, for their common sense rather than their paper qualifications, after day-long conversations that sometimes went on long into the night, valuing above all high social purpose and a readiness to try their hand at anything. An economist in charge of the finances was promptly sacked when he assumed airs implying that it was the accountants who really ran the firm. IKEA was Kamprad's family, not a family of blood kinship or of neighbours, but an ever-expandable one that included all who wanted to share in his search for a socially responsible life. Their meetings were emotional and earnest, with Kamprad showing his affection effusively with hugs, enjoying singing folk songs, holding hands, expressing a visceral pleasure in togetherness. Though he was the undisputed boss, he talked constantly about his 'defects' and apologised grovellingly for his 'stupidity' in being attracted by pro-Nazi views in his youth. (His family only migrated to Sweden from Germany just thirty years before his birth: 'I was brought up by a German grandmother and a German father.') His first marriage ended in divorce because 'I was a shit.' 'Lack of self-confidence, difficulty making decisions, disastrous organisational skills, and horribly poor receptivity are all faults I fully recognise in myself . . . I am never satisfied. Something tells me what I am doing at the moment has to be done better tomorrow . . . I am such a nervous person, I have to be at the airport an hour and a half to feel safe and I am fearfully ashamed if I arrive at a meeting a minute late.' He was not ashamed to admit that he was an alcoholic – 'a good way of forgetting' – and also dyslexic. All he claimed for himself was 'a certain nose for business and a reasonable dose of peasant common sense' .

'Faults I fully recognise in myself'

Unresolved contradic-tions

Though he urged his employees to innovate and use their own judge-ment, in reality they were surrounded with strict rules as to what they could do. So, like Walmart, IKEA grew and grew and remained the same. It became international because its competitors in Sweden boycotted it for undercutting them, and the only way it could survive was by going abroad for supplies, and getting them much more cheaply there, first in Poland and then in other low-wage countries. Kamprad's sympathies were more international than Walton's: 'I was in Prague the day the Russian tanks crushed a protesting student, arousing the wrath of the world. I arrived two days after the fall of the Berlin Wall.' He 'fell in love' with the people of Poland, 'their good hearts and their skills', theirs was 'a second home' to him. He taught his children to speak four languages. But the panacea of low prices depended on buying from poor countries with low wages, which could not continue forever; and most people in the world have remained too poor to afford IKEA furniture. The clash between the values of thrift and the business need to tempt customers to spend as much as possible awaited resolution.

To create a unique business brand, Kamprad insisted on the firm iden-tifying itself as quintessentially and unchangingly Swedish, but that did not necessarily appeal to everyone in old civilisations with different ideas of elegance. The suppliers in India, often highly educated in both their own and Western traditions, resented it that IKEA's buyers spoke to them only about delivery dates and prices, avoided making friends and refused to come to their weddings, because that might suggest bribery and corrup-tion. Though Kamprad worried that the emotional bonds that kept his

company together would fade as it got ever bigger, he liked growing bigger because it gave him a sense of achievement, but then he lamented that the results we not those he had hoped for. Economies of scale and mass production have meant that stores
all over the world look very similar and contain the same goods.

'I wish', said Ingvar Kamprad, 'I was a bit cultured, like Margaretha [his wife, who used to be a primary school teacher]. She reads novels. The best I can do is to take a few catalogues and leaf through them.' He sensed there was something missing, but was unable to see precisely what culture could do for commerce. That was because the flirtations between business and art have not yet matured into asking what more they could achieve together if they thought harder about where else their differences could lead them. Commerce means not just buying and selling but communication too, which is also what culture seeks. Business is not only about making money: originally the word 'business' meant anxiety, and anxiety certainly dominates it still. The most precious commodity that is traded is not gold, but time, deciding what can most usefully be done each day. But because culture has been largely relegated to providing entertainment or consolation after work, rather than being recognised as the ingredient that gives meaning to it, business has done little to exhibit the inspiration that can be extracted from the vast range of its experiences. So long as business is treated as a technique, which can be taught, it cannot offer what is popularly known as a 'philosophy', meaning a vision of what life is for. A technique is a procedure used to accomplish a task, whereas a 'philosophy' involves a lifelong pursuit of a broader understanding beyond

Commerce, Communication, Culture

A new philosophy of business

one's particular occupation. So long as business is obsessed by its balance sheet, it forgets that wealth without wisdom is bread without water, and thirst kills more quickly than hunger. Because financial success does not give moral authority, business has been grounding its prestige on borrowed ideologies, as when it 'conquers' markets in the military tradition, or encodes its practices in the language of the social sciences, or reinterprets the teachings of religions to suit its purposes. It remains ambushed by contradictory attitudes to work, uncertain whether leisure is the ultimate goal, or whether some kinds of work are nobler than others, or whether fulfilment is to be found in the performance of a single mastered skill. Is business still in its adolescence then, delighting in youthful bravura, with each generation trying to outrun its predecessor, and is full maturity reached only when it has comprehensive thoughts about 'busy-ness', what it is worth being busy about and what to do with time? Saving time in the name of efficiency, fighting time because there is never enough, killing time because it moves too slowly, spending time as though it is money, when time is obviously more precious than money, these are all preliminary dalliances with the mystery of 'busy-ness', which has still to reveal how the infinite variety of each moment of life can be meaningful and memorable.

Business based on borrowed ideologies

What is it worth being busy about?

Time is no longer what it was in the aftermath of the Second World War, when Walmart and IKEA defined their ambitions. Never have humans had such long expectations of life (thirty more years than in 1900), and never have they had so much leisure (the thirty-seven-hour or even forty-eight-hour week, spread over the year, taking account of all weekends and holidays, equals only four or five hours of work a day). And yet never have humans complained so much that they do not have enough time for all the demands upon them and all the temptations that distract them. When workers are segregated to perform precisely defined tasks, they are not invited to savour the multiple qualities of time as experienced by different occupations. Business is in an impasse talking about work– life balance, implying that work is not life. What people expect from work is no longer so obvious. All this provides the opportunity to redefine business, to open a new chapter in its ambitions and significance, to rethink what work could be, and to find unexplored value in those varied forms of memory and curiosity and imagination that are called culture, that are indispensable to a full life, and that every customer brings with them.

The opportun- ity to redefine business

The 'consumer society' may be only a preliminary stage in the evolution of human interaction. Being propelled by the ingenuity of a small number of people constantly inventing more and more objects, it is plunged into repeated crises by the difficulty of finding buyers who can afford them. It may seem that there is no alternative, since consumerism has survived the complaints against it, as the materialist enemy of spiritual values, for at least five hundred years, not only in the West but in the East as well; the complaints re-emerge in every period of prosperity and of wasteful extravagance, but they have little practical effect because consumers are also workers who desperately need buyers for what they produce. Shopping, moreover, has established itself as a mute language using goods rather than words to demonstrate what kind of person one wishes to be, to show affection with the gifts one buys, to impress neigh-

Beyond the consumer society

bours with the display of one's acquisitions, and to assert individual taste or group solidarity by one's choices. So long as some people have many more comforts than others, the consumer society will always have its appeal. But it is worth exploring the possibility that the ever-growing hunger for new experiences and the relentless questioning of existing practices may cause the emergence, alongside the consumer society, of other societies, challenging it both from within and without.

[23]

Are there more amusing ways
of earning a living?

WHAT WOULD HAPPEN if Ingvar Kamprad, the creator of IKEA, started reading novels, just like his wife? His *Testament of a Furniture Dealer* is already almost a novel, a fervent romantic vision of a more beautiful world, of a small group of people 'breaking free from status and convention', determined to preserve the spirit of their youth and their 'unconquerable enthusiasm', always ready 'to give each other a helping hand', always having time to talk to each other, devoted to 'kindness and generosity', refusing to work just for money, taking the football team as their model of collaboration, prizing their uniqueness, always looking for new solutions, such as going to a window factory when searching for table legs and a shirt factory to get the cheapest cushion covers, insistent that 'we will never have two identical stores' because none can ever be perfect, untroubled by the fear of making mistakes, disdaining committees, bureaucracy, statistics and 'exaggerated planning', which is 'the most common cause of corporate death', responding to a rival who steals one of their ideas not with a lawsuit but by inventing a new and better model, above all refusing to accept that anything is impossible and always looking forward to new adventures. *Lista* was Kamprad's favourite old Swedish

Refusing to work just for money

word, meaning 'doing what you have to do with an absolute minimum of resources': waste was 'one of the greatest diseases of mankind'; so he fitted readily into the ideology of 'sustainability'. However, the more IKEA expanded, the more he became a prisoner of the constraints he denounced. On the other hand, his customers are no longer neophytes in consumerism as they were when he started; they have been developing ideals which could combine with Kamprad's vision of the future of work to inaugurate a new phase in social enterprise.

Work does not have to be organised the way it is today. The struggle to earn a living does not have to be so harsh. New kinds of relationships can be encouraged in business, as they have been in private life. The young could invent different kinds of job to suit them better. It is possible to avoid falling into utopian temptations by undertaking small practical experiments to test how things could be different, without disrupting the routines of a whole organisation.

I see Ingvar Kamprad's as an unfinished life because though the IKEA stores are monuments to his memory, like pyramids, he dreamed of something more, but it became difficult to change his management structures.

Reinventing the art of furnishing a home

A home, which Kamprad set out to furnish, is no longer what it used to be. It is no longer enough for IKEA to stuff homes with its 9,500 varieties of tables, chairs, beds and household goods. A home may begin as a refuge where one can have one's own possessions around one, but it evolves into a place which one values above all because it is where it is as important to feel understood as to be physically comfortable, and to be able to share one's woes and joys with people who appreciate one another. A home is where one takes care of others and is taken care of, where one can offer hospitality to friends and potential friends, and where one can speak freely, revealing thoughts and emotions without danger. But a home can also be a solitary place. It is now one of the great personal and collective works of art that all humans spend their lives attempting to raise up and to keep from falling down; it is a cultural construct. A furniture store that promises 'a better life', which takes this evolution into account, cannot just exhibit forty-eight rooms furnished to suggest models of what a home could physically look like. It makes sense for IKEA to compete on price when customers short of money struggle to acquire the material signs of respectability, but when they have broader cultural aspirations, doing business with them could mean something quite different.

Two centuries ago there were five times more shops in Britain than there are today, one for every fifty people, some with only two or three customers a day, and many deriving only a supplementary income from trade; half of London shopkeepers took in lodgers. In the late nineteenth century, in the villages of northern France, one in every three houses sold wine or spirits. In the U.S.A., the country store used to be the hub of all local farming and craft activity, accepting payment in every kind of produce. The first department stores did not just sell goods but became agents of middle-class aspirations, organising concerts and exhibitions, and becoming public places where women could safely go out on their own, meeting one another, acquiring new tastes, and spending money as they pleased. In 1881 'the sight of women addicted to this purse-destroying vice' drove the male editors of the *New York Times* 'almost to

What is a shop?

*Shops,
bazaars,
parliaments*

despair of the future of our country'; but Gordon Selfridge, who founded his store in London in 1909, and published a book entitled *The Romance of Shopping*, presenting it as an activity to be engaged in for pleasure and not out of necessity, replied: 'This is not a shop, it is a community. Women come because it is so much brighter than their own homes.' Oriental bazaars have long been almost informal parliaments. Charity shops are now often recreation grounds, with people coming in every day in their lunch break just for a chat, because they cannot think of anything else to do. Shops have been inventive in transforming themselves in the past and are clearly not doomed to remain always what they are today.

IKEA has been keeping itself busy opening many new stores each year, but Kamprad warned his colleagues that 'a company that feels it has reached its goal will quickly stagnate': his firm now has the financial resources to be bolder in its experiments. It is mature enough to become a less timid host to the 600 million people who visit it each year, and who are not there just in search of purchases: they have emotional, intellectual and moral yearnings which are as important to them as their furnishings. They each have a story to tell and puzzles to solve around their own attempts at finding 'a better life'. It is they, the infinitely diverse customers, who have the potential to give each store the elusive originality

*Silent
customers*

that Kamprad vainly hoped for. The bright lights of cities are increasingly dimmed by a fog of loneliness, so the pathway through the store that drives the customers, sheep-like, past endless exhibits without speaking to one another, misses one of the main reasons why they have come shopping, which is to get out of the solitude or boredom of their own home.

Superstores forget that they are substitutes for the city square and market place where people used to come not just to buy but even more to socialise, strike deals, find employment and look for marriage partners. They have yet to imagine themselves as cultural and educational centres with a mission to enhance the richness of their customers' lives, rather than simply encumber them with more possessions. *Shops as cultural centres*

The exploratory trial I was allowed to make in one IKEA store to discover how such a transformation could happen revealed that customers were keen to meet other customers they did not know; and when conversations with a stranger were organised for them around an evening meal in the restaurant, with a Menu of Conversation which ensured that they did not just gossip, but discussed what was most important to them and how other people's experience could help them, the verdicts have even gone to the extent of asserting that they would remain 'eternally grateful' for the encounter. The giant stores of today have flourished in the belief that the greater the variety of goods placed before customers, the more choice they have, the freer they are because they can choose for themselves, but people are ultimately more interested by people than by things. Loyalty cards and discounts are superficial remedies for frustrated sociability. *Interest in things or people*

IKEA is not just the blue-and-yellow buildings customers see, for it has many thousands of people manufacturing and supplying goods to it from numerous exotic countries, but it is silent about the sweat and tears and thoughts of the individual maker of each object it sells. A nondescript lampshade becomes more interesting, a messenger of unfulfilled hope when it is revealed that it is made in a factory in Delhi by one of 200 women, bent over a bench eight hours a day, dreaming about how their children could have 'a better life'. The technology already exists to trace the origins of each item on sale, and it could easily be used to let the buyer see and talk to the maker, to express appreciation and to learn something of the skills used in the making. It is underestimating customers to assume that they are interested only in calculating whether the lampshade is cheap enough. And it is misunderstanding the suppliers to imagine that they want to talk only about prices and delivery dates.

Exploring IKEA

My exploratory trial in the IKEA superstore organised language lessons and conversation practice for foreigners and immigrants, not only providing a sympathetic audience for the extraordinary stories they had to tell and longed to pour out, but also enriching the customers' understanding of suffering and resilience in other lands. Restless young children, dragged around behind parents worrying about what they can and cannot afford, found a more captivating role for themselves when they were offered lessons in playing the ukulele and singing to its tunes. A parking lot does not have to be dreary, predictable asphalt; it could become open-air art gallery, each space a part of a huge carpet of designs, surrounded by hanging gardens on the perimeter walls. As online commerce expands and shops increasingly resemble museums, where people come to touch the goods offered for sale more cheaply on the web, the theatre and dances of the civilisations from which the goods originate can change the whole idea of what a 'shopping experience' is. When shops recognise that they are potentially parts of the educational system and rivals of the entertainment industry, the commercial justification for allowing cultural activities to infiltrate them becomes evident. A store need not be just a temple of consumption worshipping deal-making; it also has a congregation of shoppers who have broader ideals of conviviality. In the same way that religious reformations have been the result of congregations combining new with old rituals, so combining education with commerce has the potential to give a different character to the consumer society.

As sales assistants become more educated and ambitious but are also constantly threatened by staff cuts in the interest of efficiency, they want more scope to express their unused talents. In the exploratory trial, the woman in charge of bedding, who was formerly a bank clerk and school domestic bursar, and who has travelled widely, voluntarily began spending her lunch hour reading to young children; the man selling office furniture who had a master's degree in horticulture was eloquent about the tropical plants he grows at home; the woman on the cake stand whose real expertise was dressmaking, the head of marketing whose passion was spiritual healing, they all had much more to offer than a sales pitch. IKEA could be providing a new kind of international education to its young sales assistants if it gave them the chance to work in each of the forty-odd countries in which it operates. Commerce is inevitably focused on finance, but it also depends on reputation, and the reward to the manager of this store was the feeling that he was serving the community in a way that made him and his staff significant figures in the lives of more and more individuals. Commerce does not have to abase itself in flattery, repeating that 'the customer is always right'; on the contrary, it can inspire

The unused talents of sales assistants

the customer with new ideas. The mission of retail marketers need not be confined to establishing a relationship just between customers and the anonymous corporation, rather than between the customers themselves. Cities may not be doomed to become ever more similar, with identical branches of international retail chains and endlessly repeated brand slogans. A shopper is a person, not a purse.

A shopper is a person, not a purse

To be relentlessly pressured to work harder so as to be able to afford a never-ending stream of desirable things is a depressing kind of freedom. The big corporations have not yet devised ways of renewing themselves so that they can be a source of the personal liberation and individual creativity that so many people are now forced to search for outside their day jobs. The Consumer Society was originally a revolution against destiny and meek submission, a protest against the teaching that people had to accept their lot and that complaining would change nothing. It proclaimed the supremacy of individual desire. But desire did not necessarily liberate, it could also enslave. Business can only become an integral part of a full cultural life, rather than just a means towards other ends, when it raises its sights above giving customers what they can be persuaded to want and imposing on its workers the mundane servitudes of earning a living. Successful business people who have risen to honours and comfort may not be bothered that they have missed out on intellectual, artistic, spiritual or moral attainments, but when they see their children determined to avoid following in their footsteps, and floundering at a loss to know what to do, they realise that the system that sustains them has become meaningless to many in the next generation.

It is precisely such collapses of meaning that, in previous centuries, have spurred youth to new adventures – though not all youth, far from it, for it is always minorities who take dangerous initiatives. 'Going back to nature' is no longer an option: even H. D. Thoreau (1817–1862), the pioneer advocate of simple living in natural surroundings, had to admit that nature can be 'mean' as well as 'sublime'. However, the growing panic about the destruction of the environment revives nostalgic memories of forests where everyone could freely gather food and raise animals, and of cities which grew their own food. Henry Daniel (*c.* 1315–1385), who grew 252 different plants in his garden in Stepney, London, is a reminder of what a civilisation of offices and factories loses by its segregation from nature and by the divorce of town and country. Making the earth sustainable is only a beginning; then comes the more difficult task of avoiding having to earn so much money just to stay alive and keep warm. *Sustainability only a beginning*

Already, however, technology is giving hints that there may be other ways of feeding, housing and clothing oneself. For city dwellers, it has conceived high-rise buildings which are vertical hydroponic or aeroponic gardens, stack upon stack of automatically irrigated plants, yielding twenty times more crops than plants grown in open fields, while using 8 per cent of the water that conventional agriculture requires. NASA's Controlled Ecological Life Support System enables astronauts to be self-sufficient in food on barren planets in space. Just as the twentieth century devoted itself to installing a bathroom in every house, so it may be that eventually the smallest apartment may feel incomplete without its own internal vertical vegetable garden, possibly in that same bathroom. *How to feed, house and clothe oneself*

A food revolution

So many edible plants have yet to be discovered, so many have been discarded unnecessarily by fashions which limited taste to just a few staples, that there is a food revolution waiting to be started, and many untried ways of responding to hunger and appetite to be found. That could mean not only changing what people eat, but also where they eat it and with whom. 'We do not sit down at table to eat, but to eat together,' wrote the Roman biographer Plutarch (A.D. 46–120). Since most people spend their whole lives eating with such a minute selection of human beings, the future of food is not just a problem of physical resources and increased productivity but also of conviviality. The Incredible Edible experiments – growing fruit and vegetables communally in towns and villages on every spare scrap of land – now spreading in Europe are just one sign of the desire to be free of the constant pressure that earning a living entails and the social segregation it brings with it.

A home with a seven-year prison sentence

Finding a place to live often involves spending a third of one's wages for twenty-five years on a mortgage, the equivalent of undergoing a seven-year prison sentence. In Japan it has sometimes even meant taking out a loan repayable by one's descendants over a hundred years, a new version of inherited serfdom. Vast discrepancies in house prices have divided poor and rich into separate ghettoes. Commuting between separate commercial, industrial, recreational and residential spaces has shortened the days, as though wage earners must live in a permanent arctic winter. Lenin promised that communism would bring rent-free homes, but got no further than cramming his Soviet families into a single room in shared apartments. The housing famine intensifies inevitably each year as populations grow and expectations rise. Neither suburban villas nor tower blocks can be the ultimate achievement of architectural creativity, nor can concrete and glass be the ultimate materials. Who will pioneer new kinds of shelter created with new materials, or new patterns of migration, or new forms of transport to replace those invented for a bygone age? And what about clothing, which awaits rejuvenation from century-old methods? Is a textile revolution on the horizon? Since most people have never had enough money, the ultimate test for technology is whether it *New games, new gadgets, new jobs* can free them from the menace of hunger and homelessness, the tyranny of money and the drudgery that earning a living often entails.

When in previous centuries the young could not find work, they migrated to other continents. Today when they cannot find work they have to invent it where they are. They increasingly think: they do not want to copy their elders because the jobs on offer do not suit every temperament, do not allow the flowering of every talent, and there are never enough desirable ones to go round. When they are told that no-one has any use for them because they have no experience or the wrong qualifications, the only course open to them is to use their imagination to create new ways of living. Just as people invent new games, new gadgets, new songs, they can also invent new jobs. Dropping out is not a new way.

They may demand that work need not be dominated simply by the needs of agriculture, industry or services – whether commercial or philan- *A forgotten human right* thropic – but rather by a human right that has yet to be promulgated, the legitimate ambition to see the world and the infinitely varied forms of life it contains, to experience more of the innumerable skills that humans have developed, to be brought out of one's cocoon and to feel that one has had a full life and helped others to have one too. Though to be a respected professional is wonderful, it is no longer possible to keep up with knowledge in a single profession unless one can understand the ideas, language and methods of several other disciplines. Specialisation has been responsible for innumerable improvements in skill and knowledge, but it now only bears fruit when it is pollinated by seemingly unconnected visitors from other specialities, and when it can escape being paralysed by overdoses of bureaucratic medication. To be assured that one is particularly suited to a single career is too reminiscent of older traditions that each person belongs to a caste or has a preordained destiny. And business may outgrow the military ideals it still cultivates, with results being counted in terms of territories conquered, competitors defeated and booty brought home. It does not have to have such ambiguous relations with private life. It may prefer the analogies of gastronomy, which is about clarifying what is and what is not worth desiring. appreciating unfamiliar tastes and eliminating inherited prejudices.

A future for business schools

It is possible for business schools which sit on the periphery of universities to be the intermediaries that could give students of all faculties, whatever their subject, a chance to converse with people in many different occupations, as a basis for a reconsideration of what work has been doing, is doing and could possibly do differently in the future, to minds and hearts as well as pockets. Instead of just preparing the young for careers, universities and business schools could become laboratories which engaged in experiments by people of all disciplines and all occupations to make the search for a 'better life' more comprehensive and more imaginative. Nothing is more difficult than introducing change into institutions, but there have always been brave souls who like to think the unthinkable.

24

What else can one do in a hotel?

A LL THOSE WHO LISTEN TO THE wisdom of their contemporaries are constantly urged to be themselves, to know themselves and even to love themselves. At the same time, innumerable experts tell them that they are mistaken about themselves, that there is a lot wrong with them, and that they need help to repair themselves, educate, enrich, civilise, socialise themselves, and improve their appearance too. However, these experts are profoundly divided as to the right remedies for these many faults, and even as to what a fault is. What should one do in the face of so many contradictions? What is one supposed to make of all the people one knows, or thinks one knows, about whose characters and qualities one so often has contradictory information? Whether one agrees with Pascal that humans are 'only falsehood, duplicity and contradiction', or with Mao Zedong that all contradictions can be resolved, contradictions are part of life, and it is more interesting to know them than to close one's eyes to them.

So I turn to Dostoyevsky (1821–1881), who devoted his life to making sense of human contradictions and of the vacillations of his own mind. I choose him because he espoused, one after another, a whole series of incompatible ideals. He treated them like lovers between whom he could not definitively choose, discarding them but not forgetting them, and remaining powerfully aware of their attractions, even of those he had come to detest. His novels are conversations between characters grappling with contending diagnoses of human dilemmas, and never being wholly satisfied for long with any one. Few have described so meticulously a sky dark with different shades of doubt, gloom and guilt briefly illuminated by fireballs of hope which die out too soon. He has apparently been translated into 170 languages, which suggests that countless thoughtful people all over the world remain torn, like him, between fascination, bewilderment and repulsion in the face of Western Europe's contradictory ideologies. What other response can there be to this confusion?

Having been condemned to death at the age of twenty-eight and reprieved just minutes before the firing squad was about to execute him, Dostoyevsky concentrated with extraordinary intensity on the question of what it means to be alive. After being spared from death, he felt a 'great surge of love for life', a desire 'to immerse myself in it', a conviction that life meant 'not to lose hope, however hard things may be, that is what life is, that is its purpose'. Four years in a Siberian prison gave him another rare experience, of being able to mix with people very different from himself, 'coarse, bitter and irritable' criminals who hated him for being a member of the ruling class that had punished them and for being unsmiling, taciturn and suspicious, suffering, as he made plain, the 'terrible torment' of never being alone for a single minute, feeling that he was 'buried alive and closed in a coffin'. But gradually he made friends with some, and got to understand others. Instead of complaining that he was surrounded

Lessons from a firing squad

by 'a hundred and fifty enemies' who never tired of persecuting him, he began to think that the educated elite had much to learn from the uneducated. 'I learned to discern the human beings among the bandits, strong, beautiful natures among them, and what pleasure it was to find gold under a rough cover . . . What wonderful people; on the whole my time has not been wasted . . . so many types of the common people did I carry away . . . there's enough for volumes and volumes.' And in imagination, he became convinced, for a time, that they, uncontaminated by education, could save the world from its decadence and corruption.

Dostoyevsky's many lives
Dostoyevsky's many lives included being a romantic, a socialist, a conservative, a nationalist, an orthodox Christian appreciating both faith and unbelief, inspired by European thought but also condemning it as diseased. He despised materialism but his life was dominated by money, being always short of it, writing furiously to pay the bills, even writing two stories at the same time to meet the deadlines of newspaper serialisation, but also addictively gambling his earnings away. 'Without money you cannot take any step in any direction.' He calculated the cost of everything, and was fascinated by how those who cannot make money by conventional methods can acquire it through crime; but at the same time he deplored the obsession with money as a betrayal of Russia's tradition of generosity, brotherhood and spirituality. He was an admirer of traditional values but he also questioned the traditional family and highlighted the tragic misunderstandings to which it gave birth. Your father 'conceived you and you are his blood and therefore you must love him'. But, he replies, 'Did he love me when he was conceiving me, did he really conceive me for

my sake? He did not even know me. Why do I have to love him just because he conceived me and then failed to love me my whole life?' On the one hand Dostoyevsky has a character saying, 'Is there anyone who does not want his father to be dead?' On the other hand he insists, 'It is our duty to love our family, even though we may dislike them. That teaches us how to love all human beings.'

'I am a child of doubt and disbelief,' he wrote. 'I have always been and shall ever be (that I know) until they close the lid of my coffin.' But he was always desperately thirsting to believe in something, and yet the stronger this thirst became, the stronger the arguments against believing became. As a journalist he was decisive and dogmatic, preaching fervent nationalism, rejecting reliance on reason and scientific method: Russia's task was to civilise Europe, bring to fruition Europe's unfinished vocation, synthesise the ideas of its diverse peoples, and liberate it from atheism and socialism. But when Russia lost a war and went bankrupt, he concluded that 'Europe despises us' and turned his back on it: Russia must pursue its civilising mission in Asia instead.

A child of doubt and disbelief

As a novelist, however, he was the opposite of dogmatic, seeing all sides of every problem, the potential saintliness in the sinner, the cruelty of suffering and its universal pervasiveness but also its power to 'redeem'. Crime he regarded as one of many forms of transgression, which could be an expression of freedom, curiosity or courage: 'We are all transgressing every day; we often have to choose between two goods or two evils.' Evil was not a curable disease but inherent in the human condition. No argument could yield the truth, and truth was too elusive to be put into

Seeing all sides of every problem

words. That is why he had to be an artist, who finds some kind of truth by learning how to look at things in a way that reveals their beauty. 'It is amazing what one ray of sunshine can do for a man.'

Dostoyevsky is the poet of complexity, the painter of unresolvable dilemmas, the sculptor, in melting ice, of humanity's timid hopes. Since his death, everything has become even more complicated, with more knowledge, more diverse expectations and less conviction that any one group has the monopoly of wisdom. So I am going to approach the problem of the inscrutability and contradictions of individuals in a more prosaic way, by asking whether they are using all the opportunities available to them to penetrate into the labyrinths of unspoken thoughts. It so happens that in the year 2012 the number of tourists in the world reached one billion, which means that never before have so many strangers passed each other by, usually in silence, without revealing or enquiring what they think of each other, and of themselves. Hotels are the nearest they have to a parliament, where each one is more or less misjudged on the basis of their nationality or appearance and other trivial evidence. It may seem that only superficial encounters of brief duration are possible in them, unlike prisons where the inmates can gradually discover one another's deeper complexities concealed behind their crimes. But if the appreciation of people's contradictions is one of the necessary foundations on which fruitful human relations are built, then it is worth considering whether, now that such huge numbers are passing through hotels, they could become a significant force in promoting a better understanding of enigmatic strangers and mysterious neighbours. The idea is not too

Penetrating the laby-rinths of unspoken thoughts

Enigmatic strangers and mysterious neighbours

far-fetched, because hotels were once dominating monuments in many cities.

In the nineteenth century Americans recognised what an important function hotels could have in a new country. They imagined them as the equivalent of the Greek *agora*, where all citizens could meet. Their early hotels were hailed as Palaces for the Public, giving architectural expressions to democratic ideals by providing vast assembly halls open to everyone, with dining and entertainment spaces as well as business libraries containing shipping reports, price lists and newspapers. Whereas authoritarian monarchies were fearful of both private and public meetings, imagining revolutionary conspiracies everywhere, Americans saw themselves as a nation of strangers who had given themselves the constitutional right to meet and combine with whom they pleased to pursue common goals. They were conscious of the loneliness of *The Man of the Crowd,* portrayed by Edgar Allan Poe in 1840, where a stranger is followed all day and all night through a city, to find that he has not met any acquaintance or exchanged a word with anyone, and not even acknowledged a single person. Already in 1818 people in Pittsburgh were complaining that they rarely knew their next-door neighbour. So hotels became meeting places for every form of activity. Dinner was served at a common table, with the same food for everyone, bringing together guests and local residents. 'The charm of going to the city is dining with two hundred well-dressed people in a splendid drawing room.' Eating together in public was the pleasure the hotel offered, in contrast with the European preoccupation with safeguarding privacy and emerging only to display one's

19th century American hotels

Eating together in public

refinement. Though the hotel meal was often 'devoured with a rapidity which a pack of foxhounds after a week's fast might in vain attempt to rival', interest in one's fellow was not restrained by genteel decorum. Domingo Sarmiento (1811–1888), who later became the president of Argentina, was amused by the 'unselfconscious curiosity' of guests: 'If the buttons on your overcoat have deer, horse or boar's heads in relief, everyone who spies them will come up to you and go over them one by one, turning you about left and right to better examine the walking

The most levelling of all American institutions

museum.' An English traveller wrote, 'The hotel system is the most levelling of all American institutions.' There was no 'flunkeyism' and no room for the 'assertion of individual importance'. And this was in keeping with the way many of these hotels were (for a time) financed: owned by all classes, with shares being bought by artisans as well as the rich.

However, business ideals then destroyed this vision of conviviality. The second originality of American hotels was their adoption of the methods

Efficiency versus conviviality

of mass production. E. M. Statler (1863–1928) did for them what Henry Ford did for motor cars, reducing prices – 'a bed and a bath for a dollar and half' – by standardisation and strict instructions that employees had to memorise and follow exactly on pain of dismissal. Though some hotels became cheaper, others went the other way. When a thousand guests were looked after by 600 staff, efficiency became the first priority. Skyscraper hotels challenged the intimate atmosphere of small family ones. Hotel-keeping became a profession with graduate diplomas; hotel chains became profit centres, with just three corporations owning nearly two million rooms between them. The 'hospitality industry' was born. The commercialisation of hospitality, which monetised kindness, is another of the great revolutions in human relations. An era came to an end when a belief that prevailed in almost all civilisations was abandoned, that everyone had to offer a free bed and a meal, or several, to passing strangers.

The decisive change came when the American Hotel Plan, where the price of a room included meals eaten in common, gave way in the early twentieth century to the European Plan, which emphasised privacy, with à la carte meals taken and paid for separately. César Ritz (1850–1918), the son of a poor Swiss peasant, who rose from being an assistant waiter to owner and manager of some of Europe's most prestigious hotels, patronised by royalty and the rich, replaced egalitarianism with luxury, thick carpets, gold taps, obsequious service and exclusivity. He said, 'I want to teach people how to live.' What he meant was that he was *Idealising the upper classes* fascinated by an idealised vision of the habits and extravagance of the upper classes, thrilled by their self-assurance, and desperate to imitate them. So he created imitation palaces, allowing those who could afford it to parody aristocratic rituals of ostentatious opulence freed from the constraints of domestic realities. Posh hotels became 24-hour theatres, with staff playing the role of deferential minions, unquestioningly indulging their guests' every whim. Ever since, the rich, middle and poorer classes have been segregated in separate hotels.

However, a hotel today is a United Nations in miniature, employing and hosting people from every part of the world. Could it be a more effective peace-maker? Does it have to be, in its expensive version, a fortress protecting its inmates from the rabble outside? Is there something it could *A hotel is a United Nations in miniature* learn from Dostoyevsky and his grim abode, the prison, which protected

What hotels can learn from Dostoyevsky

those who have never been prosecuted for their crimes from those who have, and which taught him so much about human contradictions? A year I spent with a team of four researchers interviewing the employees and guests of one chain of hotels was enough to reveal a great puzzle: there was an extraordinary amount and variety of talent, experience and knowledge among the employees, at all levels of the hierarchy, but the guests

Silent chamber- maids

were never made aware of it. The chambermaids were often foreigners wanting to learn a new language, and some of them were graduates. The housekeeping staff included people training to be nurses; one barman was an accountant, another was studying for an MBA; a porter was the son of a chieftain in his own country; a receptionist was touring the world working in hotels to collect material for a novel. But the hotel's 'human resources' database contained only the most banal information about them, just a few appraisals and complaints, assuming there was no point in going deeper, because hotels have the fastest turnover of staff of almost any business. Very occasionally, senior managers did make friends with guests, superficially or not, but guests seldom had the chance to benefit from the large numbers of staff they never saw, or passed by in silence. Staff were even officially discouraged from 'fraternising', because the dogma of 'customer service' haunted them. Hotels regard themselves as having strictly limited functions; they underestimate the capacities of their staff, and do not see themselves as proactively contributing something original to the expansion of the imaginations or the enrichment of the experience of those they shelter, those they employ and the city they serve. The commercial success of hotels has been paralleled by the narrow-ing of their social purpose.

Once upon a time the English pub had a central role in public, legal, military and social activity, as the location for numerous official events, but now only nostalgia sustains its claim to being the fount of national conviviality. Since 1800, England's population has increased sixfold while the number of pubs remained constant, and the number is now falling fast; four thousand are expected to close this year. In one street in south London, the pubs have all disappeared and been replaced by six gambling shops. The pub is no longer the place that people go to for their important *What* conversations, which, according to a survey by a brewer, take place instead *brewers know about* at home with partners (74 per cent), or with work colleagues (57 per cent), *pubs* friends (56 per cent), parents (38 per cent), rarely with the boss (11 per cent) and hardly at all with shop staff (2 per cent). Pubs do indeed attract more customers than the major churches have worshippers, but two-thirds of these customers say they are shy about starting a conversation with strangers in them, and many limit themselves to gossip, banter and trivial chat; they themselves declare that half of their conversations in pubs are pointless, and only 4 per cent last more than thirty minutes. The French bistro is likewise in steep decline; there were ten times more of them in 1900 than there are today; only a fifth of the population visits them regularly at least once a week, and only two-fifths consider them as having an important role in social relationships.

The Japanese inn, though also a national icon, is even less of a place for mutual discovery; on the contrary, it is cherished nostalgically as a relic that can reconnect the stressed workaholics of today with a past which is imagined to have been more stable and more conducive to the flowering of harmony and love. An inn dating back to A.D. 718, and run by the same family for forty-eight generations, is now an eight-storey concrete building able to house 450 people, but it is valued as a shrine where it is possible to take refuge from the pressures of globalised uniformity, revive historic memories, and construct, if only in imagination, a vision of a kinder and more beautiful existence with which one can identify. Self-discovery rather than discovery of others is the goal encouraged by the still vibrant tradition of *Tabi*, which originally meant a journey on foot into the wilderness to get away from human rivalries and jealousies, in the hope that communion with nature would help one to clarify one's own true values. So today's travellers can see a stay at an inn as a step into the past, reinforcing their vague desire to escape from the temptations of conventional success and regain their ancestors' appreciation of hardship and uncertainty, the beauty of impermanence, and the sorrow of parting with people and places. Escape from the regimentation of organised tours remains the message of *The Way to Walk the World,* the favourite guide-book of independent travellers and *datsu-sara* (people who have 'abandoned salary'), but it is escape from oneself and from hard reality to nowhere very definite.

Many people have therefore been creating their own alternative to the hotel, which they cannot afford and which they find too boring or constraining. Their goal is to meet people they do not know and see places that tourists do not visit. Hajj Sayyid, who walked around the world in the nineteenth century, now has many millions of successors doing the same. There is no contact between them and packaged tourists; governments can no more control them than they can make laws to order birds to leave their droppings only in appointed places; and urban planners, obliged to prioritise the needs of residents and businesses, have to try to forget that what brings life to a city, and what distinguishes a city from a dormitory, is the presence of strangers who are not searching simply for officially publicised sights. Tourism and travel are now the world's fastest growing industry, providing one-tenth of all employment, contributing more to GDP than automotive manufacturing, but hotels continue to be ruled by out-dated assumptions, combined with a desperate search for immediate profit to compensate for the ever increasing cost of maintaining their appearances with more fancy taps and fashionable décor. They have got stuck in the nineteenth- and twentieth-century dream of rising in the social scale, becoming a 'professional' and living ever more luxuriously; they have difficulty in waking up from it because the legacy of mediaeval guilds, which jealously controlled entry into each speciality in each branch of artisan activity, still dominates today's careers. Hoteliers now constitute a distinct profession, which means they must let other professions perform tasks they could very well do themselves; nobody wants to be like peasants of old, subject to the seasons, who in winter turned their hands to many productive activities quite different from agriculture.

The difference between a city and a dormitory

So hotels have not yet discovered what to do with themselves in unfavourable seasons, even though some can have many empty rooms in slack periods and not be full even when they are supposed to be busiest.

They do not need to limit themselves to supplying beds and meals. They

More ambitious consultants

do not need to believe twentieth-century consultants who preach 'change' as the road to salvation for business, but with change always heading for the same goals of profit and happiness, and every change therefore leading to yet another change, because they are never content that they have enough profit or happiness. The alternative to change is discovery, the difference being that discovery opens paths to hitherto unimagined goals. Technology understands what that means, but orthodox business wants predictable results. The explosion of tourism and the migration of labour are making hotels increasingly international, and multiplying the proportion of tourists whose purpose is not to wallow in luxurious beds, but to discover new people. There is an alternative to spending vast sums refurbishing hotels with more luxuries, so as to be able to increase prices, and that is to take more interest in the knowledge, imagination and ambitions of each individual tourist. Hotels now have the option of becoming intermediaries pioneering the creation of more profound and informed relationships between their guests, between their guests and the inhabitants of their city, and between the guests and the employees of the hotel. Just as the early American hotels helped to bring the migrants of their continent together through facilitating personal contacts, so hotels can, with comparable but different methods, make the world more aware of the variety, complexity and contradictions that are hidden by national

Global firms do not fulfill global roles

and professional norms. There are global chains of hotels, but they do not fulfil global roles.

Hotel guests may occasionally talk to taxi drivers, but they rarely have memorable conversations with the chambermaids earning the minimum wage who clean their rooms. Their rooms are not prison cells, because they are free to go out as they please, but like convicts, they often do not know where to escape to. About half of the guests in the hotel chain I studied said they were kept fully occupied by their business in the city, and just wanted to be left alone, but half, having finished what they had come to do, or while waiting for appointments, had many empty hours to kill, and knew nobody they could visit; when accompanied, they said they would like to get to know local families; when alone they would welcome invitations to meet local professionals who might teach them something useful for their own occupation. Sitting in the lobby of their hotel, they had no means of knowing that just a few feet away there was another silent guest who shared their interests. The concierge could get them tickets for theatres and recommend shops or restaurants, but did not know enough about each guest or about each inhabitant of the city to suggest meetings that could well be more interesting.

Silence in hotels

Packaged tourism has made the masses aware of strange places, but also revealed the difficulties of appreciating them. In a Tunisian seaside resort, most hotel guests on holiday were too exhausted by their jobs to want to do anything more than rest, and never spoke to the locals; they went back knowing very little more about the country they had visited, while the locals who cleaned their rooms and served their meals felt insulted by their lack of interest. In Cancun, the guests of the two hundred hotels that have been built there know nothing of the eruption of as many slums hidden behind them, whose inhabitants complain that though

Insults to hotel staff

tourism creates jobs and brings in money, four-fifths of the money tourists pay for their holiday goes to foreign operators, in a new kind of colonialism: 'We are ruled from outside.' Mass tourism has reached the limits of its inventiveness; people are not necessarily interested simply in escaping briefly from the realities of their own countries; there is not an infinite demand for resorts specialising in sex, drugs, casinos, alcohol, and a Westernised parody of foreign food. The Germans have coined a word to express the result: 'free time stress', *Freizeitstress*. The Orthodox Church has introduced prayers for 'those endangered by the Touristic Wave'. So there are inducements to experiment with other options.

*Dangerous
tourism*

The owner of the hotel chain I studied said, 'Make my hotel your laboratory.' But hotels are not laboratories; they are there to provide strictly defined services, not to invent. Hotel schools are teaching approved methods and routines, which is a different education from that of the customers whose desires they are supposed to satisfy. The more customers are educated, the more they say that one of their major aims is to learn new things, but hotels have yet to see themselves as institutions encouraging learning. And yet many of them are situated in places where they could be significant players in international relations and in the dialogue of civilisations. Diplomats can sign treaties promising friendship between nations, but private individuals decide for themselves whom they call a friend. There is no reason why hotels should always remain just passive providers of rooms in which outside organisations can hold conferences, when they could organise meetings and conversations themselves. Instead of just providing beds for tourists who spend the day out of doors visiting

*'Make my
hotel your
laboratory'*

ancient monuments, they can organise encounters between guests and local people that can transform present-day realities by creating personal sympathies that make a memorable difference to both parties. Instead of just pampering their guests with physical indulgences, they can interest themselves in their minds and hearts and win recognition as sources of cultural inspiration. Instead of guests leaving with nothing to take back except photographs and souvenirs, they can return as ambassadors for the country they have visited, ambassadors of a new kind, who speak not as representatives of millions, but as individuals made of many contradictions, who acknowledge the contradictions not only within nations but even more within the individuals they have met. It is not that such initiatives would be too expensive that makes hotels hesitate – because a business plan has shown how they could be profitable, particularly in slack periods – but rather that hoteliers do not have the training to implement them. Graduates in the humanities from top universities rarely decide to become hoteliers, but it is possible that more of them might; a few decades ago, no-one would have predicted that so many would become celebrity chefs.

Tourists as ambassadors

    The hotel chain I studied prides itself on offering old world comfort and civility, on the model of the 'country house'. But the country house offered much more than comfort. It was where the governing classes could meet and get to know each other; they went there for conversations with interesting people, to cultivate sociability and to promote both urban and rural virtues. The more the host and hostess could dazzle their guests with art and culture, the greater their reputation. Hotels can organise

Much more than comfort

structured conversations at which their guests can get to know different kinds of people from the surrounding city, and they can create portraits of individuals from many occupations and backgrounds, revealing the diversity of interests which normally remain hidden from visitors. For hotels to become not elite salons but centres of discussion with a wider range of participants would have been difficult in the past, but it is now possible to recognise that employees of hotels include many individuals of talent who are keen to play a more significant social role as hosts and hostesses, and who are interesting persons from whose extraordinary experiences in many parts of the world the guests have much to learn; and to whom they have much to give. The superficiality of communication between the two is a relic of outdated prejudices. Learning no longer means just acquiring information, but learning with and from others, with a desire to pass on one's learning, a desire to give, and a concern for those one has helped to learn. Learning has become reciprocal, displacing the ideal of 'customer service' that still dominates the business agenda. Hotels try hard to win the loyalty of their guests, by distributing trivial gifts and little privileges, but guests would be more loyal if they could give the hotel something that only they could give, their knowledge and their experience.

Since so many hotel workers want to learn a new language, why are they not also language schools? Not just because chambermaids have to clean fourteen rooms a day, after which they are too exhausted to study, but more because the middle managers in charge of them do not think that is what hotels do; as one said, 'I teach chambermaids to be chambermaids.' Since hotels are often situated near universities, and employ students part-time, why have they not investigated what they could do together, for both guests and students? Why do they not have more active relations with professional, cultural and charitable organisations? At present they are at best only mildly flirtatious with them; they would be very different if they had the courage to couple with them and publicly assert an ambition to become a source of moral, cultural, spiritual or intellectual inspiration, to be recognised as a muse, and not simply as a Michelin recommendation. A good night's sleep is a wonderful boon, but a good conversation remains in the memory much longer and can bear more precious fruits.

The courage to couple

25

What more can the young ask of their elders?

IN 1831, WHEN TRIESTE WAS an important and prosperous free port, a sort of Mediterranean precursor of Hong Kong, a group of men of many nationalities held a momentous meeting. They were there to do business, but business, as so often happens, was not what they cared about most deeply. One wrote poetry in Hebrew, which was described as being 'of some merit'; two were Italian revolutionaries who went on to participate actively in overthrowing the governments of their country; one, who originated from Frankfurt, had ambitions to become an aristocrat and eventually ended up as a baron in Hungary. Their great business idea

The plot to abolish worry

was that it was time to insure 'the security of the life of man in all its ramifications'. They wanted to protect not just against maritime losses or natural disasters – as they and others had done before – but to remove worry about the future in general. They founded the Generali Insurance Company, which within a couple of decades had branches all over the world, from Alexandria to China and the U.S.A. Very little is known about the personal lives of the original founders; they have disappeared into almost total oblivion even amongst those who work for the company. Still less is known about what difference the company has made to the happiness of each of the individuals – numbering 85,000 today – who spent their lives in its offices. The only one of its employees the world remembers is Franz Kafka (1883–1924), one of the rare people to describe what it feels like to be a cog in the great machine that is the insurance industry. W. H. Auden called Kafka 'the Dante of the twentieth century', and indeed insurance is more than an industry; it is almost a religion, dedicated to exorcising fear, and a large part of humanity willingly makes regular votive offerings to it.

Kafka on insurance

Kafka found insurance 'highly interesting': he specialised in factory accidents, and was well regarded by his colleagues, whom he admired as 'models of stability and conscientiousness'; he was himself very conscientious too, performing his duties with exceptional efficiency. But he also hated his job, 'this horrible occupation'. In vain did he try to console himself by saying 'I suppose one must earn one's grave.' After a year he moved to another insurance company because he was disgusted by a colleague being 'upbraided in a particularly offensive manner'. His employers did not understand and explained his resignation as 'enervation connected with extreme cardiac excitability'. But the new job was no better, despite its shorter hours; Kafka still complained of sleepiness in the office and being exhausted at the end of each day, even though he spent a lot of time gazing out of the window, fantasising about girls, joking and discussing literature. He had obtained qualifications in law only because he had not known what to do with his life, but this work was not life. 'Every morning coming to the office I used to be overcome with such despair that a stronger, more consistent character than mine might have committed suicide quite cheerfully.' His dream that insurance might

'This horrible occupation'

take him to foreign parts so that he could 'look out of the office window } at sugar-cane fields or Moslem cemeteries' never became reality. And yet his energy was not destroyed. Once he got out of the office, though 'the depression of having to go back was already beginning', he had a busy social life, numerous affairs, visited brothels, enjoyed pornography, while remaining, as his best friend noted, 'tortured by sexual desire'. He had a particular passion for cabaret: 'I believe I have a deep, an immensely deep understanding for it and enjoy it with my pulse racing.' But it was in literature that he found his 'blood-brothers' and through literature he revealed the absurdities and nightmares that haunted him. 'It is through writing that I keep a hold on life', and 'writing means revealing oneself to excess.' Or else it was 'a form of prayer'.

Safer to be in chains

Working in insurance did not cure Kafka of his fears, or the dread that whoever he met would find him ugly, but it allowed him to meditate on what he could do in response to fear. He concluded that his fears were 'probably the best part of me'. Insuring against them might not be the best answer, though he appreciated that for some it was 'often safer to be in chains than to be free'. Is it possible that that insurance has still not found its full vocation?

Insurance and Enlightenment

If insurance is almost a religion, why has it not had a Reformation? Insurance companies are still following in the footsteps of their eighteenth-century founders. They are the children of the philosophy of the Enlightenment, bravely abandoning the conviction that whatever happened was God's will, and that to challenge God was to invite divine punishment. They espoused the new scientific attitude, seeking to win mastery over nature and to defeat its unpredictable whims. But at the same time as offering rational, mathematically calculated guarantees of security, they anchored their appeal in a deep emotion: fear. Insurance mitigated fear. Insurance has become the protector against an ever-widening range of fears, and also a stimulant of anxieties never before imagined. Almost every human activity is now held up as potentially dangerous and needing insurance. More profit can predictably be made from insurance against fear than from the occupations and objects that are insured.

However, newly educated generations are increasingly being moved by other emotions and ambitions which compete against fear. As the young win more independence and are encouraged to seek the immediate satisfaction of every desire, their attachment to the age-old faith in thrift, on which all previous civilisations have been based, has weakened. They may want security, but many also want adventure and excitement, now, today, and they cannot be easily interested in pensions or prudence. Moreover, money is no longer enough. They want, even more, what money cannot buy – which means, above all else, fulfilling lives and warm personal relationships.

Emotions for which there is no insurance

That is something the insurance industry has not yet caught up with. It has minimal contact with the young. It assumes the young are in any case too poor to be worth soliciting for investments. But the young are making large investments in other industries – music, fashion, mobile phones, video games – because these help them to develop personal relationships. Insurers have forgotten the long history of the efforts of rebellious young people to obtain a sense of self-worth and appreciation from their elders, to win more freedom, to expand their horizons and to satisfy their hunger for friendships that their families often judge to be unsuitable. Nor has the insurance industry made use of the energies that inspired so many of humanity's inventions. It offers a negative protection, promising monetary compensation after the event, with no relevance to juvenile aspirations. Why has it not invented a more proactive kind of insurance that would interest the young and also respond to the changes in contemporary ambitions? Why instead of Disaster Insurance, which palliates fears about property and old age, does it not offer Opportunity Insurance, when more and more people yearn for access to opportunities closed to them?

Disaster Insurance and Opportunity Insurance

Before insurance companies were invented, there were other kinds of insurance systems which contained proactive elements, with advantages (and disadvantages) over those which exist today. Families, churches, fraternities and friendly societies provided several of the services that are now so costly. What they had in common was that they placed personal interaction, and not money, at their heart. They offered practical help, emotional comfort, sociability and ritual. But now in many countries where the family is smaller and more self-contained than it used to be, and where religions have lost their once-dominant position, the friendly societies which gave the poor mutual aid and a sense of belonging have been destroyed by the impersonal welfare state. That is why fundamentalist religious organisations are the most rapidly growing insurance groups today, attracting all age and occupational categories, offering not a written contract, nor a mass solution, but face-to-face personal help to each

individual's particular needs for work, housing, friendship, social acceptance, meaning and purpose. The insurance industry, by opting to become
impersonal, corporate, anonymous, bureaucratic, and demanding that
everything should be transacted with precise documentation and accountancy, cut itself off from its convivial past.

Kafka's verdict was not that of a hostile outside critic but of one who
had played the insurance game successfully according to its own rules and
could understand why it had evolved the way it did. He protested that
bureaucracies 'transform living, changing human beings into dead code
numbers incapable of any change', and that though people could enjoy
their secure office jobs, they could also hate them for imprisoning their
imagination. Serious limitations resulted from the arbitrariness and irrationality concealed behind supposedly fixed rules, and from indifference
to the absurd injustices these could perpetrate. In what other direction
could insurance go if it took more heed of the frustrations of its own and
its customers' imaginations?

*The imagi-
nation of
office workers*

Insurance companies invented a money equivalent of chloroform that
promises peace of mind, based on mathematical calculations which
guaranteed them a profit, and they did well throughout a long period of
prosperity accompanied by the flourishing of many anxieties. The more
possessions people have, the more they have to lose; the more comforts
they enjoy, the more they want them to continue; so laws were passed
making certain kinds of insurance compulsory and others more seductive
through taxation privileges. Insurance and pension funds became highly
influential investors, determining the shape of civilisation, using the

criterion of safe monetary returns but without asking their customers what else they might want. Their focus was money, assuming money could put right what went wrong, and could ensure that life went on ticking like clockwork. But half the world's population is under twenty-five and has no money, or very little, and has rather different passions. How can insurance and youth cease to inhabit separate planets?

Keeping a life ticking like clockwork

No established industry can be expected to change its staid habits, but when such large numbers are alienated from it, when the aged become too numerous to be supported by those who work, and when therefore the continued viability, the very existence of insurance is threatened, there is a case for trying out something different; it would be no threat if carried out on a small scale, side by side with traditional procedures, just to see what alternatives there are. Science and technology are always experimenting, but organised professions are often prisoners of the vested interests of their members. And yet, though insurers are the embodiment of caution, they have been adventurous in their own way over the past 150 years, without offending the values of respectable society. Assicurazioni Generali moved on from being a marine insurer to become a landowner, a banker, an asset manager, an adviser to industry, a supplier of personal domestic assistance, and even an educationalist when its German branch established Europe's largest technical university. However, neither it nor any other insurer imagined that its function might be to get involved in the seemingly trivial ambitions of the young. So instead it was the mobile phone industry that offered insurance to young people against their most dreadful fears, which were boredom, loneliness and lack of appreciation.

Insurance against loneliness

When in 2006 the value of the youth mobile phone market passed a hundred billion dollars, insurers did not appreciate the relevance to their own future of this milestone, which indicated that vast numbers of young people were now desperately searching for friends and allies on the social networks, and that what they needed most urgently was liberation from their frustration at finding it so difficult to get satisfying jobs, better education and exciting foreign travel. Money was not enough: by itself it could not introduce them to strangers with influence who could help them and make their future more interesting. The more they looked beyond their own countries, the more they needed personal contacts to help them. But nowhere could they get Opportunity Insurance that would guarantee them access to the kind of life they craved.

An insured person has so far never been expected to have anything to say to another insured person, apart from complaining about a company's finding bureaucratic reasons to wriggle out of its promises. But it is possible to imagine Generali (or its competitors) realising that there might be advantages if they did talk. It has thirty million policy holders who are unused assets, because they have knowledge, experience and networks capable of helping the young with many of their most pressing concerns. The redistribution of knowledge between the generations requires not a revolution but a rethinking of how people spend their waking hours.

Rethinking how people spend their waking hours

The advantage that insurance companies have over social internet sites is that they can survive only by being trusted to support the life expectations of their customers, but they have so far restricted themselves to a narrow interpretation of that purpose, defining themselves as financial institutions engaged in monetary transactions. Yet even if they only communicate with customers annually or when a claim is made, their success depends on deepening mutual trust. Nothing fosters trust so much as appreciation of one's talents. All policy holders have talents of one kind or another, but they are not given a chance to demonstrate or use these within the company, to feel that they have joined a community where they can exchange their knowledge among themselves, not just for mutual benefit but also for the public good.

A chance to demonstrate one's talents

Of course, companies feel safer sticking to their 'core' business, but airline companies have been bold enough to envisage offering air travel that is completely free, earning income instead from selling other services to their customers. Major oil companies make more money from the shops they have added to their filling stations than from the sale of petrol. Google's income comes not from its brilliant search engines, but from its attractiveness to advertisers. Cinemas rely on profits from selling confectionery in the interval, not just from tickets.

Job-hunting by word-of-mouth

Insurers have not yet recognised that they command a huge and unused repository of information about three of the vital ingredients of life, a job, education and travel. It is universally acknowledged that many jobs are obtained indirectly, through knowing the right people, and that the attractiveness of a particular job cannot be discovered without inside information. And yet insurance policy holders are not given the opportunity to be useful to one another, and to the next generation whose sights are on more immediate matters than insurance. The more difficult it is for the young to obtain work that suits them, the more they need the aid of those with personal experience of the realities behind the façades. As job seekers deliberately avoid committing their whole life to one employer, the need for contacts becomes ever more important: Why cannot Generali's customers break the silence that separates those who have work and those who do not?

Or indeed the silence between the educated and those struggling to become educated? Increasing numbers are keen to study outside their home country, but have access to only very limited local guidance, and when they arrive friendless in a strange land, they often end up consorting mainly with their own compatriots. Official brochures become not just inadequate but even misleading for the sophisticated choices that need to be made. While students can safely postpone worrying about what will happen to their dependants when they die, they urgently need better ways of solving their immediate problem of being short of money, and of finding someone who will help them get full or part-time work, ideally interesting work. In China, four million students (a quarter of the student population) are classified as living in poverty. In India a bank has established that personal advice is more valued and more beneficial than mere cash or loans. The managers of insurance companies insist that this is none of their business. But are the young really none of their business?

The silence of the educated

When young people become more adventurous in their travels, whether searching for the exotic or the thrill of unexpected challenges, insurance against danger is not their main preoccupation. When they set out to explore the unknown, to penetrate the secrets of strangers, and to consciously take risks, they are not interested in mass-produced tourism

The thrill of unexpected challenges

for tired workers, in safe hotels and on safe beaches, in pre-booked packages, guaranteed by travel insurance. They need to know on whose door they can knock in whatever place they find themselves. So too do the elderly. One-third of Britons aim to retire abroad, and four-fifths want to travel abroad after retirement. Compensation for catastrophe is not enough; hope is more important, especially the kind of hope that money *The hope that* cannot buy, the hope that one's knowledge and experience might be useful *money* to people one would not ordinarily meet, and the hope that one could *cannot buy* learn from others what one never imagined could be interesting.

Insurance companies do not benefit from hiding behind meaningless names. In mediaeval times, when universities were first invented, *Studia Generali* was the name given to the courses they offered, which were very different from what universities teach today, in that they were an introduction to universal knowledge, to all the information then available. The Generali Group could make use of that coincidence, and other insurance companies could begin to choose names which reveal what really distinguishes them. To become a customer of Generali could mean being a member of a new kind of institution that is dedicated, in addition to its more prosaic commercial activity, to broadening people's horizons and *Freedom* freeing them from parochial illusions. *from*
parochial
illusions Insurance companies are among the richest but also most secretive institutions in the world. Generali's assets include ownership of some of Europe's most important historical monuments. The company would become much more than a business if its customers could feel that by investing in it, they are performing a cultural act, and becoming guardians

of their heritage too, raising the level of appreciation of that heritage, particularly if that included festivities which reasserted the vanished identification of insurance with sociability, and provided occasions for forging social and intellectual links between customers, shareholders and employees. The impersonality of modern business is a new phenomenon that goes counter to all traditional wisdom.

The most secretive institution

There is no need to treat office employees like caged animals, let out only occasionally for business-related meetings or training; and no need for that training to be so narrowly focused. Corporate universities are indeed sprouting everywhere, but they are still pale imitations of real universities, because their mission has not gone beyond producing measurable increases in profit, rather than enlivened minds. They have not yet expanded their ambition to include encouraging serious general reflection on broader issues, on how work and business could be re-invented to meet more of humanity's ideals, so that outsiders would want to attend and listen and participate, and the reward would be that they would acquire a reputation as institutions which the public values quite apart from the products sold.

Gambling is another unrecognised competitor of insurance premiums. As people become disappointed that their ambitions will not be fulfilled, gambling offers the delightful fantasy of being able to retire immediately. Gamblers are spending an estimated thousand billion U.S. dollars annually worldwide, roughly as much as the global expenditure on military defence, and gambling is expanding faster than insurance: in France, for example, stakes have doubled in real terms in the past twenty-five years.

Spending as much on gambling as on armies

Between 1 and 2 per cent of GNP is devoted to gambling in different European countries, and seemingly more in China and Japan. Insurers, however, would be able to have many more winners; they are not funeral undertakers; they serve the living, and they are able to devote a significant slice of their profits to finance scholarships, travel and adventure for the young, not just the token sums they now allocate in the name of corporate social responsibility.

'Worse things than death'

Woody Allen once said, 'There are worse things than death. If you've ever spent an evening with an insurance salesman, you know exactly what I mean.' If the insurance industry contributed more to helping people to help one another, not just anonymously by pooling their premiums, but by increasing their mutual understanding, they would give a new direction to the fight against fear. The famous phrase 'We have nothing to fear but fear itself' is not a solution. Fear cannot be permanently destroyed, but it can be smothered or forgotten when minds become wholly absorbed in new and exciting adventures. That is why insuring against fear is not enough, and why insurance companies are incomplete, and why there is a future for those of them that open up new opportunities to the isolated, the worried and the hopeful.

[26]

Is remaining young at heart enough to avoid becoming old?

T HE BRAZILIAN ARCHITECT Oscar Niemeyer (1907–2012) continued designing amazing buildings and going to his office every day until his death at the age of 104. Did he set a model for those afraid of growing old?

Niemeyer knew what he wanted at a young age and remained steadfastly loyal to the values he embraced then. Professionally, he wanted to liberate architecture from the stranglehold of the right-angle that kept buildings square. Why could houses not have curves, he asked, like the landscape, and flowers, and women, and everything else in nature; why could it not aim at beauty instead of 'structural logic' and 'functionalism', why could it not be in harmony with nature, and instead of reproducing monotonous glass boxes, why could it not 'astonish'? Architecture was, for him, an art, whose purpose was pleasure, and he remained an 'artist in concrete' all his life, devoted to 'pure invention', showing the miracles that could be achieved with reinforced concrete. Being an artist meant that he had the freedom to design as he pleased. His response to those who expressed puzzlement at the look of his buildings was: 'You have never seen a shape like this before.'

The stranglehold of the right-angle

However, he wanted not only to produce art but also to 'change society', to end inequality, injustice and poverty. He joined the Communist Party and never changed his mind about it, even when it grew old and feeble. But he combined his belief in the brotherhood of man with a profound patriotism; he was deeply attached to Brazil, furious when foreigners bad-mouthed it, insistent that what faults it had were due to its being a new country, and therefore full of promise, destined to achieve, after centuries of exploitation by Europeans, what old civilisations, encumbered with rigid traditions, could not: it was the land of the future. At the same time, he maintained an interest in all forms of 'humanism'. 'For me, reading

The impor-
tance of
reading

is fundamental. Never underestimate the importance of reading: it's neces-sary to always read, especially about subjects not related to the profession ... never let the more technical disciplines weaken or negatively influence creative intuition.' And writing was equally necessary. He designed in words as well as in drawing, alternating between the two.

When asked what his priorities were, however, he always placed family and friends first. A family was 'a lifelong friendship ... We are all very close, we stick up for each other.' He remembered with pleasure his upbringing, when parents did the talking and children respectfully obeyed, and in later years he handed over the running of his architectural practice to one of his

What
is most
important?

five grand-daughters. His autobiography is a long paean of praise for his friends, and how they were all wonderful, each in a special way. 'Life is more important than architecture ... Life is to know how to behave, to take pleasure in being amiable and just ... Life is a woman by your side.' Two years after his 75-year marriage ended with his wife's death, he married again, at the age of ninety-nine. The benefit of old age, he said, was that it produced serenity. 'In the past I often clashed with those who rejected my ideas as an architect. Not anymore. After all, they are defending what they have achieved over the years as good professionals. Time goes by, and I welcome all kinds of architecture.' It was the same with the endless disagreements within the Communist Party: 'There were so many different and controversial characters that only the common denominator of great friendship could hold us together . . . As I age, a warm feeling of fellowship is taking over my heart, overcoming old resentments, I am seeing the good side in everybody.'

Is that the wisdom that only old age can achieve? No, it was only a pretence. Niemeyer was tormented by the brevity of life. 'Death was a constant concern . . . When I was a young man of only fifteen, I was anguished to think of man's destiny . . . Over time, these thoughts have occurred with increasing frequency . . . I have tried to cast aside the disturbing thoughts that so afflicted me when I was alone. I wore a mask of youthful optimism and contagious good humour. I was known as a high-spirited and spontaneous personality, a lover of the bohemian life-style, while deep inside I nursed tremendous sorrow when I thought about humanity and life.' Only the constant company of friends could banish this gloom, and the tragedy of old age was that old friends passed away. Despite his atheism, he did not discard religion's preoccupation with death. Art was his salvation. But art that is the expression of a single imagination is the art of solitude.

Wisdom and pretence

The art of solitude

Niemeyer loved the optimism of communism, its conviction that a better world was possible and imminent, and its ability to recover from all disappointments, just as Christians have remained undismayed by the repeated postponement of the Messiah's return. But deep down he did not believe that it was possible to change people much; despite his dedication to creating a better world, there was a 'fatalism' in him that he only sometimes acknowledged: life is 'what destiny gives us'. Despite his patriotism, he did not believe that Brazil deserved its 'stereotypical image of a friendly, uncomplicated society', and he asked: 'When shall we transform Brazil into a land of friendship and solidarity? Our labouring brothers are getting poorer all the time.' Worst of all, they did not share his grand vision: 'Our people live in such abject poverty that our poorest brothers just want a small lot where they can build a miserable hut.' When asked why he designed mainly grand public buildings, he said the poor who passed by could be invigorated by their beauty, which meant 'strange and unforeseen forms'. He was more cautious than Le Corbusier, who insisted that the purpose of architecture was to change life; he preferred to say it was to give pleasure by creating beauty. But there were limits to 'the power of beauty'.

Fatalism

The power of beauty

Niemeyer's response to disappointment was generosity. He loved helping others; even if his gifts did not make any permanent changes, at least they gave a moment of happiness. He had 'a lifelong disdain for money,' he said, and often worked for low fees or no fee at all. His daughter complained, when his bank balance was low, 'Dad, just stop helping everybody.' When being a communist became a crime, and he was persecuted by the police and fled into exile, he was proud that he publicly stood by his communist friends. What was important, he said, was to remain true to one's convictions and to go on protesting. But he was conscious that with time old friends just told one another the same old stories.

Niemeyer achieved one of humanity's most ancient ambitions, to live as long as possible in good health, but it was not because he remained young at heart. Neither his bonhomie nor his architectural genius ever extinguished the gloom that infected him in adolescence and that he could never get rid of. Those who talk about remaining young into old age forget how much fear there is in childhood and how much uncertainty in adolescence. The realities of youth and old age are no longer what they used to be.

If I were living among the Visigoths after the collapse of the Roman empire, once I was over sixty-five I would be worth a hundred gold coins, the same as a child under ten. An adolescent of fourteen was worth 140, an adult man up to the age of fifty was valued at 300 and a fertile woman between fourteen and forty at 250, but after that her worth was only forty, and after sixty almost nothing. These valuations express the fundamental concerns of a society where women's function was to produce children and men's to be strong warriors. But other valuations are possible.

The stigma of birthdays

It is only a half-truth that old men once ruled the world and enjoyed universal respect. Age was never a sufficient qualification for power. Old people who were incompetent or unhealthy were frequently neglected, indeed sometimes killed off, even in illiterate societies which depended on the memory of their traditions. There are records of the young challenging the old as far back as ancient Mesopotamia. In Athens, democracy overthrew gerontocracy, and only in Sparta did the over-sixties keep their ascendancy. Though Aristotle admired some aged philosophers, he also wrote that most old people were pessimistic, distrustful, malicious, suspicious, small-minded, and continually reminiscing about their past, but so humbled by their failures that they have no greater ambition than to remain alive. The Roman aristocracy was paralysed by bitter opposition between fathers and sons. In India, the old were encouraged by their religion to withdraw from worldly activity and prepare for death. 'Better is a poor and wise child', said the Old Testament, 'than an old and foolish king.' For all the supposed wisdom that experience produced, the ancient Egyptians hated the disabilities of age: Ptah Hotep, chief minister of the Pharaoh, said in 2450 B.C. that what old age does to man is evil – weakness, forgetfulness and pain. It was his civilisation that invented anti-aging wrinkle cream.

The disabilities of age

However, remaining young can be as difficult as being old. Youth continues to be both envied and denigrated as it always has been, both loved and repressed, over-sentimentalised and underpaid, sometimes admired for energy and 'innocence' and sometimes attacked for disobedience, licentiousness, frivolity and many other sins. Does remaining young mean one never stops growing? Does it mean rejecting the lifestyle of one's elders? Is it because the old have lost confidence in their own lifestyle that they tell their children to find their own way of being happy? And if youth is the model of physical fitness, why are so many young people in prosperous countries becoming monstrously unfit and obese? Children who used to participate in adult work are now protected from its

What does being young mean?

grim realities and exhorted to play instead, but at the same time they are compulsorily schooled to acquire the skills adults demand, and punished when they fail to integrate. They are encouraged to be themselves but are subjected to ceaseless training to improve them, by experts who keep changing their theories about what is wrong with them. They do not even own 'youth culture', which is commercialised so that participation is expensive, and the profits go elsewhere. Minorities among them may be rebellious or inventive or energetic, but the majority, according to social researchers, generally adopt the same values as their parents, and inherit the same religious convictions. In countries entering prosperity, many say their goal is to become rich, as though they cannot imagine anything different to replace their parents' failure to become rich.

The distinction between young and old has recently been confused by a radical transformation of their status, with both generations being eliminated from the active working population, the young by education and the old by retirement. Never before have so many able-bodied people been paid to be professionally inactive. But the old are too diverse in health and wealth to form a single category. Not all of them appreciate being officially branded as useless: retirement is a liberation for those who hate their work, but an insult to those who do not want a divorce from active society. The meaning of pensions keeps on changing; they were invented for the working masses in the late nineteenth century by Prussian landlords as a bribe to win them away from socialist revolution; but the workers originally rejected the whole idea of retirement, and American trade unions went on strike against it – with good reason,

Young and old out of work

because hard labour ruined the health of the poor, who seldom survived to enjoy their pensions for very long, and it was the middle classes who benefited most. Now that the whole pension system is collapsing because people are living longer, the idea of retirement is ready for retirement. If people live for a whole century, they cannot spend forty years working and forty years in retirement. No amount of financial wizardry could fund them. Something else has to be invented. Besides, now that half of young people in some countries are unable to find work, remaining young takes on a sinister meaning.

A new vision of the future emerges if, instead of being fixated on the differences between the old and the young, useful though the distinction sometimes is, one asks not how many years someone has lived, but how they have lived. A human head is an antiques shop full of bric-a-brac, of memories, habits, prejudices and fairy tales dating from a variety of centuries. Each life is partly shaped by a different mixture of ideas inherited from the past, and by emotions that contain traces and flavours from disparate epochs. Each person has not one age but many. It is not even true that the body ages gradually, that 'from hour to hour we ripe and ripe, and then from hour to hour we rot and rot': there is no such steady progression. Oscar Niemeyer's obsession with death, his fatalism, his roots in family, his passion for protest, for surprise and for curves, his loyalty and generosity and humanism, each reveal him drawing sustenance from traditions and ambitions of varying antiquity, and by mixing them he acquired a unique flavour. The quality of a life depends, in part, on how skilfully, how painlessly, how elegantly memories are combined to inspire

A human head is an antiques shop full of bric-a-brac

experiences that together achieve more than their different elements could alone. None of this can be measured in the number of years one has lived.

The antiques shop may constantly be replenished, or remain immobile gathering dust. One's physical age says nothing about the age of one's ideas. What is special about ideas is that they can resist the passage of time and remain fertile, capable of generating new ideas when embraced by new questions, or they can fossilise. Whereas sexual fertility is the flower of youth, intellectual fertility is what turns the silences between the past, the present and the future into music. Confucius hoped his disciples would aim at that when he said 'a man who brings warmth to old knowledge – or keeps cherishing his old knowledge – so as to acquire new knowledge, may be a teacher for others' (*Analects* 2.11). Everybody is constantly espousing, divorcing, ignoring, misunderstanding relics from past thoughts and only occasionally begetting new thoughts. A conversation that surprises, challenges, stimulates, soothes or inflames, because it rearranges these relics, helps one to see what is missing from one's life. In each of my chapters I have found myself being pushed into thinking beyond my existing beliefs after an encounter with a figure from the past who saw the world differently from me. In the twentieth century it became fashionable in some countries to limit oneself to excavating one's own personal and family memories as a way of reducing one's anxieties. But more interesting results come from exploring, outside one's own head, the ideas of people one never imagined could be one's ancestors, and the legacies of places far distant from any that one has visited. To aim to know only oneself is to

The age of one's ideas

Sexual fertility and intellectual fertility

choose to close one's ears to the screams that echo throughout history and to be unable to distinguish which are of joy and which of pain.

How alive a person is, not how old

How soon people become impervious to what others say is the second criterion by which one discovers how alive a person is, as opposed to how long they have lived. The interaction of a baby with its mother, the meeting of children and playmates, of adolescents and their heroes, of students and teachers, of lovers with their partners, are decisive steps in gradually becoming more aware of how others see the world. The process may slow down when one finds it difficult to make new friends or acquire new interests, or when one relies on social networks that create only superficial links. Very recently MRI scanning has suggested that the most important part of a meeting is what happens after the meeting ends: its effects depend on how much reflection is devoted to penetrating its significance,

Sleeping as a skill

and it is in sleep that this reflection is pursued with the greatest perseverance. When a person is asleep and is supposedly doing nothing, parts of the brain remain intensely active, using 20 per cent of the body's energy, a mere 5 per cent less than the brain uses when it is awake and attentive to specific problems requiring immediate attention. This activity is apparently dedicated to reviewing personal memories, present experiences and future possibilities as well as attempting to understand other people, constantly evaluating hypotheses about what might happen in the future, and trying to find ways of avoiding painful surprises. The implication is not just that what people do in their sleep may be as decisive as what they

A time for musing

do when they are awake, but even more that they do not give anything like enough time to musing on what they see and hear.

So the question Oscar Niemeyer raises is not how he succeeded in being
so active for so long, but how much he was reshaped by the people and   *Provocation*
ideas he met during his 104 years, how long he remained receptive to ideas
other than his own, how the books he read confirmed his own thoughts or
injected new ones. He only very partially answered these questions himself, but enough to show how valuable his early mentors were in making
him realise where he did not want to go; their importance was that they
were different from him, inciting him, by the strength of their personalities
and convictions, to discover what mattered more to him than their ideals,
and what he could do that they could not. He began as a pupil of the urban
planner Lucio Costa and as an admirer of Le Corbusier, twenty years his
senior, but he then made his own way independently of them, and became
more his own person. He moulded his own individuality under the provocation of others. When he moulded the concrete of his monuments he was
not just expressing his tastes, but creating them in the process of interacting with his mentors, his staff and his materials. Le Corbusier, whose
real name was Jeanneret, adopted his pseudonym saying everybody needed
to invent themselves. But this is not something one can do on one's own.
How it can happen can be seen more clearly by looking at Niemeyer's
fellow artists.

He was born in the same year as the first Cubist painting was publicly
exhibited, and while he was liberating architecture from the rectangle,
Cubism liberated painting from perspective. Georges Braque (1882–1963)
has something to add to Niemeyer's story, in that he too, in gradually
defining himself, needed a mirror, a mentor, a muse to clarify what he

was searching for. What Le Corbusier was to Niemeyer, Cézanne and
Picasso were to Braque. Discovering Cézanne forced Braque to 'rethink
everything' and 'fight against much of what we knew'. For six years, Braque
and Picasso met almost every evening, discussed each other's painting,
experimented together, even tried on each other's clothes and exercised
themselves painting in each other's style. Through this endless conversation, gradually Braque discovered that what he was interested in was
not painting which imitated nature, but creating a canvas that was an
independent entity, that had a life of its own, and that did not even need a
frame. He then decided that it was not the objects in his painting that
interested him, but their relationship, and he went on to realise that what
concerned him most was relationship, the gaps and the links between
people and objects and between them and him. This change in sensibility
was not just a new fashion in art. It was also the expression of a desire to
look at people or objects and appreciate them not by how much they
resembled ideal forms of beauty or respectability, but by their relationship
with oneself and with others, and by what they could contribute to one's
understanding of oneself and to the way one behaved. After looking at
Braque's paintings, a visitor exclaimed, 'I would go round the house and
say, my God, everything looks like a Braque.' There are many more possible connections in the world than those that custom and convention
notice. Seeing the world as others see it does not need to mean seeing it as
one age group supposedly sees it.

The undeniable fact that the young are generally considered to be
more beautiful than the old shows that the Visigoths' criteria are not dead.

*Cézanne
forced
Braque to
'rethink
everything'*

*Gaps and
links between
people and
objects*

The old who pretend that they are young may or may not be as beautiful as those who are really young, but they have other more interesting options   *Concealment* apart from copying the appearance and manners of a different generation. Ancient civilisations have used cosmetics and clothing, for example, to emphasise the dignity of individuals as hunters or warriors or communicators with the supernatural, often with great artistry. In more recent times, by contrast, as soon as middle age is reached, conspicuous personal decoration is abandoned, discreet dressing is adopted, as though no longer able or willing to proclaim what an individual experience can offer to the rest of society. Those who are ashamed of their failures congratulate themselves instead on giving the next generation a chance to do better, letting each person do their own thing. Whereas in the past the young were expected to copy the old, now the old are copying the young, but neither makes clear where they are going.

It has become more difficult to uncover what hides behind the façade of youth that has become fashionable, and behind the sagging faces of the elderly, but the world looks slightly different every time one does succeed. It sometimes requires no more than a smile to change what one understands about another. In a flea market outside Paris, I once came across an old woman standing all alone, poorly dressed, trying to sell a worn pair of shoes that she had placed before her on the pavement, but nobody was paying any attention to her and she looked the very image of misery and despair. But when I spoke with her, her eyes lit up and gradually she was transformed: she became animated, and the animation made her beautiful.

In 1415, one of the first books ever to be printed with movable type was *The Art of Dying*, a bestseller all over Europe for several centuries, because what happened after death was the subject everybody wanted to know about. People were all heading for an afterlife, and vast numbers still are. How old or young you were had less importance than it does now, following a steady hardening of expectations from different age groups, increasingly segmented. There is no longer anyone to compare with Shunzhi Fulin (1638–1661), who ruled the huge Chinese empire, quite effectively, when aged between twelve and twenty-two, or William Pitt (1759–1806) who became prime minister of England at the age of twenty-four, and was one of the most competent the country has ever had. Today, instead of asking people their age, it is more useful to discover how alive they are, and when they stopped having new thoughts. Age is often a disguise.

I do not ask people their age

Age is often a disguise

Niemeyer's extraordinary legacy is to be found not in the length of his life, nor in his inability to free himself from youthful fears; it survives in his buildings, but also in the equally original reconstruction of himself that he achieved through his collaboration with Le Corbusier, old enough to be his father.

27

What is worth knowing?

I LIVE IN THE INFORMATION AGE, the Knowledge Economy and the Lifelong Learning Society, and nevertheless feel profoundly ignorant. I am assured that with better technology, better management and better education, I will be cured. But it may take some time.

While I wait, I should like to know how to cope with ignorance. I shall try to decipher the little I know about the habits of my own brain, in the hope that it will encourage others to reveal what they know about theirs. Brain-life has more secrets than sex-life.

Brain-life has more secrets than sex-life

I have pursued knowledge since my earliest years, with unquenchable passion. I have embraced it in different ways at school, at university, as a teacher, author, researcher, and as an adviser to corporations and governments obese with information but still hungry for more. Nevertheless, I am incapable of understanding even a small portion of what there is to be known. I cannot remember half of what I was taught. Many of my students have probably forgotten the other half too. I am not writing the confessions of one who believes he can remain forever young by being a perpetual student rejuvenated by every new piece of knowledge. Rather, I am trying to reconstitute the itinerary of a truant, who has no illusions about knowledge. Education has been a panacea for virtually all human ills for many centuries, and yet, despite all the marvels it has brought,

some of humanity's worst follies have been perpetrated by highly educated individuals and nations. Minds crammed full of information have not always known what to do with it. The managers of knowledge have not been innocent of deceit. Politicians constantly respond to criticism by saying 'lessons have been learnt', but the mistakes do not stop. Faith in Lifelong Learning dates from at least the time of Hsun Tzu, who died in 238 B.C., and who wrote, too optimistically: 'Learning continues until death and only then does it stop.' If it is so difficult to avoid being led astray by what one learns, or to be sensible in putting what one learns into practice, where else does hope lie?

I could blame my failure to learn all I should learn on having been born too late. Around 1600, I could almost have read all the 400 English books published each year as they came out. Renaissance Men had an easier time than us. But today I am confronted with 200,000 new books annually, besides all other kinds of publications, journals and broadcasts. That figure excludes everything that is produced outside my little island. Half a million new books are published in the world each year. So human-

*A new phase
in the history
of ignorance*

ity is clearly entering a new phase in the history of ignorance.

Twenty years of my youth were spent writing my *History of French Passions*, reading almost non-stop; I could plausibly believe then that I had come fairly close to having seen most of the significant evidence available on my subject. But it would be impossible for me to write such a book today, because so much new evidence has been found, no individual can hope to master it. My experience should perhaps have warned me off expanding my ambitions still further to trying to understand what being alive has meant in all centuries and in all civilisations. I did not foresee, however, nor did anyone else, the huge cloud of ignorance that the explosion of university education would spread across the world. A tsunami of doctoral theses and professorial monographs has changed the landscape of knowledge. The widening of scholarly interests in many directions means that every time I want an answer to some question, however tiny, I risk being buried under a torrent of responses, a hurricane of facts never imagined before, and an onslaught of ever more ingenious explanations, each from a different point of view. The more information there is, the more ignorance there is.

What being alive has meant

I am by no means the first to realise this. Humans have always suffered from there being too much information (as well as too little, because one can never know enough). The ancient monuments that reveal this best are encyclopaedias. I first became aware of their magic when, barely eight years old, I received two of them as gifts from my father; and I have derived pleasure since then studying their varying criteria for selecting, manipulating and plagiarising facts and opinions. From the earliest times, the most significant encyclopaedias have been those that have not just tried to make information available in an easily digestible form, but have given it meaning, to ensure that it leaves people feeling nourished rather than bloated. Facts by themselves are worthless, mere grains of sand and spikes of seaweed on a beach, unless they are collected and their edible part extracted and cooked to make knowledge. Between the third and eighteenth centuries, over 600 Chinese encyclopaedias were compiled;

The digestion of information

Chinese en-cyclopaedias

they are almost the equivalent of the pyramids of Egypt: the Yongle encyclopaedia (1408) was the work of 2,169 scholars; the Encyclopaedia of 1726–8, 'the Imperially Approved Synthesis of Books and Illustrations Past and Present', was 852,408 pages long. The Chinese called their encyclopaedias 'classifications' (*leishu*), because they were essentially compilations of ancient texts presenting all existing knowledge about Heaven, Earth, Humans, Events, Arts and Sciences in a form that would ensure that the supposedly learned men who ruled the country knew what traditions needed to be followed, and so that examination candidates for public service (there were over a million of these every year in Ming times) knew what they had to remember. These encyclopaedias gave lonely facts a sense of purpose, and, incidentally, compiling them kept potentially subversive scholars absorbed by the minutiae of editing texts instead of questioning tradition. Putting information in order meant giving it a slant and a message, and the emperors devoted a lot of energy to controlling the message.

Islamic encyclo-paedias

The great mediaeval Islamic encyclopaedias did even more than that. They boldly attempted the synthesis of all known cultures, Mesopotamian, Greek, Indian, Iranian, Jewish and Arab, while at the same time propagating the particular opinions of the scholars involved: one of the most famous, the tenth-century encyclopaedia of the Brothers of Purity, for example, written in Basra, expressed their hope and expectation that government would soon wither away. By contrast, European philosophers like Bacon, Descartes and Leibnitz wanted information to be presented so that it could be used to make new discoveries. Diderot's Enlightenment

Encyclopaedia in twenty-seven volumes (1751–72) carried this ambition to an unprecedented level of subversion by attempting not a summary of existing knowledge but original research and social criticism aimed at reinventing government, religion, economics, education and much else. However, it had only limited success. Literacy failed to turn most people into philosophers or revolutionaries. Today, many encyclopaedias are timid summaries of what everyone believes, aids to help people converse politely, and to make superficial comments about fashionable names and Isms, concealing their ignorance. Harold Macmillan said the encyclopaedias he published aimed at no more than 'alleviating bewilderment'. Knowledge does not necessarily eliminate ignorance.

The failures of literacy

The internet is the heir to this long ancestry. Though it opens information of all kinds to a much wider audience, it does not make any sense out of it. Wikipedia, like the Chinese *leishu*, rejects facts which have not been previously printed, imagining that a footnote reference to a previous publication guarantees respectability. The internet has not diminished, far from it, the vast numbers of people for whom all knowledge originates in one book. The arrival on the scene of armies of Chief Information Officers and Knowledge Managers reorganising data so that it contributes to the prosperity of corporations and the survival of governments still leaves unanswered the question of what is worth knowing by ordinary people wanting to lead more interesting lives. These information experts are concerned with the processes by which information can be stored and handled, not by its detailed content, let alone its moral value. Savouring its poetry is not part of their job, and they are neither seers nor sages. So it

The limitations of the internet

is not surprising that humans today are no wiser than their ancestors.
What use is information if there is no wisdom? No-one claims that this is
the Age of Wisdom.

Where to find wisdom

However, my experience of struggling through the blizzards of information that make it so difficult to see ahead does not lead me to despair,
nor to pine for the supposed calm and simplicity of ancient times, nor
to feel any less excitement and satisfaction while learning. On rare occasions, the fear of revealing what is contained in the invisible encyclopaedia
that individuals carry in their head does vanish: in Paris in 1968, for
example, when state authority suddenly collapsed, I saw people unburden
themselves to complete strangers and say what they would normally
conceal; but they soon clammed up again. In this book I have tried to open
up the pages of the encyclopaedia inside my own head. I need to discover
what other heads contain, but not just to understand what is peculiar
about mine, or to prevent me bumping dangerously into others. I cannot
consider myself fully alive if I know only my own thoughts.

The invisible encyclo-paedia in one's head

The information I have accumulated in my head does not all point in
the same direction. Instead of disturbing me, this gives me a sense of freedom. Learning is only a beginning. Writing history, I have always searched
for truth, as honestly and diligently as possible, but when I finish, I realise
that I have written a work of fiction, for I have selected fragments of what
I perceive as the truth and pieced them together in my own way to create
a picture that seems plausible to me. Nobody can re-create or remember
the past exactly as it was. I applaud artists who have shown that the world
is much more than it appears to the casual glance and who have had the

Writing fiction

courage to rearrange its elements as a way of extracting more profound messages. Like them, I have also sought to liberate the memories of the past from the iron chains of chronology, by juxtaposing events and ideas from different contexts so as to illuminate their universal significance. The past for me is not a string of stories but an imaginative creation of beauty and horror out of the totality of human experience. Creating knowledge is an art. That is very different from imbibing information or eliminating ignorance.

Inventing beauty and horror

One day, I received a cutting from a Chinese business magazine. It had interviewed a famous visitor from the West, one of those rare people who has influenced almost everyone's life all over the globe. He had been my student some thirty years earlier; he became the venture capitalist who was the first to invest in Google, Yahoo, eBay, humble start-ups that eventually changed the world. He was asked who had been the greatest influence on his career. He named me, and gave this reason: I had taught him that things are not what they appear to be. It is unusual for a teacher to be understood by a pupil. But he saw precisely the true measure of my ignorance. Every time I encounter an object, a person or an experience, I do not see only it, but also how else it could be. I am always asking myself: How could it be otherwise? This is the question that has made humans what they are today, for without it we would still be living in tree-tops. Which is why I ask what else can be done about ignorance, apart from battling against it with yet more information and endless learning.

Things are not what they appear to be

My answer to the question 'What is worth knowing?' is this: what matters is not just how much knowledge I have, but what I do with my knowledge. The process of creating something useful and beautiful out of what I learn does not resemble building a house out of bricks that have been ordered in advance. It is more like painting a picture which gradually takes shape. As I add and subtract colours and contours, each opens up possibilities that I did not imagine beforehand, and I rush off to deepen my understanding of them, and research new territories, which in turn open up new vistas and new meanings for the too naïve or simple thoughts I began with. I usually end up with a creation quite different from the one I originally envisaged. That is how I select what I want to know, a process that is all the more unpredictable in its outcome because it draws me to places of whose existence I might previously have been unaware. The excitement reaches a peak when the people or places or ideas that hitherto seemed unrelated or irrelevant come together to suggest some new insight to me, and are able to do the same for others.

Unpredict-
able thoughts

I owe to my wife Deirdre Wilson an appreciation of the importance of relevance. She is the co-inventor of the theory of relevance which has helped to overturn what people have believed about communication ever since Aristotle. Communication is not a simple matter of sending messages and having them decoded and understood in the way the sender intended. Messages are understood and new knowledge acquired depending on how much relevance the receiver can find in them, given that each person has a limited background of knowledge, and a varying amount of willingness or energy to extract their implications. The more numerous the implications, and the less effort required to find them, the greater the relevance will be. Inevitably, there is an element of guess-work in understanding

The theory of
relevance

what implications others intend us to find. Communication is a battle with uncertainty. So I am aware that much of the knowledge I deal with is malleable or diluted. I have no use for dogmatism. This does not mean that I consider all opinions as equally worthy of respect and all truths relative. The discoveries we make are indeed always subject to revision, but we can strive for the truth, even though it is so often beyond our grasp. That endless search on the frontiers of ignorance is as much one of life's great delights as constantly expanding one's taste for strange foods.

Though I express my excitement at the imaginative possibilities that knowledge offers by using metaphors from art, I am sustained also by the rather similar attitudes that scientists have recently adopted, abandoning the certainties of the nineteenth century for an almost poetic interaction with the mysteries of the universe. 'Even the mathematically formulated claims of physics', wrote Heisenberg of quantum fame (1901–1976) 'are in some sense only word-paintings in which we try to make the experience of nature known and understandable to ourselves and to others.' 'What we call scientific knowledge today is a body of statements of varying degrees of certainty . . . It is of paramount importance that we recognise this ignorance and doubt,' added Richard Feynman (1918–1988); 'the first principle of science is that you must not fool yourself . . . I always live without knowing.' The Principle of Uncertainty can apparently be inter-preted in at least six different ways. The Principle of Complementarity was announced in a lecture that is considered to be a landmark in the annals of physics but also one of its most incomprehensible texts, a 'juxtaposition of several coexisting arguments addressed to different quantum theorists

Science as 'word painting'

about different issues'. It was not only Dostoyevsky who wrote 'polyphonic novels'.

So I do not regard ambiguity as an enemy, nor do I consider disagreement a pest to be eradicated. New ideas almost inevitably excite disagreement. Knowledge is the child of disagreement. I do not expect people to agree with me, which is why I am not preaching to you. When the historian Braudel, whose biography I was once invited to write, said wistfully that there was only one person in the world who fully understood him, he was uncharacteristically forgetting that misunderstanding is the eternal companion of most human relationships.

Misunder-
standing is
the eternal
companion

For long, I did not understand the education I received. It taught me to sharpen my critical faculties, but was less interested in imagination, even though only imagination could turn criticism into a constructive thought. Academia is a zoo where different species of minds irritate and exasperate one another saying 'I do not think like you'. It is not easy for heads of different shapes, with contrary opinions, to imbibe new thoughts from one another. And yet, 'Science is rooted in conversation,' as Heisenberg said. His memoirs, *Physics and Beyond*, written in the form of dialogues, have as their subtitle *Encounters, Conversations*. The two greatest discoveries of the twentieth century, in quantum physics and genetics, are now documented as having been the fruit of long, long conversations between people of differing points of view. 'Science rests on experiments; its results are attained through talks among those who work in it and who consult one another about the interpretation of these experiments.' Full agreement brings invention to a halt. Niels Bohr (1885–1962)

'Science is
rooted in
conversation'

was famous for growing his ideas out of innumerable conversations with students and colleagues, inviting over 400 visitors to his laboratory to stay for over a month. He insisted that ideas acquire life when they are conveyed and understood by others. He even concluded that 'the task of physics is not to find out how nature is but what we can say about nature. Humans depend on words. Our task is to communicate experiments and ideas to others. We are suspended in language.' And he devoted the rest of his life to the language of science and the way people communicate.

These revelations strike a chord with me. Though I enjoy suddenly finding something significant in what superficially seems trivial, I only appreciate what I have learnt from a conversation or from a book the *In praise of* morning after. Some ancients have found the solution to problems in their *the morning* dreams. Not I. It is in the first moments of wakening, after having gone to *after* bed puzzling over information I cannot make sense of, that I have flashes of thought in which ideas that have been floating around in my mind link up and assume a meaning I had not suspected; but these sudden intuitions do not necessarily produce an answer that can be reconciled with all the facts; and I may go through the process many times before I am satisfied that I have something coherent. I do not offer this as a method to be copied, any more than I quote the great scientists as examples to be imitated. I find it comforting to read about the struggles that other minds have had and the many years of rumination that have preceded a discovery.

It is therefore impossible to know in advance what is worth knowing; only when one piece of knowledge meets another piece of knowledge do they discover whether they have anything to say to each other, and the link is made by the unpredictable spark of an individual imagination. As it is, most ideas that spring in human heads never meet what could be their muse. So every morning I would like to include in my breakfast a taster of a new book from any part of the world, in any subject, summarised in a thousand words, whose author has something to say that may be of universal interest, though it might escape the attention of most people because it is imprisoned in the category-cage of a speciality. It would require some effort on the part of the authors who may have spent years writing their fat books to say in a couple of pages what their message is, since it is hard to guess who might find relevance in their work. But those half million books that appear each year are part of humanity's struggle with ignorance, and they are part of the world I want to connect with. I have put my breakfast idea on my website, and will discover where it leads.

The sieve in my head

What is very much worth knowing is the shape of the pattern that I impose on the facts that pour into my head, and the shape of the sieve that discards so many of them. That becomes visible only by comparison with other people's patterns and sieves, which is why I need you to tell me what you have discovered about your predilections, what you see and what you do not, though you will not know that until you compare this with those of many others. But in addition, I can never have enough of the practical know-how which enables me, for example, to grow vegetables or repair broken objects; I delight in the company of those who have mastered many such skills and find unexpected solutions for the myriad dysfunctions that afflict daily living. Nothing has been so damaging as the separation between abstract and practical knowledge. The great advantage that people had until about 1830 was they were able to participate actively in numerous branches of science and the humanities, with Leonardo da Vinci's famously varied inventions demonstrating how beneficial that could be. Now that each branch of learning has become so specialised, demanding that attention should be concentrated for many years on a few minute details, the interaction between amateur skills and expert learning has become more precious than ever. The most influential discoveries have been made unexpectedly, and have depended on freedom from preordained targets and freedom from too much certainty about the inevitability of things being the way they are.

Freedom from targets

The Lifelong Learning Society may not be the ultimate goal. Endlessly consuming knowledge is highly pleasurable, but to be obese with knowledge can be damaging to mental health. If I get the chance to try out my alternative to academia, I shall describe it in my next book, together with all the other themes on which my thoughts still need to mature, under the influence of practical trial and error.

My alternative to academia

28

What does it mean to be alive?

'STRANGER, MY MESSAGE IS SHORT,' says an ancient Roman inscription. 'Stand by and read it. Here is the unlovely tomb of a lovely woman. Her parents called her Claudia. She loved her husband with all her heart. She bore two sons, of these she leaves one on earth; under the earth she has placed the other. She was charming in converse, and gentle in bearing. She kept house, she made wool. That's my last word. Go your way.'

Inscriptions on grave-stones

Two thousand years later, gravestones say much the same, and usually less, about what having lived means. What else can people say today? This Roman text summarises the ancient common sense view that the purpose of life is life, the survival and transmission of life. It recognises that nature has gone to seemingly irresistible lengths to ensure that life does not stop. Women are born with two million eggs. Men produce forty million sperm in every ejaculation, or at least did before pollution maimed them. The humble wasp can produce between 800 and 3,500 young from a single egg. It was 'natural' for Genghis Khan to believe that his mission was not only to conquer most of Asia, but also to 'hold the wives and daughters of his enemies in his arms' and father as many children as he possibly could, so that there are apparently sixteen million individuals descended from him.

But humans are also nature's heretics. They often devote as little as a quarter of their lifetime to raising children, and delegate many of the tasks of parenting to experts outside their family. They have encouraged their children not to be mere copies of their parents, and every new generation represents a slightly altered version of humanity. From time to time they forget that family is what they care about more than anything else, that children are what has given them the most joy, and that to have brought them up well is what they are most proud of. Throughout history there have repeatedly been huge, sudden and sustained falls in birth rates. Mesopotamia's population trebled in its days of glory, but then descended to one-tenth of its peak when its inventiveness and optimism were extinguished. Egypt's population, which was less than a million in 3000 B.C., rose to five million at the time of Christ, and then fell to 1.5 million by A.D. 1000. Mexico's population was reduced to one-tenth of its former size after the invasion of the Spaniards, not just by disease but also by despair. China's one-child policy has been regarded as an assault on natural instincts, but many countries – like Greece, Italy and Spain – have simultaneously and voluntarily reduced their birth rates to well below China's. In Germany, 30 per cent of women are childless and an even larger proportion of graduate women. Vast numbers of humans have been nuns and monks. The roster of the childless who have chosen to create only spiritual offspring includes Leonardo da Vinci, Bacon, Descartes, Newton, Locke, Berkeley, Hume, Kant, Keynes, Handel, Beethoven, Tchaikovsky, Louis Armstrong, Maria Callas, Georges Brassens, Jane Austen, William Blake, Ruskin, Oliver Wendell Holmes, Magritte, Susan B. Anthony, Florence

Humans are nature's heretics

The sudden despair of civilisations

Nightingale, Simone de Beauvoir, Coco Chanel, Katharine Hepburn, Greta Garbo, and of course Jesus himself. They found other ways of responding to the warning of the philosopher Mencius, who was sorry for those without a family because they had 'no-one to tell their grievances to'.

Humans are like locusts

When it rains heavily and the deserts suddenly bloom, so that there is plenty to eat, locusts multiply rapidly. The more crowded they become, and the more physical contact there is between them, the more their legs rub against each other, the more excited they become, changing their colour from their normal drabness to yellow and orange and black, as though discovering fashion and cosmetics. They join in bands when young, and as adults they form swarms, a single one of which can contain sixty billion locusts, consuming every bit of vegetation over thousands of miles, until there is none left and they die of starvation. Humans have also been multiplying while denuding the earth of its forests and the oceans of their inhabitants, but they have never been quite convinced that they will die like locusts when prosperity ends.

When life begins at death

The originality of humans is that they (or most of them) have believed that their life only begins with death. When Mozart said that the purpose of life is death, he meant that life on earth was a brief journey to the eternal afterlife elsewhere. Some believe the journey leads to heaven; some that it involves a series of reincarnations in other bodies. For the ancient Egyptians, the dead become space tourists accompanying the sun on its daily ride. The purpose of life, said Buddha, is to escape from life and its inevitable suffering, but it might require several deaths to become free. The reward of life, said the Jewish prophets, was to be 'gathered unto their fathers', and many civilisations have given ancestors the role of watching over their living descendants. Dying became the supreme art, more challenging than living. The Spanish playwright Calderón concluded, 'Man's greatest crime is to have been born'. The focus on procreation and the afterlife had a more powerful meaning when life was a brief candle than when marriage is postponed to the age of thirty and it is increasingly possible to survive for almost a century.

However, humanity's most subversive rebellion has been to overthrow the notion that the 'meaning of life' is fixed for ever by nature or by God, and exists independently of the wishes of ordinary people. It challenges this with a different conviction, that each person has to find an interpretation of the gift of life to suit their own ideals and desires. The question is rephrased: 'What do you expect from your life, and how do you shape your life?' rather than 'What do you have to accept?' What purpose would you like not 'life' but your own life to have? That makes the idea of the purpose of life in general meaningless; it is up to you to give a purpose to your own life. Desire dethrones obedience.

A purpose for a life

Suddenly, the idea of progress becomes very useful, because it provides a framework into which each can give significance to a personal struggle that can otherwise be very lonely. Previously you expected to do as your parents did, to work, marry, eat and dress as they did. Now you have to better yourself. Life is no longer a journey on slow-flowing rivers that have been there since the beginning of time; instead it is a maze of long and steep ladders, and your future depends on your ability to climb them and not fall off. Instead of seeing yourself as merely a link in a long chain of ancestors and descendants, you have to compete to attain qualifications and achievements beyond the dreams of any member of your family. But how to choose? How to spend the next month, year, decade?

Humans have 135 different goals, according to a precise professor at the University of Southern California. One way of coping with that profusion is to follow the psychologist Abraham Maslow (1908–1970) who reduced ambition into a simple picture of a pyramid. You start by satisfying your physiological needs, like food, sex and sleep, which are at the base of the pyramid; the next step up is your need for security, and then you go up one step to love, then self-esteem, and finally at the peak you seek 'self-actualisation'. That means your ultimate goal is to develop all the qualities hidden within you, but which could not manifest themselves because you were too busy satisfying the preliminary needs. 'Man has infinite potentiality, which properly used could make his life very much like his fantasies of heaven,' wrote Maslow. He studied the biographies of famous heroes to discover how they reached excellence. 'Why are we not all Beethovens?' he asked. The implication seemed to be that we could indeed all be Beethovens, or almost so, and that is how Maslow's theory prospered. It was refreshing to hear something more optimistic than Freud's dire warnings about neurotic memories. Moreover, Maslow was not just a professor in an ivory tower: he was the son of a Jewish Russian couple who had recently migrated to the U.S.A. with little education, but eager that their seven children should do better than themselves, and he could claim some experience of ordinary working life, for his family eventually owned a wine barrel factory in California. His achievement was to

Why are we not all Beethovens?

compress into five straightforward ambitions that everyone could identify with the vague aspirations for a better life of a generation that did not know what to do with its freedom. Elements of his diagnosis are to be found today in almost every sphere of endeavour, from work and business ideology to education and feminism.

Maslow is an excellent illustration of how a writer's message – as so often happens – is vastly oversimplified by disciples. Privately, he regretted that he could find very few self-actualised people in real life; perhaps only 2 per cent of the population could reach that state, he said, and on closer examination they were sadly 'imperfect' and 'not well-adjusted', suffering from anxiety and guilt, 'capable of extraordinary and unexpected ruthlessness and surgical coldness'. Though they were wonderful lovers, 'good marriage is impossible unless you are willing to take shit from the other'. Maslow's childhood, battling against anti-semitism and against his dogmatic mother, had left him with few illusions: even though he was devoted to making the world a better place, he was also sceptical about the possibility of turning his hopes into reality. He was disappointed that his students did not measure up to his ideal and he complained he could not understand how Hitler, Germans or Communists fitted into his theory.

The ideal person 'sadly imperfect'

Besides, he said, very few people could understand his theory. Each of his colleagues, clever professors from Europe who had found refuge in the U.S.A., had their own theory, and did not quite agree with anyone else, for that is how academia encourages the critical spirit; they took from each other what suited their purpose. The neurologist Kurt Goldstein (1878–1965), who had not long before popularised the term 'self-actualisation' in America with different connotations, disapproved of Maslow's appro-

priation of his language. In reality, the idea dates back to Aristotle, and numerous philosophers had advocated different varieties of it ever since. Maslow was unusual because he insisted that he knew how 'shaky' were the empirical foundations of his own theories, which were based on the study of only 'three or four dozen people carefully and perhaps a hundred or two but not as carefully or in depth'. This was a 'bad or poor or inade- quate experiment. I am quite willing to concede this – as a matter of fact I am eager to concede it, because I am a little worried about this stuff which I consider to be tentative being swallowed whole by all sorts of enthusias- tic people.' The practical application of his theories also left a lot unclear. He recognised that 'self-actualised' creative people tended to be wayward, disobedient and 'crazy because every really new idea looks crazy at first'. 'I told this to a company – but I don't know how managers can work with creative people, who tend to cause trouble. This is not my problem.' He left it to the managers to solve it, hoping they would see management as 'a psychological experiment' and encouraging them with the thought that they were as 'spiritual' as 'professionally religious' poets or intellectuals, except that they had a 'different jargon' and 'conceal their idealism under a mask of toughness, calm and selfishness'.

These reservations and obscurities did not deter large numbers of Americans, and then people of many nations, from seizing on the idea

of self-actualisation or self-realisation as the key to the successful life and to profitable work, as though an El Dorado of talent was suddenly being discovered and everyone would soon become wonderfully rich and

fulfilled. The failure of sages in both East and West to transform the
ignorant and the sinful into models of self-realisation was forgotten when
a new generation of management experts, led by Douglas McGregor of
MIT and Peter Drucker (just becoming famous for his study of General
Motors), gave this universal panacea their blessing, and it is now embed-   *Universal*
ded in every human resources training programme that claims to convert   *panaceas*
ordinary people into exemplary leaders. The New Age gurus of the 1960s
turned Maslow's psychology into an instant fast food that they could add
to their mystical recipes, and through them it percolated, variously diluted,
into a myriad self-help books promising wealth, happiness and fame. As
one advertisement explained, all that was needed was 'awareness that you
can be, do and have anything you want'. Betty Friedan (who majored in
psychology at the very time when Maslow's 'humanistic psychology' was
just becoming fashionable) used its language when she famously wrote in
The Feminine Mystique, 'The problem that has no name – which is simply
the fact that American women are kept from growing to their full human
capacities – is taking a far greater toll on the physical and mental health
of our country than any known disease.' 'Positive psychology', which is the
successor of 'humanistic psychology', and acknowledges Maslow as one of
its inspirations, is now an academic discipline which teaches people to be
happy, to 'nurture their strengths' and 'find niches in which they can best
live out [their] positive qualities'. Not least, Maslow's hierarchy of needs
gave captains of industry a ready formula that could convince employees
that their jobs were helping them in 'self-development'. Feeling good
about oneself, and being oneself, became the ultimate goal of life. It is as

though the only possession of which individuals now have full ownership

is their feelings, and they need protection from criticism because judgement which would make them feel bad. But is asserting and defending one's identity the supreme ambition? Where does cultivating self-esteem lead?

It is not clear that there are more Beethovens today than in the past, or fewer tyrants, or fewer fools. Nor, as yet, has anyone produced a theory proposing that since so many geniuses, prophets and artists have suffered poverty or persecution, the best preparation for attaining the summits of eminence is to live on bread and water in a garret or a prison. This is not the first time in history that humans have embarked on this friendless journey, searching for meaning inside themselves. It has happened whenever official institutions fail to satisfy anxious minds. The twentieth century made the journey more arduous by persuading many individuals that they had only their own solitary ego as a companion, leaving it to the lonesome sperm and the frustrated egg to make peace between them.

Attaining self-realisation is not the same thing as having a full life. Can anyone conscious of their limitations be satisfied with having nothing more to hope for than the fulfilment of their obviously inadequate 'potential', using only the meagre talents they were born with? Though self-realisation has become an officially endorsed orthodoxy of many nations aiming to liberate individuals from the obstacles that prevent them from being 'truly themselves', it may not be humanity's final goal. Those who govern the world, having variously tried to make people happy, or wealthy, or empowered, or free, but seldom giving them all they wanted, may sooner or later search for some other elixir. Happy people can be self-ish. Becoming wealthy does not automatically make one a better person. Power not only corrupts, but is the virus that spreads megalomania. Freedom, however essential, can be blighted by uncertainty about what to do with it. Only very rarely have official prescriptions to improve human welfare produced the expected results. Climbing pyramids, one step at a time, knowing where each foot must tread, is a restrictive metaphor for life. At the age of twelve, I climbed to the top of the Great Pyramid of Egypt, and wrote my name on its roof as all tourists do, but then there was nothing left but to climb down again.

Happiness and selfishness

I shall not know what life signifies until each person reveals what they have found or failed to find in their life. I can only see a minuscule corner of the universe, and I cannot begin to construct a bigger picture until I discover what others see. Being alive is not simply a matter of having a heart that beats, it is also being aware of how other hearts beat and other minds think in response to one another. The fatal disease that attacks the living is *rigor vitae*, rigidity of the mind, which burns up curiosity and replaces it with repetitive and numb routine; it is more dangerous than *rigor mortis* because it gives the illusion of being alive. One is only nominally alive if one is incapable of giving birth to thoughts one has never had before and of being inspired by what others think.

Rigidity of the mind

There could be no change in understanding life until there was a change in understanding death, and that at last has happened, now that microscopes have watched closely the process of dying. Death is not what we thought it was. Fruitful conversation is not only what makes it possible

A new understand-ing of death

for us to enjoy one another's company, it also takes place, in a form only recently discovered, silently and invisible to the naked eye, inside our flesh and blood. Our physical survival depends on a dialogue between the cells out of which we are made. A cell is kept alive by the links it establishes with other cells around it. Billions of cells die every day inside my body, but old age is not enough to kill them; on the contrary, most cells commit suicide. They are born with a capacity for suicide, which they trigger when they fail to exchange signals with their neighbours; they survive when they succeed in combining with other cells to produce something more than themselves. Cells are constantly transforming themselves by fusing with other cells, different from themselves, and the proteins in them adapt to the other proteins around them, like dancers joining a ballet. Every cell has the power to destroy itself in just a few hours, and the suicide is decided after a whole series of attempted conversations between it and those around it fail: when it cuts off all contact with its neighbours,

*The punish-
ment for
silence is
death*

the punishment for silence is death. This process means our bodies are perpetually renewing themselves, with huge quantities of cells vanishing like autumn leaves falling off a tree. Our minds, too, acquire and discard ideas we borrow from others.

*Missing out
on life*

It is not just cells which commit suicide by shutting themselves off. Humans who become absorbed in the contemplation of their own navels miss out on life too. The gift of life includes an invitation to connect with the limitless variety of the natural world and with the imagination and ingenuity of others, appreciation of which can grow to become affection; and expanding the radius of affections makes one more alive. When

I discover interesting qualities in another person, and am able to give that person some kind of inspiration that no-one else can, I add something to life. Each meeting between two people that is not merely superficial is an opportunity to enlarge it beyond the banal, through discovery and invention. When others inspire fear in me and I do not know how to speak to them, nor they to me, or we have no sympathy for each other's needs, we are in the same state as cells for whom existence no longer has any purpose. But though fear is as unavoidable as hunger, there are more or less elegant ways of responding to them both. Exploring fears is one of life's missions, as is redrawing the map of one's fears.

Adding something to life

Redrawing the map of fear

Institutions, governments and businesses, whose purpose is to iron out the irregularities caused by temperament, anger, boredom and accident, and all the other misadventures of each day, may continue to think that private conversations have less influence than mission statements and rules of conduct that everyone must follow. Orators may still on occasion be able to suddenly transform crowds of humans into swarms of locusts. But the world has new possibilities when the interaction of individuals sharpens minds, softens fears and creates unexpected synergies. There is no shortage of talk, but talk is not conversation, which is the engine of thought. There are more opportunities for interaction today than there ever have been, and also more obstacles. Technology, though its inventions may work perfectly, has not eliminated the fears that make humans break down. That is why every person's experiences, their trials and errors, are an essential part of the understanding of life.

Conversation the engine of thought

In 1085, the king of England 'had deep speech with his counsellors and

*A new
Domesday
Book*

sent men all over England to each shire to find out what or how much each landholder had in land and livestock, and what it was worth'. The result was the Domesday Book, a record of what mattered most in those days, property. Today there is room for another kind of investigation. How well others understand you, and you them, makes more difference to your life than what you own. There is a much longer book waiting to be written, composed by individuals saying what they value, believe, dread and hope. Giving people the vote was only a timid beginning. Everybody has much more to say than can be summed up in a cross on a ballot paper. Eighty-one per cent of Americans have told pollsters that they have an idea for a book and would like to write one. That need not remain a pipe dream. Public libraries, which contributed so decisively to the self-education of the masses, can turn the threat to close them down into a spur propelling them into a second phase, not only lending books but also creating them. They can facilitate and store self-portraits in which people record what their lives signify and what they would like others to know about them; and be the place where it is possible for them to discover how they can benefit from the talents and hopes of neighbours they know only super-ficially or not at all. Already the public librarians of one of the greatest cities in the world have agreed to embark on this adventure.

This book is my contribution. I hope that eavesdropping on my con-versations will make my readers want to interrupt and disagree, and feel impelled to start their own book, from their own perspective, evoking the past that is most meaningful to them, and imagining a future that would give more hope to the present.

Where can one find nourishment for the mind?

All the people I have ever met, all those who have been kind and sympathetic, and who have opened their doors to me, as well as all those who have puzzled, shunned, terrified or horrified me, all the books by the dead or the living that I have read in my life, all that I have ever seen and heard are the co-authors of this book. All have been muses to me, though usually they do not know it.

Unlike the Giant Panda which likes to eat nothing but bamboo, human beings can turn almost anything into mental nourishment. This book is my attempt to expand our tastes, which involves discovering the tastes, opinions, experience and hopes of others. You can discover practical ways in which you can participate in this endeavour by looking at the website of the Oxford Muse Foundation (www.oxfordmuse.com), a charity established to encourage the kinds of conversations, portraits and experiments in work and culture described in these pages. Though you may feel that you are powerless to diminish the absurdities and cruelties that plague our lives, you can undoubtedly make the world a very tiny bit wiser by enabling it to understand you, your ways of thinking, the vagaries of the occupations by which you have earned or failed to earn a decent living, and the methods you have developed to respond to your misadventures.

Every literate person is a writer as well as a reader, and this is an invitation to you to write down what you normally keep to yourself. By placing your self-portrait in our gallery, as anonymously as you wish and in visual form if you prefer, you become a muse to others.

The website also invites you to participate in a new project to demonstrate that what distinguishes humans is their capacity for thinking, and that thinking can be as exciting and as satisfying as any entertainment.

Finally, just by buying this book, you are sustaining a charity whose ambition is to remember the past in more useful ways, its illusions as well as its achievements, so that it becomes possible to do more than repair potholes on an old road strewn with contradictory signposts.

The Oxford Muse website records more fully my gratitude to the very many people who in different ways have encouraged and contributed to our activities through the years. But every object deserves to have the names of its creators engraved on it, so on this last page I wish to mention those who transformed my writing into a physical book, with delightful imagination, and made publication such a pleasurable and interesting experience: Christopher MacLehose, Katharina Bielenberg, Auriol Bishop, Paul Engles, Bethan Ferguson, Lucy Hale, Corinna Zifko and their colleagues, Rukun Advani and Michael Salu, and Andrew Nurnberg and his colleagues, and not least the indispensable booksellers who have expressed a willingness to act as foster parents to the book until it finds a gentle reader.

Index

Soviet Communism 219, 237, 338

Sparta 378

species classification 238–40

Spectator 40

Spencer, Herbert 85–6

Spinoza 157–8

sport; the consolations of 26; women's
    tennis 313–4

Stalin, Joseph 60–1, 110

Statler, E. M. 348

Sterne, Laurence 190

strangers 16

stupidity; origin 77; fear of seeming
    stupid 306;

students 369; sexism among 75; and
    hotels 358

Sufis, 255–6

suicide 99–100, 108–10, 175, 183;
    of reputation 33; voluntary 99;
    by abandoning ideals 106; by
    humorists 175; a virtual suicide 183;
    and the strain of work 294–5; and
    cells 410

superstores 333–5
    see also IKEA; Walton, Sam

T

Tagore, Rabindranath 141–50,
    151–2, 153–5, 156, 160; ideals
    141; prejudice against 142–3; as
    reformer and environmentalist 143;

and the arts 144–5; as educator
    146–7; in politics 147–8; and
    relationships 148–40; influence
    on England 149; as inventor 152;
    thoughtfulness 153; memory 154–5;
    reconciliation 156

Taizu, Emperor 130

Tamerlane, Emperor 189

Taoists 269

Tarlton, Richard 184

tax evasion 108–9

Taylor, Frederick Winslow 292–4

Temple, William 188

The Times 157

Theophrastus 253

therapies 21

thinking 387; and sleep 382; brain life
    and sex life 388; ignorance 388;
    being alive 389; wisdom 392;
    ambiguity 396; misunderstanding
    394–6; in science 395–6; and
    freedom 399; rigidity of the mind
    409; conversation the engine of 411

Thoreau, H. D. 337

thought; contraceptives against 42;
    fear of 12; how I think 51

thoughtfulness 12–13, 153

Tillich, Paul 57

time 161–65

Tocqueville, Alexis de 53

toleration, limits of 126, 139